Spring 2004   Vol. XXIV, no. 1
ISSN: 0276-0045   ISBN: 1-56478-364-2

THE REVIEW OF CONTEMPORARY FICTION

Editor

JOHN O'BRIEN
Illinois State University

Senior Editor

ROBERT L. MCLAUGHLIN
Illinois State University

Book Review Editor

TIM FEENEY

Production & Design

N. J. FURL

Cover Illustration

SAMUEL BERKES

Cover Photos

LAURA VON ROSK (Douglas Glover)
SANFORD ROTH (Blaise Cendrars)
JEAN BELLEC (Severo Sarduy)

www.centerforbookculture.org
www.dalkeyarchive.com

The Review of Contemporary Fiction is published three times a year (January, June, September) by the Center for Book Culture, a nonprofit organization located at ISU Campus Box 8905, Normal, IL 61790-8905. ISSN 0276-0045. Subscription prices are as follows:

Single volume (three issues):
    Individuals: $17.00; foreign, add $3.50;
    Institutions: $26.00; foreign, add $3.50.

DISTRIBUTION. Bookstores should send orders to:

Review of Contemporary Fiction, ISU Campus Box 8905, Normal, IL 61790-8905. Phone 309-438-7555; fax 309-438-7422.

This issue is partially supported by a grant from the Illinois Arts Council, a state agency.

Indexed in *American Humanities Index, International Bibliography of Periodical Literature, International Bibliography of Book Reviews, MLA Bibliography,* and *Book Review Index.* Abstracted in *Abstracts of English Studies.*

The Review of Contemporary Fiction is also available on 16mm microfilm, 35mm microfilm, and 105mm microfiche from University Microfilms International, 300 North Zeeb Road, Ann Arbor, MI 48106-1346.

www.centerforbookculture.org

THE REVIEW OF CONTEMPORARY FICTION

BACK ISSUES AVAILABLE

Back issues are still available for the following numbers of the *Review of Contemporary Fiction* ($8 each unless otherwise noted):

DOUGLAS WOOLF / WALLACE MARKFIELD
WILLIAM EASTLAKE / AIDAN HIGGINS
CAMILO JOSÉ CELA
CHANDLER BROSSARD
SAMUEL BECKETT
CLAUDE OLLIER / CARLOS FUENTES
JOHN BARTH / DAVID MARKSON
DONALD BARTHELME / TOBY OLSON
BRIGID BROPHY / ROBERT CREELEY /
   OSMAN LINS
WILLIAM T. VOLLMANN / SUSAN DAITCH /
   DAVID FOSTER WALLACE
WILLIAM H. GASS / MANUEL PUIG
ROBERT WALSER
JOSÉ DONOSO / JEROME CHARYN
GEORGES PEREC / FELIPE ALFAU
JOSEPH MCELROY
DJUNA BARNES
ANGELA CARTER / TADEUSZ KONWICKI
STANLEY ELKIN / ALASDAIR GRAY
EDMUND WHITE / SAMUEL R. DELANY
MARIO VARGAS LLOSA / JOSEF ŠKVORECKÝ
WILSON HARRIS / ALAN BURNS
RAYMOND QUENEAU / CAROLE MASO

RICHARD POWERS / RIKKI DUCORNET
EDWARD SANDERS
WRITERS ON WRITING: THE BEST OF *THE
   REVIEW OF CONTEMPORARY FICTION*
BRADFORD MORROW
JEAN RHYS / JOHN HAWKES /
   PAUL BOWLES / MARGUERITE YOUNG
HENRY GREEN / JAMES KELMAN /
   ARIEL DORFMAN
JANICE GALLOWAY / THOMAS BERNHARD /
   ROBERT STEINER / ELIZABETH BOWEN
GILBERT SORRENTINO / WILLIAM GADDIS /
   MARY CAPONEGRO / MARGERY LATIMER
ITALO CALVINO / URSULE MOLINARO /
   B. S. JOHNSON
LOUIS ZUKOFSKY / NICHOLAS MOSLEY /
   COLEMAN DOWELL
CASEBOOK STUDY OF GILBERT
   SORRENTINO'S *IMAGINATIVE QUALITIES OF
   ACTUAL THINGS*
RICK MOODY / ANN QUIN / SILAS
   FLANNERY
DIANE WILLIAMS / AIDAN HIGGINS /
   PATRICIA EAKINS

NOVELIST AS CRITIC: Essays by Garrett, Barth, Sorrentino, Wallace, Ollier, Brooke-Rose, Creeley, Mathews, Kelly, Abbott, West, McCourt, McGonigle, and McCarthy

NEW FINNISH FICTION: Fiction by Eskelinen, Jäntti, Kontio, Krohn, Paltto, Sairanen, Selo, Siekkinen, Sund, Valkeapää

NEW ITALIAN FICTION: Interviews and fiction by Malerba, Tabucchi, Zanotto, Ferrucci, Busi, Corti, Rasy, Cherchi, Balduino, Ceresa, Capriolo, Carrera, Valesio, and Gramigna

GROVE PRESS NUMBER: Contributions by Allen, Beckett, Corso, Ferlinghetti, Jordan, McClure, Rechy, Rosset, Selby, Sorrentino, and others

NEW DANISH FICTION: Fiction by Brøgger, Høeg, Andersen, Grøndahl, Holst, Jensen, Thorup, Michael, Sibast, Ryum, Lynggaard, Grønfeldt, Willumsen, and Holm

NEW LATVIAN FICTION: Fiction by Nora Ikstena, Paul Bankovskis, Guntis Berelis, Arvis Kolmanis, Andra Neiburga, Rimants Ziedonis, and others

THE FUTURE OF FICTION: Essays by Birkerts, Caponegro, Franzen, Galloway, Maso, Morrow, Vollmann, White, and others

NEW JAPANESE FICTION: Interviews and fiction by Ohara, Shimada, Shono, Takahashi, Tsutsui, McCaffery, Gregory, Kotani, Tatsumi, Koshikawa, and others

Individuals receive a 10% discount on orders of one issue and a 20% discount on orders of two or more issues. To place an order, use the form on the last page of this issue.

www.centerforbookculture.org/review

The *Review of Contemporary Fiction* is seeking contributors to write overview essays on the following writers:

Felipe Alfau, Chandler Brossard, Gabrielle Burton, Michel Butor, Julieta Campos, Jerome Charyn, Emily Holmes Coleman, Stanley Crawford, Eva Figes, William H. Gass, Karen Elizabeth Gordon, Carol De Chellis Hill, Violette Leduc, Olive Moore, Julián Ríos, Esther Tusquets.

The essays must:

- be 50 double-spaced pages;
- cover the subject's biography;
- summarize the critical reception of the subject's works;
- discuss the course of the subject's career, including each major work;
- provide interpretive strategies for new readers to apply to the subject's work;
- provide a bibliographic checklist of each of the subject's works (initial and latest printings);
- be written for a general, intelligent reader, who does not know the subject's work;
- avoid jargon, theoretical digressions, and excessive endnotes;
- be intelligent, interesting, and readable;
- be documented in MLA style.

Authors will be paid $250.00 when the essay is published. All essays will be subject to editorial review, and the editors reserve the right to request revisions and to reject unacceptable essays.

Applicants should send a CV and a brief writing sample. In your cover letter, be sure to address your qualifications.

Send applications to:

Robert L. McLaughlin
Dalkey Archive Press, Illinois State University, Campus Box 8905, Normal, IL 61790-8905

Inquiries: rmclaugh@ilstu.edu

Contents

a nexus of politics and the arts

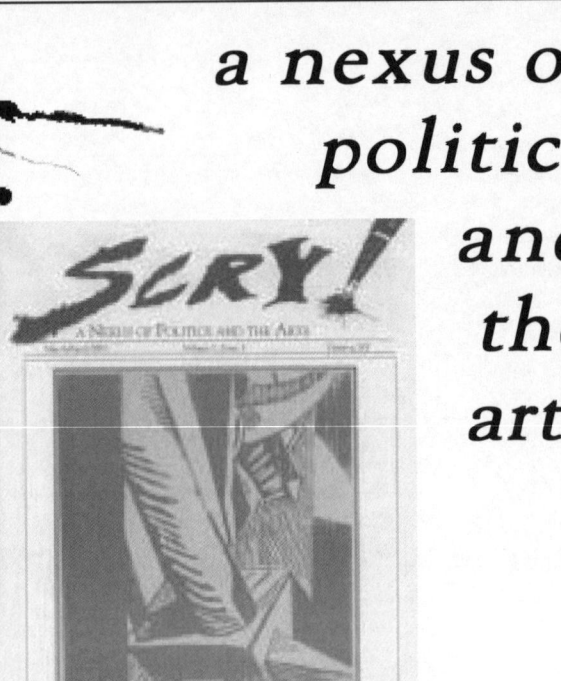

Douglas Glover

Bruce Stone

Douglas Glover's characters are a persecuted lot. They suffer from cracked skulls, diseased lungs, digital amputations (both elective and compulsory), aesthetic constipation, nymphomania, toothache, chronic masturbation, amnesia, Kierkegaardian despair, alcoholism, and are sometimes politely homicidal. Squeezed between an intolerable past and an equally intolerable future, they are driven by desire and literally driven mad by its perversions. For these characters, suffering is the primary ontological condition. As one narrator in Glover's most recent collection observes, "It seems impossible that a human being could suffer this much and live. And just when you think you can't stand any more, it gets worse and you discover new possibilities of living" (*16 Categories* 174). It might sound excessively bleak were it not for the fact that pain, in Glover's universe, is very often the instrument for transcendence and redemption, if only temporarily and incompletely. What's more, Glover's prose radiates a blistering irony, by turns wickedly comic and sublimely affective, which, coupled with a broader compositional mastery, further leavens the agonizing climate; in his studied pursuit of stylistic estrangement, Glover knocks edgewise, as it were, even the weightiest drama—on the battlefield or in the bedroom—transporting the reader, if not always the character, to an entirely other plane where pleasure is, in fact, the norm.

To be clear, Glover's protagonists are not often characters in the conventional sense; rather, their identities regularly undergo a variety of distortions, involving slippages in point of view as well as other subtler and more radical dislocations that call to mind William Gass's formulation, "Characters are those primary substances to which everything else is attached" (49). To redirect Glover's terminology slightly, characters are the "essential furniture" in a work of fiction (*Notes Home* 36). They frequently exist in the space where text and selfhood overlap, well versed in the malign influence of semiotics, very much aware that their subjectivity is a by-product of linguistic systems. In this regard Glover is thoroughly, almost stubbornly, postmodern, a stance he defines broadly as having one's aesthetic "options open" (*Notes Home* 102). And his work capitalizes on this ultimate latitude, at once technically experimental and viscerally experiential, which entitles him, one would think, to a readership much larger than he currently enjoys.

On the whole Glover's aesthetic might best be characterized by the rift that his works generate between predominantly two interpretative strategies; it almost seems as if there are two Glovers, forking along the lines of deconstructionist theory and formalist praxis. As Glover's fiction openly flexes its philosophical muscle— one character remarks, "Structuralists would characterize my style as 'robbing the signifier of the signified'" (*Dog Attempts* 107)—his work inevitably triggers one's theoretical reflexes, broaching issues of subjectivity, agency, and the much-ballyhooed problem of language. This programmatic philosophizing, partly borne out in the essay collection *Notes Home from a Prodigal Son,* tends to give the prose the weight of an "ethical injunction" (107); against the machine of language, Glover is scatological and anti-Zen, offering a nearly Blakean concept of libidinal energy, and on this level his fiction can be configured to provide, as the title of his third collection seems to indicate, *A Guide to Animal Behavior.* That title is, however, ironic, and to read Glover this way is, at least for some of us, to construe narrowly the scope of his achievement. Rather, there's another Glover who operates solely on the aesthetic level, for whom the deconstructive autocommentary is as much a stylistic opportunity as it is an ideological necessity, for whom both suffering and its temporary alleviation, transcendence, are figurative textual requirements as much as they are literal worldly critiques. Glover is making a career out of exploiting this slippery divide between Arnoldian imperative and Paterian possibility, but I would argue that it's his aestheticism that equips him to outlast any potentially faddish interest (or disinterest) in theory mongering.

A partly expatriated Canadian, Glover has written to date four collections of short fiction, four novels, and a book of essays. His most recent novel, *Elle,* was published in April 2003 by Goose Lane Editions; Dalkey Archive Press has seen fit to release a book of selected stories, *Bad News of the Heart,* which appeared in March of the same year. His short fiction has been nominated for the Governor General's Award (Canada's version of the National Book Award) and has been anthologized in both *Best American Short Stories* and *Best Canadian Stories* (where he has been the editor since 1997). His criticism has appeared in the national juggernauts of, among others, the *New York Times Book Review,* the *Washington Post,* and the *L.A. Times,* and he currently teaches writing at Vermont College. All of this places him, on the literary chain of being, somewhere between Shakespeare and you (depending). To get the full measure of Glover's singular achievement, we must of course examine the work itself.

*   *   *

Notes Home from a Prodigal Son is an assemblage of interviews, aesthetic meditations, and stylistically knowing literary criticism: good-humored, dispassionate, and pugnacious in more or less equal parts. Like Kundera's *The Art of the Novel* and Todorov's *The Poetics of Prose,* it offers writers of so-called experimental fiction, almost incidentally, some of the most cogent commentary on the practice of writing to be found. However, *Notes Home* is also an authoritative source for Glover's biography, most directly and definitively in the autobiographical essay "The Familiar Dead," but also in the variegated glimpses that surface throughout.

On 14 November 1948 Glover was born in Simcoe, Ontario (in the post-NAFTA world, roughly equidistant between Toronto and metropolitan Detroit), where his parents owned a tobacco farm that had been in the family since the turn of the century. In a moderately affluent household, his upbringing was cultured—his mother helped import to Simcoe a traveling Shakespearean troupe, and the Glovers lived within nearby Toronto's artistic penumbra (e-mail 24 Dec. 2002)—but not privileged, as tending the crop was a hands-on experience, both onerous and beautiful. Glover writes, "what I remember best is . . . the terrible pain of the cold dew on my hands late in harvest, those chilling September mornings with the sun just coming up, and the smell of horse manure and sweat and the jingling of the harness . . ." (*Notes Home* 156-57). Understandably, the Canadian landscape—and indeed what it is to be Canadian—has consistently been one of Glover's writerly obsessions. In 1968 he wrote his first short story—"Hail" in *The Mad River*—while in Freiberg, Germany, where he was training to make a bid for the Canadian Olympic track team (e-mail 28 Dec. 2002), yet the story is set at home on the farm and depicts the devastation that nature can wreak on human endeavor. Glover continues to return, literally, to the farm in Ontario as often as possible, but over time, his fiction graduates from these experiential roots to a more complex take on his native land. In his most recent collection, *16 Categories of Desire,* the unnamed narrator of "The Indonesian Client" remarks, ". . . I will not gainsay the fact that Canada had become a symbol of everything about myself I wished to leave behind, that my constant dream of snow, glaciers and, occasionally, amnesia was a childish dream of grace and redemption . . ." (68). As this passage begins to suggest, Glover's relationship to Canada as figured in his fiction is markedly ambivalent. His characters can both deplore its "barren culture" (*16 Categories* 57) and succumb to an inevitable patriotic nostalgia.

What's more, Glover suggests that his Canadianness might offer a unique cultural perspective surprisingly attuned to a postmodern vision; in an interview he remarks, "We Canadians, disturbed as we are by memory and identity, are, by the backdoor, closer to the cutting edge of postmodernity than say the Americans next door. . . . At any rate, the equation 'Canadian=postmodern man' sometimes almost makes sense to me (late at night after two or maybe three glasses of bourbon). As I say this, I know it can't be true" (*Notes Home* 144). How seriously we should take this assertion is less important than the fact that Glover paints himself as a writer on the margins, an exile, an outsider: a position with its own subversive advantages, for which his Canadian roots are, if not cause, then metaphor.

Glover's seeking out of intellectual and societal fringes was part of his nature from the earliest stages of his career. In 1966, when his mother had arranged for him to attend Trinity College at the University of Toronto, "nurturing ground of Canada's Anglo elite" (*Notes Home* 158), Glover responded by abruptly enrolling at York University. In his words, "I fled tradition and the stodgy elitism of Trinity for a half-built, inchoate institution with no identity" (*Notes Home* 158). At York, he completed a degree in philosophy and, owing to a bureaucratic oversight, later matriculated as a graduate student at the University of Edinburgh despite a minor deficiency in his undergraduate qualifications. He wrote a Master's thesis on Kant and Schopenhauer, then returned to Canada, where he taught philosophy for a year at the University of New Brunswick. In general, *Notes Home* tends to downplay the significance of Glover's formal education—at one point he remarks that he sometimes fell asleep during classes—but philosophy is rarely far away in his fiction and often verges on the theological, spanning historical eras and cultures.

After he'd left off teaching, in 1972 Glover took up the first of what would be a series of newspaper jobs, starting as a reporter for Saint John's *Evening Times-Globe* and concluding as a copy editor for Saskatoon's *Star-Phoenix* in 1979. His journalistic experience plays out in his writing in numerous ways, but perhaps the most fun is Glover's occasional taste for magnificently ludicrous headlines. The title story of his second collection, "Dog Attempts to Drown Man in Saskatoon," is a case in point, as is "Woman Gored by Bison Lives" in *A Guide to Animal Behavior.* But more broadly, his experience with newspapers dovetails with another of his primary fictional concerns, namely, the insufficiency of fact and the myth-making or general delusiveness (for Glover, a particularly Canadian quality) that most of us call reality.

At this time, Glover was writing both his first collection of stories and his first novel, in what appear to be radically disparate aesthetic modes. The stories of *The Mad River* include two technically stable or conventional pieces ("Hail" and "Horse"); the remaining five stories all to varying degrees disrupt and unsettle the traditional elements of plot, character, and point of view, as we'll see. However, *Precious,* the first novel, while containing vestigial elements of vintage Glover, bears little relation to the more ambitious stories of the same period.

Precious was published in 1984 and, according to Glover, went out of print almost immediately. Today, copies are difficult to come by—it seems to require a minor act of Providence to obtain one—and those few that remain linger on in the collections of a handful of Canadian libraries (the public library in Madison, Wisconsin, preserves one anomalous copy, stamped with a noncommittal "Unique" on the title page). The novel opens with protagonist Moss Eliot's down-and-out return to Toronto; after significant wheedling, he lands a job with a provincial newspaper where the murder of a local gossip puts him on the trail of a big scoop, involving land-wrangling, identity-shifting, intermittent sexings, and one auxiliary murder. The tenor of the book is largely gumshoe, and technically it shows Glover mastering the plot devices of traditional novelistic practice. In an early survey of Glover's work, Louis MacKendrick suggests that *Precious* "is a studied parody or a pastiche of a literary manner," and concludes, "It is a distinctive—and sadly little known—novel of character and style, smooth in development, knowing in its journalistic particulars" (126). Certainly, *Precious* is in many ways an accomplished performance, but it contains a variety of stylistic features that can only seem anomalous in retrospect: bales of expositional dialogue, high-ordinance similes of varying efficacy, and a unidirectional narrative line. As a result, the appeal of *Precious* for fans of Glover's later fiction might be largely archeological.

Nevertheless, as the book verges on extinction, here we might remark on some of those features that render it Gloverian. First, there is Eliot's suffering—both spiritual and physical: at times his skull seems like a veritable piñata—and his incorrigible binge drinking, which secure him a place in the rogues' gallery of Glover's protagonists. Also, some of the early chapters show a technical proficiency, interpolating past events with present action: a demonstrated if transitory rhetorical savvy. In addition, for the climactic scene, a showdown involving firearms and snowmobiles, the scrupulous first-person narration begins to waver and slip, and Eliot recounts the action, for the first time, as if providing an objective news account. He consciously establishes a bullet-point chronology and sometimes relates the event as witnessed by two constables playing sniper in an overlooking tower, thus stretching the parameters of the first-person narration. In fact, periodically the novel intimates a potentially interesting connection between the reporter's task and the novelist's; however, the implications of such a thematic possibility are largely turned under in the course of the linear events.

Glover was revising *Precious* while he was a student at the Iowa Writers' Workshop (he enrolled in 1980, after leaving the Saskatoon newspaper). In keeping with his habitual outsider status, Glover identifies only Robert Day, a one-time replacement instructor, as having been particularly helpful to his development as a writer. According to Glover, Day was the only teacher whose pedagogy was hospitable to the kind of formalist aesthetic that Glover was refining. To this day, Glover remains critical of his MFA alma mater, where he felt that "subjective mystification," also known as the school of psychological realism, was the pedagogical norm (e-mail 28 Dec. 2002). The result is that, for Glover's growth as a writer, it's not possible to locate influential mentors among his familiars, only those that he cites in *Notes Home*: notably Vladimir Nabokov and Milan Kundera, but also the Canadian writer and radical Hubert Aquin, who committed suicide in 1977, and R. D. Laing, who introduced Glover to a postmodern perspective on culture and acculturation.

Iowa did however have a lasting impact: as negative example. Since 1987, Glover has been teaching creative writing, first as a writer in residence at several Canadian universities, then at Skidmore College and State University of New York-Albany, among others in this country, and since 1994, he has been on the faculty of Vermont College's MFA in Writing program, a low-residency format that offers distance learning and individual mentoring rather than requiring a year-round campus presence. His pedagogy is remarkable for its emphasis on rhetorical structure; indeed, he takes pride in having developed a "globular" approach to writing fiction, training his students to recognize that rhetorical patterning is the sine qua non of a literary work. Against the conventional arrow of the plot, he offers the "net" (*Notes Home* 66), incidentally ultracontemporary in its terminology: a network of repeating elements that can be modulated to achieve effects ranging from a verisimilar emotional wallop to a chill conceptual distancing. Among the students at Vermont College, Glover is somewhat legendary for his aggressive and lucid take on structure, he is regularly honored for his pedagogical practice, and his lectures are invariably a crowded affair.

Still, excepting his post at Vermont College, Glover's position within the ranks of academia has been largely as journeyman itinerant, generally unsecured. Unfortunately, the same can be said for his record of publication to date. Since the 1989 collection *A Guide to Animal Behavior,* Glover has been publishing sporadically with Goose Lane Editions, and the genesis of this relationship is representative of Glover's ongoing struggle to bring his books into print. At the time, the story collection was slated for release with Viking Canada as part of a two-book contract; however, at the eleventh hour, Viking balked, wanting to hold off publication and offering, in the face of Glover's irritation, to terminate the contract. Glover countered by phoning Goose Lane editor Susanne Alexander, whom he had previously worked with in her capacity as award officer with the Canadian Arts Council. Her response was diffident; she said she would have to run the proposal by an editorial committee. Glover had time to hang up and make a sandwich when Alexander called back, telling him Goose Lane would take the collection. The second book from the Viking contract was *The Life and Times of Captain N.*; eventually, Glover sold the novel to Gordon Lish at Knopf (e-mail 20 Jan. 2003). With *16 Categories* and *Elle,* Glover has resumed publication with Goose Lane, and it seems as if he has found at least a temporary harbor there. Still, like most Canadian publishers, as Glover explains, Goose Lane has few resources to foster an American audience for his fiction (e-mail 12 Jan. 2003). This is lamentable. At fifty-five, Glover is at the top of his prodigious game, churning out midcareer masterworks that too few readers in this country will enjoy. He currently resides in New York State, just outside Saratoga Springs.

From the outset, Glover's career reveals a surprisingly linear trajectory, each work significantly advancing from and trumping the last. The novels in particular manifest a distinctly steady movement both into historical subject matter and away from linear narrative. From the largely conventional *Precious,* which is wholly contemporary in its Canadian locale, Glover progresses to *The South Will Rise at Noon,* a book with more stylistic aplomb, in which the central narrative event is a staged reenactment of a Civil War battle. With *The Life and Times of Captain N.,* Glover pushes the line further, setting the novel directly in the north woods of the American Revolution and employing an aggressive, perspective-shifting narrative technique vaguely reminiscent of Faulkner. Now, *Elle* presses still deeper into the European invasion of the New World, reworking and radicalizing the historical record of a woman marooned on a Canadian island during a French colonial expedition in the sixteenth century. Still, to characterize Glover as a historical novelist, a loaded term, is slightly misleading since Glover essentially transports ultramodern concerns into the past. That is, Glover's novels exist less as sources of historical information than as artifacts of a most contemporary aesthetic vision.

Between the novels and the short stories, there is for Glover a qualitative difference; in *Notes Home* he remarks, "A novel is not an extended short story" (139). The primary distinction seems to be that for the novel, Glover imposes on himself a more stringent set of specifications for the depiction and scope of the narrative action. The short stories, by contrast, reflect an absolute design freedom that Glover exploits to the utmost advantage. Despite all thoroughgoing differences, the devices Glover favors are largely shared in either mode; in particular, his works feature an obsession with his fundamental compositional element: rhetorical patterning. On occasion Glover will submerge a text's formal devices to the vanishing point, but more often his is an aesthetic of revelation, openly airing its technical inventiveness. Structurally, his fiction is elegantly modular, multilayered, fugal, generating both stylistic harmonies and dissonances that are central to the impact of his prose.

Surprisingly, reviewers have been largely (and consistently) receptive to Glover's postmodern aesthetic cosmology. Among the Canadian press, his books draw favorable coverage throughout the provinces: Lorna Jackson, in her review of *16 Categories of Desire*, turns one of Glover's fictional devices to her own advantage, emphasizing that "Patterns of rhythm, imagery, structure—even punctuation—are the esthetics of writing." Another reviewer says of *The Life and Times of Captain N.*: "It's a tale that will smack readers upside the head like a warrior's club and leave old preconceptions about historical fiction in a muddy, bloodied heap" (Horton). In this country the critical attention has been far less extensive: both *The South Will Rise at Noon* and *Captain N.* received brief endorsements in the *New York Times Book Review,* and *Captain N.* garnered additional enthusiastic attention in the Midwest, including in this journal (Graham, Malin). However, such limited ink, it seems, has been insufficient to generate an audience capable of cementing Glover's relationship with American publishers.

As with the novels, the short stories, from collection to collection, reveal the considerable growth and development of Glover's primary aesthetic concerns. From the earliest works in *The Mad River* that foreground narrative action to the extreme, Glover graduates to increasingly more subtle and flexible compositional approaches, where the action can be largely expeditious, and the prose acquires a strong "told" quality. In addition, the stories cover a vast geographical range, varying historical periods, and feature a stylistic diversity that plays freely with the precepts of plot and point of view, splintering pronouns and verb tenses, occasionally approximating verisimilitude. Perhaps here we should note that for Glover's brand of postmodernism, "literary realism," or whatever name it goes by, isn't necessarily stylistic anathema. While his works often self-consciously reject the historical and epistemological worldview of a conventional compositional model, at the same time Glover recognizes that such a limited aesthetic is simply one particular stylistic constellation, one that he is free to sample from as he chooses, usually within the framework of a highly subversive narrative. The result is that Glover's fiction is at once radical-minded and reader-friendly, revealing once again that these do not have to be contradictory assertions.

His prose style also contributes to his ultimate accessibility; while he is capable of an impressive syntactic range, his prose on the whole reflects a succinctness of expression, a predilection for direct declarative sentences, that might owe in part to his experience as a news writer. At its most mature, his style often attains an icy aphoristic clarity, without a lot of adjectival trappings—the prose equivalent of a magnesium burn, at once searing and subtle. Yet Glover changes idioms so frequently that it seems difficult to pin him down; his narrational modes veer from the erudite to the colloquial, from an articulate writerly despair to the cracked eloquence of a narrator in whom literacy is itself surprising.

Despite the undeniable substantive and technical variety of Glover's prose and despite the evidence of a linear developmental trajectory, Glover's oeuvre is perhaps even more distinguished by the myriad interconnections—stylistic affinities, situational correspondences, and image sharing—that exist from work to work (at times, whole stories appear to germinate spontaneously from a solitary phrase in one of its predecessors). Given the prevalence of this latent self-referentiality, frequently it seems that Glover is writing not several, but one big book, making for a body of work that resists a chronological approach. Some of these instances can, for our purposes, be dispensed with broadly. For example, Glover writes with equal facility from either side of the gender divide—many of his protagonists are women—and he also delves into the interstices with narrators who are, often equivocally, homosexual: an assertion of considerable interest for a gender-sensitive thematic approach to his work. Also, despite their tortured circumstances, Glover's characters often achieve a markedly upbeat perspective, however tenuous, by the close of the narrative: which is to say that Glover, ironically, is not averse to the happy ending. However, other shared features better illustrate, perhaps, the rich pageant of Glover's compositional habits, offering a viable inroad to a comprehensive stylistic survey of the works. What follows is such a typology of some of Glover's primary structural devices, one that, admittedly, can be only provisional, offering one possible configuration for the dense constellation of Glover's prose.

The Split Story

The first of Glover's hallmark devices is at once situational and stylistic; it is perhaps the one Glover works with most regularly at present and which he has been interrogated about in *Notes Home*: namely, many of his protagonists are in the grip of amnesia. However, as a condition, amnesia seems to carry connotations too benign to describe the severity of these glitches in identity. Often the crisis is a full-blown dissociative split, a form of fugue-state psychosis, rather than the more photogenic and functional soap-opera variety; correspondingly, these stories regularly feature Glover's structural penchant for splintered narratives and fugal patterning.

Of the numerous stories of this type, "A Guide to Animal Behavior" offers the most innocuous instance, relatively speaking, of mislaid identity. Despite the complexity of the situation, this slight story opens, as many Glover stories do, elegantly unobtrusive, with the simplicity of a welcome mat: "I am in bed with a woman who looks like a movie star, and I have lost my memory" (*Guide* 131). Nameless and fittingly naked, the narrator nevertheless reveals those qualities of character that we associate with identity; that is, despite his fundamental dislocation, he offers a fully personalized response to his sensual environment, commenting on his bedmate, "I find the combination of her beauty, her shamelessness and her snores moving in strange and delightful ways" (131).

As the story progresses, we swiftly learn about his partner's family history (she is pointedly named Tracy Mondesire), some of her bizarre sexual predilections (she can blow air from her vagina), and occupational skills ("She sells real estate to Arabs, nothing under a mil and a half" (132)). And quickly we realize that the narrator is equally trying to understand himself as an amalgam of material and behavioral attributes: he notes, "Our swimming pool has an undertow. I have set off the burglar alarm eighty-two times since moving in" (132). When Tracy has her publicist invent a tabloid-issue past for the narrator as fingerer of drug kingpins, he obligingly plays the part and takes to driving "a pink Fleetwood with zebra-skin seatcovers and an oog-gah horn" (133). On the thematic level, here Glover is posing fundamental existential questions, conflating two responses to a self constructed from the outside—Tracy who, if unlikeable, is existentially at home in such a universe, and the narrator who is lost within the same relativizing system. For the narrator, the only constant is sexual desire, which leads him into bed with Tracy, and with their maid Juanita, as well as with numerous other women in unidentified liaisons. His promiscuity notwithstanding, the narrator's condition is obdurate, and identity in any meaningful sense evades him.

Stylistically, this theme is perfectly suited to the present tense; as the narrator muddles through the flux of experience, little seems to hold, to adhere to him categorically, to invest him, simply, with a past. However, three times in the story, events trigger a treatment in the past tense: the first is the recounting of Tracy's biography, the second is the story Tracy's publicist disseminates about the narrator, and the third is the incidental encounter that closes the narrative. The narrator relates, "A woman stopped me in the street the other day. . . . She said she was my wife. She said she had married my brother Daken after I left like that. . . . We have three children, all brought up Christian" (133). This third shift to the past tense is multiply significant, providing closure both thematically and stylistically. On the simplest level, it functions as a structural return, giving a technical shapeliness to even this three-page work, but also it suggests that this alternate version of the narrator's past, while more homely and apparently less artificial, is equally powerless to remedy his condition. The emotionally uninflected distancing of the repetition ("She said") and the final reversion to the present tense in the last sentence indicate that, while the narrator seems willing to entertain the plausibility of the stranger's story, the existential malleability endures, and the crisis is unalleviated.

Nevertheless, the narrator of "A Guide" is surprisingly well adjusted to his dilemma, as he can remark about his new marriage, "I don't know how this happened, but we are having one hell of a time together" (133). Other similarly afflicted protagonists are not so fortunate. For example, *A Guide to Animal Behavior* contains another even more virtuosic rendition of the split story, "A Man in a Box." The situation is virtually identical, but "A Man" picks up where "A Guide" leaves off, as is clear in the story's first lines: "A woman followed me home to my box today, claiming to be my wife. I did not recognize her" (103). However, where "A Guide" offers a technically univocal, distanced narration, "A Man" offers a greater range of rhetorical effects and is, finally, a work of both greater difficulty and greater mastery.

Given this work's pervasive italics, segmentations, editorial intrusions and personalized shorthand, "A Man" can appear less like
a story than an orthographical event. However, such a surface level
response discounts the undeniable charge of pathos and the diaboli-
cal fun that the story delivers. The text consists of essentially two
disparate rhetorical strands, one recounting in its idiosyncratic way
a plot of escalating events, the other providing the fruits of the
narrator's writerly obsession, a staggering collection of numbered
"stick 'ems" with hyperbolic epistemological ambitions. On the level
of the plot, the narrator literally inhabits a box; he shares an alley
with another homeless couple who are by turns hostile and friendly.
He refers to himself as It and, like the narrator of "A Guide," lacks
both past and identity. Certain incidentals of his life crop up: he has
a job donning a sandwich-board advertisement for a Times Square
strip club that caters to bizarre tastes, and he frequents a nearby
mission for purported monthly showers, though he takes to visiting
daily. But the primary narrative trigger involves the repeated and
insistent visitations of the woman (named Hester, with a likely nod
to Hawthorne) who claims to be his wife; we learn that she has left
him for the store manager of Paramus, New Jersey's Toys R Us, and
she is currently trying to get him psychiatric help for the dissociative condition that keeps him box-bound. For her troubles, she receives a black eye, gets doused with a milk carton full of urine, and
is called into service to rescue It's compatriot, the other homeless
man, from a sanitation truck when he is inadvertently thrown out
with the trash.

The second strand, involving the catalog of Post-Its that cover
the interior walls of It's box, becomes progressively more elaborate
as the story progresses and more ambitious in its reach. The first
referenced stick 'em offers a tidbit of helpful commentary: "Stick
'em #131108 . . . mentions a theory about the verbal origins of certain diseases (shingles, bad smelly farts, fibrodisplasia ossificans
and plantar warts) and advises against exchanging words without a
physician's certificate" (103-04). In general the notes reflect a similar coarse hilarity, juxtaposing discursive registers, but they graduate to even more complex purposes. By the story's start, the narrator is no longer simply penning and affixing such notes to his box,
but he is already immersed in a second involuted stage of
"boxological research" (130), collating and renumbering the numbered notes in what he calls the LOAT, or List of All Things, project,
which entails additional emendation: "The LOAT system itself
raises a host of philosophical and grammatical—not to mention
medical, lexicographical, numerological and gnostic—questions,
questions which I intend to deal with in a separate preface to the

LOAT Concordance" (108). The goals of the project become clear later in the story, as the narrator remarks how it might ultimately approximate Textual Totality, or TT: "At TT, for example, it will be possible, at last, to decide if life (L) is meant to be read as a comedy or a tragedy, as romance or thriller, or some combination of genres, styles and points of view" (120). To this purpose the narrator even derives an equation, surprisingly intelligible in context: "the meaning of existence: $(t)n/AOAT=L$" (121). Gradually, the story suggests that in addition to such an absolute reach, the LOAT project subsumes every aspect of the text; the narrative segments, the visitations from Hester, are themselves stick 'em artifacts. Appropriately, the disparate rhetorical strands, despite their segmented alternation, are inextricably intertwined; the Post-Its illuminate the physical action, and the action even crosses literally into the LOAT project as Hester leaves a uniquely blue note to inform It of a psychiatric appointment she has scheduled for him (later giving rise to the beautiful line, "eyes the colour of blue stick 'ems" (126)).

The gorgeously crazed intricacies of the Post-Its probably indicate some of the complexity inherent in the story. However, on both the structural and thematic level (in a story like this one, such a distinction becomes pointless), "A Man" has even more in store. First, It's subjective displacement is so far advanced that he attributes the writing of the stick 'ems to multiple personages, none of whom are him, but one of whom might have been the Tom that the ex-wife Hester seeks (another is transparently named Ed Note). Second, the condition is here transferred onto the other characters as well as the locale; It confuses his New York with Weimar Germany, simply owing to a Teutonic news article he encounters and interpolates into his own experience, and for similar reasons he takes to calling his alley cohort Schalck-Golodkowsky (who might turn out to be one of the narrator's split selves). Further, at one point It remarks, "She was clearly deranged. I was not Tom, though I felt myself begin to acquire a veneer of Tom-ness through repetition and association" (113). Here we begin to see again something of the thematic import that "A Guide" offers as well, but with even more profound implication; for It, the problem of an externally constructed self becomes an overt meditation on the literariness of that outer/other self. For It, everything is a text to be decoded (characters, himself included, occasionally are tattooed with prose); his identity is partly determined by the rules of the system and, as such, is malleable, constantly recontextualized and reconstituted by an ultimately hostile universe. His box, then, is both a physical aggravation and a metaphor for an existential condition of textuality from which he can't escape.

On the structural level, the story's asymmetrical alternations between rescue efforts and boxology are all prefaced by an odd section heading, "1," from the start. This first numbered section includes all of the alley-action through the recovery of Schalck-Golodkowsky, but then we reach heading "2" (a much shorter section) and read: "It did not fulfill his goal of translating the Croatian stick 'ems with Prof. Schalck-Golodkowsky's help. Old S-G returned to Wandlitz [the alley], but he had clearly lost heart after his accidental run-in with the city sanitation truck" (127). Here, the first-person narration has veered into the third person to recount the end of the tale: It does avail himself, briefly, of the psychiatric services that Hester offers, but he clears out and leaves town after he reads (on the buttocks of a man in the mission shower) a newspaper story of the burning down of the Paramus Toys R Us. This last section is signed at the story's end, "Edward Note," whose name we recognize from the numerous parenthetical editorial intrusions. The implication is that It's dissociative split was triggered by heartbreak, that he really is Tom, and that even the provisional It identity collapses following his act of arson, now submerged within one of the multiple selves who has achieved a lyrical tranquility (as well as a vision capable of simplifying the LOAT project: the section headings offer a reduced version of the collation process). In the final paragraph Note relates, "It will step out on his tiny balcony, wipe his glasses and peer upward, marvelling at the innumerable pinpricks of light which spangle the firmament. At such moments, he feels the deepest peace. For in his heart, he knows that what he sees is nothing but the ceiling of yet another vast and mysterious box" (130). Like "A Guide," this story closes with the confirmation that the subjective nightmare, while inescapable, nevertheless retains its own unique consolations.

As an instance of the split story, "A Man in a Box" shows Glover at his most winningly radical (and, we might add, Nabokovian); however, as a structural and thematic program, the split develops to these heights from comparatively humble origins. "There Might Be Angels" in Glover's second collection offers what looks to be the genesis of this aesthetic preoccupation. Set on a Spanish train, the story is outwardly conventional, relating a compartment-sharing encounter between a complacently pious cheese-making abbot and a ruined tramp who manifests the dissociative state of so many Glover characters. Slowly, the abbot recognizes that the repulsive, hollowed out and nearly dead tramp (he seems a kind of Bartleby) is a former classmate and promising theological scholar, Silvestre. When pressed about his current condition, Silvestre relates a story about angels traveling in disguise and the temptation of a wife, all of which is thinly veiled autobiography revealing that Silvestre had failed, like It and the narrator of "A Guide," as a husband. The abbot finds himself confronted by a test of his own faith, his own capability to alleviate another's suffering, and he responds by legitimizing Silvestre's angelic hallucinations, claiming to be an angel himself, and ushering the scholar to a more peaceful death. What's interesting here is that, as the inception of the split story, the dementia is presented from an exterior third-person perspective; the later stories are narrated from within the subjective rift, freeing up more radical technical effects. Also, as the abbot takes it upon himself to decode and respond to Silvestre's madness, he seems to anticipate the reader's role regarding the later stories, which require similar decoding on our part. As a result, "There Might Be Angels" offers an early, never so explicitly repeated and possibly disavowed intimation that there is an ultimate sanctity in such a relationship, even if ultimately futile, in Glover's aesthetic.

Glover's most recent collection brims with stories of this type, all offering unique variations on the theme. In "Bad News of the Heart" (title story of the Dalkey Archive collection) the narrator, Hugo Tangent, is mildly amnesiac and magnificently deranged; upon his release from Bellevue, he engages in a despairing tryst with the discharging nurse and one of her friends (he continuously suspects they are automatons or aliens) and regularly lapses into recitations of stories that illuminate his unhappy life. In "State of the Nation" the unnamed narrator embarks on a voyeuristic relationship with a woman who lives across the street—an unstable situation that further deteriorates when the woman attempts to slash her wrists. As she recuperates in the hospital, she mistakes the narrator for her long-lost brother Buddy, a role the narrator assumes ambivalently and never really corroborates, but in Glover's universe we have to suspect the likelihood of unacknowledged kinship. Similarly, in "Abrupt Extinctions at the End of the Cretaceous," we are ostensibly allowed insight into the demise of the brontosaurs, as the saurian narrator kicks off the story with the anticlimactic explanation for the extinction, "We were tired. Yes, it was as simple as that" (*16 Categories* 119). The narrator proceeds to relate the poignant and tragic romance involving his friend and a third enormous herbivore: a premise with its own inherent charm, but again, since this is Glover's universe, it's likely that what we have is a narrator so deeply schizoid that the text is only analogically human.

Of the lot, perhaps "La Corriveau" is the consummate Glover fiction, as it highlights his deconstructive linguistic energy and his obsession with Canadianness and most clearly evinces his fugal approach to composition. Like "A Guide," the story opens postcoitus in the nude; however, this time our amnesiac narrator, an English Canadian tourist in Quebec for the winter carnival, is female, and the situation possesses a further distinctive nuance in that her partner is dead. Despite certain evidentiary niceties (she admits it is her knife sticking out of the man's back), she is unable to own up to the murder, but instead props the corpse in a chair on the subzero veranda of her hotel room and sets out on a tour of the town, hoping equally to account for his death and remedy a pretty bad headache. At length, the police take her into custody (she gets nabbed at the zoo—an event not depicted in the text's present action), and when a detective leads her to reconstruct her activities of the previous day, her memory of her culpability is restored and the text closes with an ironic plea of extenuating circumstances that falls on the detective's (and possibly the reader's) deaf ears.

Such is the plot of the story, which is remarkable for its touches of dark comedy and the crisp staccato cadences of the searingly brief sentences and paragraphs. However, what happens, as with many Glover stories, doesn't accurately reflect the work's structural ambitions. Rather, "La Corriveau" is a dense matrix of repeating elements, each modulated and variously inflected to create variety and movement in the ostensibly static wavelengths.

The most distinct of these constituent parts is the series of references to Quebecois tourist brochures that document morbid incidents of the city's history. As she ambles through town, the narrator reflects on the veranda-propped dead man: "Does he hear the lurid song of La Corriveau, the Siren of Quebec (see those tourist brochures), who murdered her husband and was hanged and exposed in an iron cage above a crossroads till her body rotted? (Later the cage became a minor exhibit in Mr. Barnum's circus—you can make whatever you want of this outré fact.)" (*16 Categories* 17). Given the correspondence between this legend and the story's title, clearly here we have an explicit clue that our narrator is herself a murderess. However, even while resolving most directly the story's primary mystery, this passage is just one of five such brochure references. The others include mentions of Hélèn Boullé, who was Champlain's preteen bride, Bishop Laval who died of penitential frostbite, Marie de l' Incarnacion, who abandoned her children for the convent, as well as a broader prophetic vision of severed heads on an ice-bound river. Collectively, these other brochure references might act as false leads, taking the pointed edge off of the Corriveau reference; however, on a structural level, they exist solely as a stylish mechanism of coherence that runs counter to the traditional narrative emphasis on linear action. At the same time, on the thematic level, they further suggest that the narrator's subjective displacement here implicates national issues of identity. Just as the narrator is self-divided, so is the country: between French and English heritage, between versions of history and heroism, between simply male and female. The personal here dovetails with the political, without sacrificing any of the situational ambiguity, the punch of the narrator's discrete suffering, or lapsing into conventional moralistic truisms. And finally, as these passages regularly alternate with the exposition of the narrative events, they seem to stripe the text like the rhetorical shadow of the cage bars that imprison La Corriveau; like It from "A Man in a Box," this narrator is in her own way box-bound, the story constituting her cage at the crossroads.

Even on the level of the physical action, "La Corriveau" again features a conspicuous element of recurrence: the nearly continuous references to ice, particularly in the form of the ice sculptures the city has commissioned for the celebration. The first mention of ice occurs in the context of the narrator touching the dead man's earlobe, which is simply "cold as ice" (12). Later, as she circulates through town, she encounters the sculptures at every turn (both immediately following the murder and in the company of the detective), and near the story's end, this image undergoes further development. The narrator recounts how "People walking in the streets take on the aspect of ice statues. Ice statues begin to resemble ordinary tourists, shoppers and dead calèche drivers" (20), and later she complains that "A gusty wind drives swirls of ice particles round the lampposts and into our faces" (22). In the story's climax, "the ice statues come alive, wounded soldiers piled in heaps, dying generals, weeping savages, fatherless children, widows touching themselves in ecstasies of loneliness" (22). This modulation in the treatment of the recurring image establishes the story's developmental trajectory, not finally all that different from Aristotle's model of rising action: a progressive escalation that simultaneously radicalizes and serves traditional narrative requirements. What's more, given the correspondence between the ice sculptures and the tourist-brochure passages (both depict images from French Canadian history) and the swift, nonchalant prose style, the story is at once multiform and fluid, elastically prismatic: it's as if the reader peers through those ice crystals that sting the self-estranged narrator.

Glover refers to such recurring rhetorical elements as, in student-friendly terminology, "globs"; in *Notes Home* he clarifies: "A glob then is just a chunk of information that fits somewhere into a narrative. . . . Globs can be scenes, scene fragments, bits of dialogue, digressions, interjected stories, descriptions, summaries, anything"

(39). And most Glover fictions, even those most outwardly conventional, are frankly globular constructions. To discuss an aesthetic composition in these terms tends to elide the scintillating potential implicit in the design strategy; it sounds bluntly mechanical, and it is, partly, if we buy into the stigma that has long plagued Viktor Shklovsky's brand of formalism in the annals of literary criticism. In his landmark essay on *Tristram Shandy,* when Shklovsky identifies discursive digression as one of the novel's primary structural gambits, he is indifferent to the maneuver as an offshoot of social commentary. Instead, he concerns himself only with the aesthetic necessity to defamiliarize literary conventions, to breathe fresh life into forms that immediately grow stale. Such an approach generally holds more appeal for writers (interested in how it's done) than for readers (interested in what it means); in fact, it's possible that, in addition to iron-fisted Bolshevik opposition, this hothouse aestheticism contributed partly to the demise of formalism—its descriptive stylistic insights contain precious little humanistic argumentative traction. While Glover's fiction offers considerably more in the way of an organic/humanistic response, at the same time his formalist disposition testifies to the enduring necessity to continually reinvent prose poetics: a constant recalibration of the textual equalizer, balancing well-worn and newly minted devices. And one has to concede that a good part of the pleasure his prose delivers stems from the "simple" appreciation of a work's compositional design; in Glover's fiction we are invited to marvel at the infinitely nuanced possibilities of literary form.

Repeated Action/Recurring Event

Just as Glover's penchant for fugal structural schemes is his way of exploring alternative narrative possibilities, his work features additional devices that serve the same innovative purpose. To circumvent, disrupt, or undermine linear action he sometimes subjects his characters to a cycle of repeated events, a kind of behavioral redux that punctuates the narrative course. In *Notes Home* Glover suggests that he might have learned the device from Hubert Aquin; about Aquin's fiction he writes, "This repetition of the same event is the antithesis of plot because it denies uni-directional time; it is an anti-plot" (49). And we should note that in the split stories discussed above, this device surfaces from time to time, in the repeated box-visitations of Hester, in La Corriveau's retracing of her narrative steps. However, Glover was plying this device perhaps most strenuously earlier in his career, particularly in his second novel, *The South Will Rise at Noon.*

Set in the rural backwaters of gulf-coast Florida, the novel is narrated by Tully Stamper, a cracked eccentric whose interests include taxidermy and ornithology. He owns a curio shop, is an earnest dabbler in the fine arts, and is also pursuing romantic liaisons with three women. One is his ex-wife, Lydia (blonde and leggy to boot), who is currently remarried to a celebrated Hollywood producer, and the novel opens with Stamper's unceremonious return (after a stint in jail) to the town of Gomez Gap, whereupon he immediately climbs into bed with Lydia and her husband, attempting to have sex with her while she sleeps.

The other two women whom Tully pursues gracelessly are Danger Babcox, a sultry tough and mother to two poignant daughters, and Ruth Appledorn, a candidly unattractive animal-behaviorist whose research project involves firing a paint cannon at the gulf-coast laughing gulls, daubing them in neon colors. As Tully cycles through his potential inamoratas, the town prepares simultaneously for the staged reenactment of the Battle of Gomez Gap (a Confederate defeat, according to the novel's history). The action is madcap, with numerous vying plotlines, and the book is eminently readable. Tully seemingly moves from crisis to crisis: from his unabashedly horny mother, who thinks she has murdered a would-be bedmate, to a local sheriff who is a periodic menace, to Tully's own efforts to secure a role in Lydia's husband's film, hampered by bouts of self-medication (bourbon and barbiturates) and ongoing paroxysms of conscience. As the book reels toward its conclusion, the smaller, more intimate set pieces escalate into the swell of humanity preparing for the mock-battle. But once the director delivers his rousing exhortatory speech, cuing the action by intoning the novel's title line, the playacting slowly grades into genuine conflict, owing to some directorial incentive ($200) to rewrite history as well as the presence of an all-black Union platoon of which Tully has been given command: the artificial construct poses a real threat. Throughout, Tully is a bumbler, a ne'er-do-well, a loser, but under duress, he comports himself admirably, for the first time unselfishly, and narrowly averts a massacre, sacrificing himself in the process.

Ultimately, Tully's redemption from his characteristic failure is presented in terms of the recovery of his aesthetic vision, and all along the novel is exploring this question, conflating differing aesthetics. First, there is Tully who suffers from painter's block and has only his taxidermy as a surrogate art form: programmatically imitative and tinged with morbidity, at one point this art produces a monstrosity that repulses its audience (i.e., Lydia). Lydia's husband, the director Otto Osterwilder, supplies a second aesthetic alternative, advocating a not-quite-mimetic art form, as is clear early on when Tully apes the film reviewer: "Osterwilder's rigorous psychological realism is combined with a style that is baroque and operatic—naturalism and neo-realism have no attraction for this child of the cinema. . . . In form, his films are invariably corrosive melodramas. . . . They are technical funhouses, cinematic carnivals" (30-31). While this passage applies equally to the book Tully is writing, still this aesthetic too is ultimately a doomed enterprise. In the avowedly scrupulous re-creation of the battle, despite the visceral response it provokes in the participants, such an aesthetic operates solely at the level of parody or as a parody of itself. Tully's antagonists are distorted caricatures of the worst human impulses—racist, cruel, and violent—and even Tully's mock-heroism seems to stop just short of the poetic legitimacy that Nabokov, for example, ascribes to a parodic aesthetic in *The Real Life of Sebastian Knight* (91). What's more, since Tully's metatextual aesthetic here aligns with that of his antagonist, we have to suspect that there's another option.

The novel does present a third aesthetic alternative in the person of Kinch, Tully's curio-shop assistant, whom Tully commissions to ghost-paint a canvas in an attempt to win back Lydia's affection. Kinch's art is a collage of styles and materials, partly representational and partly surreal (or suprareal) in its formal incongruities (one of Ruth's painted gulls is the central focus, a portrait of Tully occupies a corner), and again, we can't help but recognize in Kinch's painting a metaphorical extension of the book we're reading: an aesthetic moment by which Tully recognizes the true thematic undercurrents of his surface agonies (the Polaroids pasted to Tully's hands are as subtle as stigmata). Tully sums up his response, "It was strange to see, like meeting yourself coming around a corner. For a moment I felt stunned, empty, near tears" (140-41). However, this aesthetic also invites the reader's skepticism as it is undermined by the novel's poetic denouement. Of his time in Gomez Gap, Tully reflects in the novel's last paragraphs:

> I will always remember this: Half-tide. A pair of Ibises hunting in single file in the shallow bayou behind Danger's house. . . . Against the cotton-batting clouds that stand low offshore and obscure Dog Island and Corrigan's Reef, I can see fishermen motoring up and down the channel, standing in the sterns of their open crab boats, looking comic in baggy pants, Wellington boots and baseball caps. And everywhere there is the sound of boat engines, birds calling and the gentle insistent tap-tapping of an oyster hammer. (265)

Here Tully has attained an aesthetic vision that is transportive, transcendent, rendered in a Wordsworthian present tense. Ultimately, it seems the only legitimate aesthetic option, as suggested by the sacramental tone and Tully's absenting himself, for the most part, from the composition, as if he has finally broken clear of the self-pity and self-absorption that drove him to distraction, both losing and finding himself in his new vision. Even if there remains a certain interesting irreducibility in the handling of the conflated aesthetics, the process doesn't quite yield the scintillating experience that characterizes Glover's later works. In stories like "The Canadian Travel Notes of Abbè Hugues Pommier, Painter, 1663-1680" (*A Guide*) and even "La Corriveau" with its Pygmalion overtones, Glover continues to explore the metasubject of aesthetic creation, generating even more satisfying and provocative ambiguities.

Still, there is much to commend this novel, which is at present out of print, as it reveals another facet of Glover's talent and provides a benchmark for his stylistic development. Most interesting here are the glimpses of the novel's formal architecture. The vast majority of the action spans a mere three days in Tully's down-and-out Gomez Gap—on the night of the third day, there's a crucifixion of sorts in a pine tree that occupies far more time temporally than textually. However, the three primary days all seem to have similar rhythms: with Tully awaking in the throes of conflict—Day 1 attempting to violate Lydia, Day 2 aiding his mother with her nearly dead bedmate, Day 3, more sedately, perusing postal testimony that he has bottomed out—then cycling through crisis moments with Ruth, Danger, and the townsfolk, not necessarily in the same order. Moreover, each of the first two days ends with Tully bedding down alone in a dilapidated boathouse, where he contemplates his ruinous existence and is visited by an unidentifiable lover in the dark. Tully writes, "I lay where I fell, staring into the Gothic vaults of night frescoed with the after-images of my desire, taking uneasy, faltering stock of my day. Had I done anything I could be remotely proud of?" (177). Given this recurrence and the images looted from Christian symbology of Tully's regeneration, it's as if he is locked in a cycle of persecution with nightly returns to an eroticized Gethsemane. Of the sexual congress, Tully remarks, "I wanted it always to be like this, all secrecy and ignorance. Without names, without words to give us definitions and rights. I wanted my love to be always separate from the world of daylight, this drunkenness of limbs, this ghostly presence, absence of guilt and ties" (178). Just as the self-analysis provides the ethical terms (and therefore the trigger, in a way) for Tully's gradual change, the sex is similarly replenishing, restorative. The result is that while the returns to the boathouse effect a kind of narrative stasis, a disruption of linear progress, at the same time these returns contain the forward-looking seeds of Tully's freedom from the cycle.

Another character of roughly the same period finds herself in a similar situational redundancy: the female protagonist of "Fire Drill" (*Dog Attempts*) is mildly neurotic, incapable of responding in crisis situations and also unable to have sex with her husband. In the course of the story her instability is tested and finally alleviated by way of her daughter, Erin, who has recently started kindergarten, where the first curricular requirement, apparently, is to teach fire safety or, in the narrator's words, to instill a "morbid and abnormal obsession with fire hazards" (120). On consecutive days Erin is put through the drill, first on the bus, then, for practice, in the school, and then Erin relates that there's a third drill scheduled, "a real fire drill" timed by the faculty (120). In broadest terms this is a story built out of fire drills. However, the third go-round raises the stakes considerably in that a real fire obliges the cautious administrators by sparking on the scheduled day. Erin finds the drills frightening initially, although she remains much cooler than her mother throughout, but in the fire she acquits herself admirably, overcomes her fears, and helps console frightened classmates. When she sees her daughter's level-headed response and resources of strength, the narrator is herself jostled slightly out of her anxiety and the story ends with her phoning the husband to rush home from work for a "quickie" (126).

This phone call is itself a less overt kind of repeated event, as it represents the narrator's knee-jerk response to the fire drills; she first calls her husband, asking him to come home for crisis-management, later grapples with not calling him, and at last does call him for their sexual reconciliation. As with *The South Will Rise at Noon,* the recurrences here certainly mark a departure from the conventional model of linear action; however, the disruption is not so severe that the story loses temporal and developmental momentum. It would be considerably more baffling if the return involved, not a subsequent installment of the event, but the same installment: if the first fire drill were to happen over and over, with little to no variation in the particulars. But on the whole Glover tends to favor stylistic distortion rather than the more thoroughgoing textual ruptures and involutions that might characterize high-modernist practice.

Glover continues to use "Fire Drill" as a pedagogical guide to effecting structure in short fiction; however, Glover's most recent work reveals how far he has extended the possibilities of the device, especially in the story "Iglaf and Swan" (*16 Categories*). "This is how it goes:" the story begins, "a boy named Iglaf . . . met a girl named Swan at a potluck supper and open mike poetry reading in the basement of the Estonian Church on Broadview the summer of 1969"

(47). Both partners have literary ambitions—Iglaf becomes a writing teacher; Swan ultimately achieves a measure of poetic notoriety as the interfering "guardian" (57) of her daughter's work—so again, we see Glover broaching the subject of aesthetic failure in the course of an artistic success. But more important for our present purpose, the story is narrated from a seemingly maxed-out, distanced third-person perspective that alternates irregularly between the nascent lovers' points of view (as well as their daughter's, eventually). After some initial gestures at scene-setting or grounded narrative action (". . . Swan woke up, wrapped a sheet around her breasts, sniffed the smell of burnt ticking . . ." (47)), the story reads as very nearly pure exposition, only occasionally rising to fully rendered scenes: a narrative stripped bare of its conventional trappings, wholly told (as opposed to shown, in the old dichotomy).

From this, their first sexual encounter, it's clear that the affair is doomed; nevertheless, the two marry, have a child, Lily, engage in extramarital affairs, separate, survive the suicide of their daughter, and grow old, periodically coming together to resuscitate the spent remains of their affection. All told, the action, if one can call it that, spans nearly two decades, and the characters' lives seem to be slowly evaporating over time (one could call this distanced effect a hyperrealism). In fact, crucial narrative events are often rendered by implication, rather than depicted as concrete scenes: for example, Lily's method of suicide is alluded to (pills and a plastic bag), but receives no stage time (54). Similarly, Glover overtly disavows any pretensions of a traditional climactic scheme. The story concludes with a brief summational addendum (a frequent textual maneuver in Glover's work): a section that begins, "All the rest is twilight, bits of life manufactured without hope. Iglaf and Swan are not old; there are no dramatic exits available," and proceeds to lapse in and out of the future tense (59). The narrative technique here is as hollowed out as its characters, generating an evanescent poignancy rather than a chill indifference.

Lacking all else, the story proffers sentences of a devastating beauty. In the aftermath of Lily's suicide, the lovers briefly reconcile, an optimistic gesture pierced with enervating qualifications: "They both knew there was some trickery involved; they had acted so long, they no longer yearned for an end to the acting but for clear and simple parts, as close as most of us come to honesty" (55). And, "They only wished that the moment could go on and on, that they could exist forever on the cusp of someone else's death, that they could always feel this important, tragic and redeemed" (56). However, on the structural level, despite the textual cavities and pervasive ephemerality, there are certain organizing principles in the form of recurrences. One could argue that the lovers' affairs and their temporary reconciliations are themselves a pattern of repeated behaviors that here, ironically, stabilize the narrative against a hypertrophied linearity. Further, there's an even more overt element performing a similar function: the lovers' first sexual encounter, which opens the story, returns twice, once from Iglaf's perspective and once from Swan's, as both characters remember their relationship's hopeless inception. Iglaf is said to reflect, "He saw himself and Swan reading their poetry nearly twenty years before in the church basement on Broadview, remembered making love, the smell of burnt ticking, the sultry resonance of Swan's voice and the long, shameful years that followed, and making love again on the night Lily died" (58). With the repeated returns to the primal scene, as it were, it's as if their first meeting haunts the narrative, working against the swift advance of years, effecting a structural coherence and underscoring their relationship's characteristic impossibility, which had been present from the start.

Disjunctive Threading

Another of Glover's formal devices, disjunctive threading occurs largely within the short fiction and usually entails skewering a representational or experiential narrative (distinguished by grounded action, scene-setting, and the like) with a second, much more slender discursive vein. It might be a dialogue with the dead or something even more tenuously related to the narratorial consciousness of a given story, in either case developed incrementally, the thread remaining not fully disclosed until very near the story's end. We might say that this technical maneuver is merely an emaciated version of the broader-scale interpolations of, for example, "A Man in a Box." And like the device of repeated action, this one reveals a similar evolutionary trajectory, appearing predominantly in Glover's first and second story collections, virtually disappearing in *A Guide,* and resurfacing almost unrecognizably in the title story of *16 Categories of Desire.*

Of the seven stories in *The Mad River,* three feature threading devices in various guises. First, there is "Panther," which presents an alternative version of the Gospels' postcrucifixion Christian account: according to MacKendrick, a reworking of "an apocryphal legend of Christ's Roman heritage and of His death in Britain as a crippled healer who literally takes on men's particular ills" (121). Narrated by a captured priestess, the experiential detail of her hard use by the Romans and ultimate salvation is periodically interrupted by italicized assertions that stand outside the story and give it an incantatory edge: *"Yea, this I saw"* (110). It's as if the story doesn't exist in one linear, completed circuit, but is instead cyclical and infinitely repeated.

In "Wild Horses" the experiential facade of the tale is itself a bit more complex, disjunctive in its own right. The story consists of three sections, two narrated from Lucy's point of view; lulled into near-dementia by her marriage, she sits by the hospital beds of terminal children. The third (middle) section is narrated from the perspective of Father O'Donnel, who presides over the hospital ward and experiences a spiritual regeneration through his contact with Lucy. Here, the threaded device, again italicized and addressed to a now-defunct lover, involves the halting elaboration of a narrative subevent, recounting an incident when Lucy's father razed a corral fence to admit the passage of a herd of wild horses: *"Julio, my love, did I ever tell you about the wild horses? How they would go scudding across the plains near our home like ships at sea"* (80). However, the device, by the story's end, is co-opted by the experiential segments: "And so she sits whispering her vision in the darkness. It is good to say it. It has been in her mind all day" (81). Surrounded by her "Flowers of suffering" (80), the disease-ravaged children, she receives the concluding narrative benediction: "She is not sure what [her threaded story] means, is vaguely aware it is sentimental. She knows she is not a special person. . . . But the direction is there. The fence is down and she is free to move off toward the sunset" (82). Lucy might be in the dark, but for us the implication is fairly clear: she has found a kind of redemption through a gesture of *"extravagance"* (81), like her father's making way for the horses, enduring sacrifice in the name of beauty. Thus in this story the threaded device both establishes a fitful linear continuity among the isolate segments and supplies a radical complement to the text's primary discursive register.

In each of the preceding stories, to varying degrees, you might feel as if you're watching Jacob wrestle with the angel; the clenches tend to be tortured, running short on the grace that characterizes Glover's recent achievements. Nevertheless, the third threaded *Mad River* story, "Between the Kisses and the Wine," provides, surprisingly, an ur-"La Corriveau" and illustrates another category of textual interpolation. The experiential segments are wildly disjunctive, a design the text appears to flaunt from the outset: the episode headed "Marsha's Subway Train #1" concludes, "I hold little parties for myself at which I make punch and sing for entertainment. . . . My punch is different every time I make it. I go to the liquor store and buy three or four different things and pour them all into the silver ice bucket I got from father's estate. . . . And voila—Marsha's

Subway Train" (83). The text is just such a concoction, its modular form partly chronological but nowhere linear, including decontextualized quotes from the narrator's brother, a philosopher-poet driven to the madhouse after witnessing his father's self-immolation. The narrator recounts some of the circumstances that have led to her solitary alcoholism—not quite incestuous relationships with her brother and stepfather, her bizarre first date and first sexual encounter, as well as a short trip with her mother to Florida in which she nonchalantly opts for suicide ("I got sunburned the second day and slashed my wrists on her bed" (97)). In their technical handling, these disclosures range from concrete moments that include dialogue and scene-setting to ultradistanced reflections. But at the same time, among the segments a recurring italicized voice (the narrator's, possibly in another orbit of consciousness) appears, slowly gaining momentum: *"Last night I got twisted on Negronis and Angel Dust. I slept with Brian, the dobro player . . . "* (84). Near the end of the story, we get the conclusion of this event more or less in full. The narrator coerces the gay dobro player into having sex, after which he kills himself; the ensuing complications with the authorities and her conscience then drive the narrator deeper into despair. As a result, in this story the threaded element is of considerable narrative moment—one might argue that if there's a story to be told, a present action, it exists on this textually subordinate level, the rest offering a disjunctive biography (not entirely without its own narrative impetus) of the psychological construct that surrounds her becoming an accomplice to suicide. Here the threaded device inverts a more conventional narrative treatment.

In Glover's next collection, *Dog Attempts to Drown Man in Saskatoon,* the device doesn't enjoy quite as much narrative force. "The Seeker, the Baba, and the Snake" is set in a powerfully rendered Indian locale: "The heat stunned him. In the square outside Puri Station beggars, brandishing their stumps, swarmed like maggots. A pyre smouldered by the river as kites swung expectantly on the thermals. Bearded mystics, caked in blood and ashes, skewered with nails, staggered in ecstasy" (71). Kenneth Malory has arrived on the subcontinent to be with an old lover, for whom he feels partly responsible, on her deathbed in an ashram; ultimately, her condition is terminal, and, excepting glimpses of the lovers' backstory, she never rises to consciousness in the text. This grounded discursive level has an overt allegorical reach as Malory finds himself between vying cosmological systems, at a cultural crossroads with eternal ramifications: he insists upon his lover's drug abuse to comprehend her death, but the baba explains her suffering in theologically loaded terms, as if supernatural powers are in play. The story's threaded discourse further exacerbates this tendency. Again told incrementally and distinguished by italics, the threaded discourse broaches an alternative narrative register, a loose textual approximation of Malory's nightmare involving cobras and an existential dissolution: *"He imagined the snake emerging downward from the wattles of the roof, lengthening in the emptiness of night . . ."* (83). MacKendrick calls this discursive level "the real truth" (128) of the conflicting systems at the ashram, and it does have that feel, apparently corroborating Hindu cosmology, partly because in this story the threaded element, presented in full, provides the concluding textual unit, rather than a return to the grounded discursive register.

After a long hiatus spanning two novels and a story collection, the device resurfaces only vestigially in "16 Categories of Desire." No longer italicized, the threaded vein here consists of the segmented disbursement of the title catalog: a list of sixteen "bad" desires imparted to the narrator by Sister Mary Buntline, a Catholic nun and also the narrator's former lover. And the list is seamlessly interwoven with the story's action, which opens with the narrator's mother crawling up the church steps towing her oxygen bottle in a show of religious prostration, while the narrator herself idly looks on, pointedly smoking cigarettes.

"16 Categories" bristles with sexual and destructive energy, a combustible atmosphere rendered nonchalantly through the narrator's idiosyncratic and charming pidgin-speak that finesses distinctions between past and present tense. Again, as Glover's fiction so often does, this story conflates two ethical constructs. On one side, there is the narrator's mother, a comically distorted figure of Puritanical denial. When prodded about the circumstances of her daughter's conception, the mother replies, "I let him do it under the covers and only lifted my shift high enough so he could put it in" (178). Currently, between her ritualistic attempts to scale the church steps, the mother is chastely courting Mr. Bennett, a decrepit neighbor; her sexual inhibitions and general hatefulness contributed partly to the suicide of the narrator's father (he slit his own throat), and Bennett too is doomed by her company (a jealous nurse murders him).

On the other side, there is Sister Mary Buntline, who exists only in the backstory of the text—the lovers' relationship concludes after they are discovered in a tryst and beaten nearly to death—and her categories of bad desire: "The first bad category of desire is the desire to have a baby with a man. And the second is to put warm peeled carrots up your ass when you come. She laugh, laugh. And the third is to learn to French inhale when you smoke a cigarette. And the fourth is martyrdom. And the fifth is to relieve yourself in public" (179). The narrator sheds light on the import of the list when she recollects how Sister Mary, "say sometime she just want, not even knowing what she want, that she want only to submit to the wanting, just say to life anything any way and close her eyes" (180). That is, while she might pay lip service to the condemnation of bad desires and even punish herself with her "whippy thing," Sister Mary's worldview is eye-poppingly receptive to the urges of the flesh, sanctifying her affair with the twelve-year-old narrator, and permissive even of the beating that the lovers receive at the hands of their assailants. Similarly, like a good novitiate, the narrator's signature response to events—a minor recurring gesture—is the terse and expansive affirmation, "Surely" (179). While in a sense moralistic and damning to the mother's ethical tenets, this is a place beyond moralizing, an experiential openness that is finally the only source of emotional comfort in the text. Additionally, Claire Wilkshire notes how the narrator's nostalgia for the Sister's companionship is a "doubled desire, since it represents not merely longing for the past, but for that particular past because it was full of longing" ("Story"), which further deepens the text's thematic register: the storytelling impulse itself appears to endorse the Sister's position beyond the dichotomy.

As a threading device, the list in this story is remarkable for both its lunatic substantive excesses and its graceful structural deployment. Rather than accruing textual space as they unfold, the progressive installments gradually diminish in size, never to be reiterated in total. For example, after three multiple-item returns to the list, the narrator revives the thread succinctly, "She say the fifteenth category of desire is the petty cruelty of the weak and the disappointed" (182). Interestingly, the last, equally succinct installment near the story's end—"the sixteenth bad category of desire is the desire for Our Lord pure and simple" (186)—reprises the story's opening lines, providing narrative closure of the most technical variety. However, to say that the list alone dominates the structural design is slightly misleading in that the text does generate significant momentum through the depiction of the lovers' affair (of which the list is a part) as well as the mother's repeated sallies up the church steps. That is, both plotlines manifest overt escalations in pitch—for example, the mother's concluding foray incites an orgy of like-minded penitents (184)—yet so far removed from a linear/causal development that the mother's repeated ascents seem to wink slyly at the convention of rising action. As a result, then, the threaded device, rather than standing outside of the narrative as complement, has here burrowed in, occupying a more fluid and integral discursive plane; it comprises one facet of a textual universe that is brutal, comic and perverse, that is to say, a universe of cracked and enduring beauty.

Embedded Metaphorical Event

While all of the preceding devices are fairly clearly delineated in text—distinct topographical features, as it were—Glover's use of embedded metaphorical event is slightly less apparent to the eye as it enacts, as much as it subverts, the discursive habits of verisimilitude. These embedded events, or subevents, consist of narrative moments that encapsulate in microcosm a story's primary narrative impetus. For example, in "Woman Gored by Bison Lives" (*A Guide*), the dominant narrative involves a woman whose lover, Susan, is stricken by and finally succumbs to cancer, and the story recounts the nuances of their preparation for the imminent tragedy (the narrator compulsively photographs Susan, Susan attempts to make arrangements for her daughter's well-being). Before the cancer is well advanced, the couple takes a trip to a bison farm where they watch as another visitor climbs into the paddock to photograph a bull and is subsequently gored (not fatally) in the thigh. The encounter with the bison is telling in that it provides a bitter counterpoint to Susan's condition; one woman does something terminally stupid and survives, another does nothing ostensibly to provoke the proprietary divinities and is nevertheless condemned. As the text asks, "WHAT IS WRONG WITH THIS PICTURE?" (183). However, the encounter with the bison also speaks to the narrator's position regarding her lover's illness as she similarly confronts the advance of an overpowering natural force, which maims her in a way perhaps even more lasting. On this level as well, the minor event acts as a metaphor, mirroring, reproducing, or allegorizing the dominant event.

Spread broadly over Glover's career, stories of this type sometimes grade into near-conventionality on the one hand and radical narrative instabilities on the other. Among them is "My Romance," which Claire Wilkshire calls "by far the most striking" story of *16 Categories of Desire* ("Story"), and again the embedded event verges on the ludicrous. While the narrator struggles to stave off suicide after the death of his infant son (his marriage falls to pieces, he embarks on a sadomasochistic affair with his son's doctor), he befriends Mike, the son of motel proprietors who own a pet Brazilian monkey. On a drunken binge with the narrator, Mike nearly shoots the monkey, but then, through a change of heart or perhaps incompetence, allows it to escape out the window. In this story the narrative subevent doesn't offer quite the same situational equation as

"Woman Gored," but rather provides a more ambiguous correspondence: one of tonality as much as anything else. We might say that the narrator's loss of his son is similarly ludicrous, an event so pointlessly tragic that it defies reason and indeed causes rationality to buckle. Also, while the monkey's fate is never resolved, the narrator closes the story by remarking, "Mike . . . believes the monkey just kept walking, and somehow is on his way back to Brazil, home" (45). In this, the monkey's fate appears to mirror the narrator's equally touching, unlikely, and possibly temporary reconciliation with his wife. As with "Woman Gored," the nuanced handling of the embedded event by no means exhausts what "My Romance" holds in store technically; rather, in every instance the embedded event is simply one particularly luminous stellar mass amid a complex structural constellation. The works that result from this intricate coordination are among the most poignant and viscerally affective in Glover's oeuvre.

Perhaps the early masterpiece "Dog Attempts to Drown Man in Saskatoon" is the most illustrative case. The story again presents a marriage on the verge of dissolution as its primary subject; however, here the situation is tinged with a lyrical irony. The story begins, "My wife and I decide to separate, and then suddenly we are almost happy together" (97). The action then purports to describe an eleventh-hour visit to the Saskatoon art museum (which is itself the source of significant irony in that the building was formerly a slaughterhouse), but instead the narrative forks considerably in the course of the isolated, lengthy paragraphs that comprise the text. Rather than pressing the narrative potential of the trip to the art museum, the narrator consciously rejects this event in favor of a self-reflexive compositional process. He continually returns to the story's first sentence and subjects it to metaphysical qualification. As MacKendrick points out, such a story "asks the reader to distrust narrative as well as the tendency to fictionalize experience" (131). The narrator offers a blunt description of his method: "Traditional story writers compose a beginning, a middle and an end, stringing these together in continuity as if there were some whole which they represented. Whereas I am writing fragments and discursive circumlocutions about an object that may not be complete or may be infinite" (102). Among the fragments, we receive vignettes, veering between past and present tense, that flesh in Lucy's character, which is "composed in the sense of being made up or put together out of pieces" (104): for example, the couple's first meeting after Lucy's surgery to have supernumerary toes removed (101) or a definitive visit to an outdoor puppet-show (109). Another fragment, near the story's end, recounts the singular embedded event in which the narrator helps rescue a blind man and his seeing-eye dog from a freezing river.

Isolated from the chronology established by the visit to the art museum, the rescue attempt (that is, the structural device, the embedded event) supplies the most sustained verisimilar experience in the text, and, positioned at the end, it likewise provides an oddly dislocated escalation of drama. The precisely rendered narration includes, "He is a strange bearlike creature, huge in an old duffel coat with its hood up, steam rising around him, his face bloated and purple, his red hands clawing at the ice shelf, an inhuman 'awing' sound emanating from his throat" (111). As the blind man and the dog are swept by the current, the dog locates its owner in the water and places its paw on the man's shoulder, thus giving rise to the newspaper headline and the story's title; ultimately, the man is rescued while the dog drowns. The narrator begins to broach the metaphorical implications of the event when, after positing competing explanations for the interpretive dilemma of the dog's paw, he remarks, "man and dog together are emblematic—that is my impression at any rate—they are the mind and spirit, one blind, the other dumb; one defeated, the other naïve and hopeful, both forever going out. . . . [T]he act is full of a strange and terrible mystery, of beauty" (113). However, the final metaphorical implication is reserved for the story's concluding lines. The last paragraph again reprises the story's first line, then passes through the dichotomy that characterizes the narrator's failed marriage—"There are two kinds of courage: the courage that holds things together [Lucy's] and the courage that throws them away [the narrator's]"—before disclosing the final circumlocution: "sometimes I remember . . . well . . . the icy water is up to my neck and I hear the ghost dog barking, she tried to warn me; yes, yes, I say, but I was blind" (114). Here, unlike the stories discussed above, the narrator lays bare, to use Shklovsky's term, the embedded event as an overt metaphor for the primary narrative layer. What's more, this brief, terminal paragraph successfully fuses the story's varied rhetorical energies—the repetition of the first line, the marital vignettes, the embedded event—generating a surprising harmony out of the narrative dissonance.

If one story could be said to explode the Aristotelian devices of "realistic" narrative, it would be "Dog Attempts to Drown Man in Saskatoon." Here the conventional configuration of plot and character is exposed as a kind of institutionalized dishonesty, and the radicalized narrative, the narrative that is suspicious of its own inadequacy, is rendered by default that much more honest, closer to the kind of truth that the narrator, and humanity in general, hopes to achieve. This is the story's supreme irony: the narrative that overtly disavows a representational aesthetic is most readily accepted as factual. However, we should keep in mind that "Dog Attempts," no matter how sincerely it reads, is posed in lieu of honesty. The embedded event is inevitably a contrivance, a forced conjunction, and is therefore an abortive gesture insofar as truth is concerned: beauty is as close as we get. The same holds more broadly for all stories of this type. It is nevertheless appropriate that for stories in this heart-wrenching vein, in which Glover faces unstintingly the most excruciating, emotion-laden subject matter, his favored structural device (or at least the one these stories share) should be the most congenial to verisimilar precepts. Insofar as pathos is the desired end of a fictional work, a subtlety of artifice (at times paradoxically engendered) seems in order. As such works tend to privilege, in this qualified manner, *fabula* over *suzhet* in Shklovsky's terms, content over form, they might tender a legitimate claim on the attentions of the broadest possible audience. In any case, they surely provide an object lesson in the impressive range of Glover's arsenal.

Subjective Fission

At times Glover plays his fiction technically close to the vest, producing works that outwardly imitate the conventions of literary realism with its thoroughgoing discursive stability. However, we should note that even in such works, Glover's fiction often strives for an archetypal resonance, dredging the maximum existential profundity from a limited narrative moment. In "Horse," "Hail" (*The Mad River*), and "The Irredeemable" (*Dog Attempts*), the vehicle for an experience of such magnitude is an insane act of violence, be it meteorological or human. Perhaps the most starkly conventional story in his fiction is "Red" (*Dog Attempts*), which concerns the marital harmony discovered by a woman who was once on the verge of suicide, her current felicity being tested and ultimately reaffirmed by the overtures of her ex-husband and the enduring misery of her children. Ironically, it is this story that has been the subject of a rigorous discursive analysis titled, with Bakhtinian overtones, "The Voices Voice Comprises" (Wilkshire). More recently, "The Indonesian Client" (*16 Categories*) too presents an outward narrative stability, at least regarding voice, if not always verb tense, but in the Kafkaesque machinations of an international manufacturing concern, ambiguously named eTrans.com (a surge in its stock value is tinged with existential import), the characters are able to change personas, adopting new incarnations as easily as they change their attire: a process that is explicitly revealed to be a willful imposition, one of self-creation or rather a fictionalization of self.

Such works are relatively few in number, and, as "The Indonesian Client" begins to suggest, even when his fiction draws upon the array of so-called representational effects, Glover aims expressly to disrupt the ways and means of conventionality, particularly regarding the concepts of character and point of view. In *Notes Home* Glover devotes a chapter to razing the traditional Jamesian mandate for a unified narrative point of view, and, since his earliest collection, his fiction has set out to demonstrate that a perspectival instability, far from being a narrative faux pas, is a generative textual possibility, perhaps even a necessary rupture in stylistic complacency. For example, the title story of *The Mad River* depicts a kayaking excursion undertaken by Hunter, the protagonist, and two equally committed friends along the eponymous rapids. From the outset, the prose makes a bid for complete experiential immersion in the drama; the sentences froth and churn, providing a rhetorical echo of the action underway, and the text underscores this connection as Hunter's identity merges with the appurtenances of the narrative he inhabits. Glover writes, "Hunter is aware of himself, his body and its extensions: a paddle, a boat, a river, a rock" (9), and the mantra becomes an overt refrain in the dramatization of a prolonged ecstasy, a transcendence of self, that concludes with the final ecstasy: a narrative terminus indistinguishable from death. Similarly, "Pender's Visions" begins, "Pender is a bottle, a glass, a table, a gun, a house" (50), and here the protagonist is also on the verge of self-annihilation. A psychotic half-Indian, Pender stages what is described as an artistic production of sorts: he conducts an armed stand-off of the local police force from the living room of his homely residence. The story additionally veers between Pender's point of view and that of Chief Shaw, who commands the containment operation from the street. Although the two men are seemingly distinct personages, Pender's orchestration of the drama so explicitly doubles the creation of the text— "The telephone on the table rings, stabbing into Pender's consciousness like silver icicles in the brain pan. And Pender becomes a telephone. Chief Shaw again, he knows. He won't answer. And the act of not-answering adds a line or two to his piece" (51)—one might easily suspect that the lapses into Shaw's point of view are themselves a by-product of Pender's megalomania: Pender becomes Shaw, so to speak.

In both stories independent subjectivity is smeared into a kind of textually contingent amalgam (the Bernini sculpture *Apollo and Daphne* provides an apt illustration as the chaste maiden is depicted on the cusp of arboreal transformation, her hair and limbs morphing into vegetation). And as we began to see in the split stories above, weighty theoretical implications pervade these deconstructions of persona. The distinguishing feature here is that the protagonists, their deranged behavior notwithstanding, are largely in possession of their cognitive faculties, having not fully lapsed into the amnesiac territory of their split-story counterparts; they are both conscious witnesses of and contributors to their own subjective dissolution. Given a greater, albeit vitiated, subjective stability, such fictions generally adopt extensively some of the discursive habits of representational narratives, generating a textual immediacy: richly depicted landscapes and thoroughly rendered action. Perhaps the most conspicuous of the lot is *The Life and Times of Captain N.*, Glover's third novel.

In the long view *Captain N.* is like a distant thunder that rumbles periodically throughout the other fictions, finally erupting in the 1993 novel. The book received more review attention (at times partly hostile—see Chidley) than any other in Glover's catalog and also spawned two scholarly studies. The first positions the novel within a dense theoretical matrix, establishing the linkages between *Captain N.* and *A Thousand Plateaus* by Giles Deleuze and Félix Guattari: an intertextual conversation that prompts Glover to ask, "What the fuck is a rhizome?" in an interview postscript (Cowdy Crawford 26). The other, an academic appraisal by Don Sparling, characterizes the book as a unique postmodern blend of historical fiction and the bildungsroman of the nineteenth century, noting how the novel reinvents the form on both fronts.

The title itself is pointedly ironic as the novel offers little in the way of the stable, continuous chronological narration of its "life and times" tradition. Set in the wildernesses of upstate New York during the American Revolution, the novel adopts the perspectives of three characters to depict the conflict, which is itself a forked event. The war represents simultaneously the birth of independent America, as well as the birth of English Canada with its settlement by displaced Tory loyalists on the side of the defeated. It's this lame-duck perspective that Glover is most interested in as all three characters are ultimately in the service of its backward-looking cause. What's more, the novel is even less concerned with the Tory guns than it is with the cultural conflict between Europeans and Native Americans. The text explores the fundamental dichotomy of the vying epistemological systems—Western culture's progressive-minded rationality and the native culture's temporally ambivalent spirituality—and records the ideological violence of their collision. The question of who wins is largely a secondary concern, excised from the novel's pages; here, victory and defeat become irrelevant. What matters is transformation, which engenders fractures—cultural, psychological, physical, and textual—for which the hero's ambiguous initial is a titular sign.

As the novel's three primary characters take turns narrating the events they're immersed in, each makes an equal bid, in a way, for authorial preeminence. First, there is Mary Hunsacker, a young girl who tells her story largely in the past tense: of her capture by a band of Native Americans, of her eventual adoption by their community, of her marriage and rise to prominence as a shamanic seer, and of her ultimate expulsion from the community as the fate of the indigenous peoples becomes clear. Another first-person narrator, Hendrick Nellis is the leader of a mixed division of Native Americans, colonial loyalists, and English soldiers—his primary concern seems to have less to do with battle strategy than with the "redemption" of Europeans captured by the natives (as well as simply enduring an excruciating and thematically loaded headache). Finally, there is Oskar Nellis, Hendrick's son, who is loyal to the revolutionary cause, repeatedly drafting letters, sometimes strategic and sometimes digressive, to General Washington. Nevertheless, he is captured by his father's company, and strangely he becomes a respected, if suicidally courageous soldier on the Tory side while never wavering from his original loyalties—it's as if in war, one's allegiances are less important than the simple necessity of violent conflict: it's all the same. What's more, unlike the other characters' stories, Oskar's tale is rendered in the third-person, and his narrative is further split in that he also speaks from a first-person perspective, positioned well after the revolutionary conflict has ended. From this distanced vantage point, Oskar suggests that his identity is, literally, an amalgam of his novel's diverse populace (157). Fittingly, then, all three characters are depicted in the throes of cultural fusion, all of them explicitly adopting the habits of Native Americans. Ultimately, Oskar and Mary are thrown clear, partly reassimilated by white society, while Hendrick succumbs to madness, disease, and death.

In the characters' limited time between cultures, as it were, the action of the book focuses, and there's little in the way of developmental escalation. If the traditional Aristotelian model of rising action resembles a spike in the wavelengths of a heart monitor, this book offers a considerably flattened line: not near the base level of the moribund, but maybe a few degrees below the traditional triangular apex. In addition to the sporadic musket-play and the privations of military encampments, the action features scalpings, executions, self-mutilations, and a vague kind of necrophilia. At this pitch of slightly restrained ferocity the book simmers, alternating among the voices of the three narrators. Even the moments of quietude bear the pall of death as, for example, Oskar's letters express his fears that he will "be terrible kil't soon" (53). Shedding light on the pervasive brutality, the dwarf Witcacy, who possesses a surprisingly Renaissance cast of mind and who teaches Oskar to read and write, offers the maxim, "In art . . . there is only form and the extremity of utterance" (21). Similarly, Hendrick Nellis, as he nears death, is said to comment, "violence has its own strange and perverse beauty—at least it makes you pay attention" (168). *Captain N.,* as with many Glover fictions, epitomizes such an aesthetic vision.

It has been famously speculated that the Nighttown episode in Joyce's *Ulysses* represents the book dreaming self-reflexively, and a similar kind of logic pervades *Captain N.,* as the characters ostensibly blend into one another, confronting nearly identical crises, assuming similar postures. The book's governing image is that of Hendrick Nellis's war mask, adopted from the Native American totemic pantheon: a face divided, split down the middle, half-red, half-black. Gradually, Oskar too assumes the same mask, additionally tattooing his body with Native American symbols. Elsewhere, on her first appearance, during the gruesome raid that results in her captivity, Mary Hunsacker tosses an infant child out the window, to safety she hopes; later, she discovers a large discolored welt on the infant's head. Shortly after, she too is brained by one of the natives, an injury that ultimately requires a no-less-gruesome operation in which a military surgeon installs a silver plate in her skull. It's as if the infant's injury accrues to Mary (incidentally the infant dies on the native bayonets), and further, Mary's wound leaves her with an obdurate headache nearly identical to Hendrick Nellis's. While this imagistic diffusion is posed at least partly in lieu of a linear chronology, the action of the book is wholly intelligible, lucidly rendered, and unstinting in its particulars. In many ways *Captain N.* provides the quintessential decentered novel, the various narrative vantage points cycling around the absence of a narrative continuity (battles of bullet and of heart) that typically governs the novel; for these characters the war is an experience of discontinuity, requiring a correspondingly discordant form, relying on dissonant imagistic overlappings to create an alternative compositional methodology.

In this broad-scale subjective interface, here we should mention that most Glover novels share a plot device that might best be described as Dickensian: through at times sudden twists, identities turn out to be duplicitous, disingenuous assumptions of persona. In *Precious* the murderer Eliot pursues is right under his nose: his boss, Burton Spandrell, formerly Brian Oxley, a low-level hockey star involved in an earlier unsolved murder. In *The South Will Rise at Noon* the curio-shop assistant Kinch is the famed New York artist Horne Tooke incognito. And in *Captain N.* Tom Wopat, Oskar's Native American friend and supposed rebel sympathizer, is discovered to be Scattering Light, Hunsacker's Messessagey husband and one of Hendrick's loyalist scouts. Glover's handling of this time-worn literary device is uniformly skilled, never the jarring cliché of ostensible convenience that it is in the worst kind of novel. In fact, it's possible that Glover has tuned into the device's immanent metatextual import: such densities of character construction are perhaps an inevitable by-product of a narrative coercion or corrosion.

The aspect of *Captain N.* that has drawn the most critical fire is best illustrated perhaps by the narration Oskar's older self offers. Identified as excerpts from "Oskar's Book about Indians," which seems to be and not to be the book we're reading, these passages include explicit commentary on the book's major thematic currents. For example, Oskar writes, "The book about Indians can't be a book at all. . . . It is a break, a rupture in the whole cloth of normal discourse. It is an antibook meant to destroy all books" (121). In such moments, Glover appears to have no compunction whatsoever about strip-mining major deposits of postmodern thought (nor should he); in fact, it's possible to read *Captain N.* as an imaginative ménage à trois involving the franchise representatives of deconstructionist, postcolonial, and (specifically) "postindian" theory. That said, the primary complaint, not surprisingly, seems to be that such passages disrupt the novel's narrative texture and preempt the reader's interpretive processes. However, we should keep in mind that the self-reflexivity serves the novel in vital ways. First, the existence of this vocal layer enacts one of the characteristic native ideological maneuvers, namely to extend the action of the novel "laterally, as it were, across the axis of time" (83). The crisis the action represents endures long after the battles have ended; indeed, it has taken philosophy and art two hundred years to catch up to what happened. (It's probably more accurate to say that over time the nature of the event itself has changed, and continues to change with the times.) In addition, such passages bring into sharp relief the novel's primary subject: the cultural conflict and the degree to which writing itself is implicated in the destruction. And finally, since the text strives as much as possible (writing is here a preclusive condition) to accommodate the transrational Native American epistemological system, it seems inevitable that the novel must explicitly preempt many of our second-order hermeneutic gestures, predicated as they are on Western rationalism. What remains is the quiddity of the book itself as an experience rather than a deductive exercise.

However, the road to this quiddity passes through at times nettlesome terrain. Oskar writes, "If you read the book carefully enough, it will change your life" (121), and Hendrick, shortly before his death, leaves the mandate, "Love difference" (173), which is ambiguous in that love is itself a destructive force. More broadly, this antibook pursues its agenda with an unalleviated evangelical severity that makes for a high-acidity environment, an atmosphere defiantly overradiated. Even the touches of humor are of the gallows variety, as in the chapter title, "Oskar Beds a Widder" (111)— an unhygienic tryst offering little emotional solace. Such an atmosphere seems at least partly at odds with the other facade of Glover's Janusian mask; in *Notes Home* Glover remarks of fiction in general, "Form is its message" (59). At best, the apparent moral urgency of *Captain N.* is a paradoxical proposition. All objections aside, Oskar's first-person narration, his book about Indians, does provide the text with perhaps the only conceivable endgame, short of simply petering out. In the book's concluding segment, Oskar visibly lapses from his older persona into the antiquated idiom of the younger and writes, "I put these down as random Thoughts, in no particular Order, reflecting my State of Mind wch is now chaotic & unformed as the Earth on the First Day" (185). Here, the terminus is a leap into the book, into the rift between cultures. On the whole, it seems fitting that such a novel should engender hostility and division in the aesthetic response of its readers, as it does for those who would like to keep the visceral and engaging polyphony and pitch the autocommentary. But whatever one's tastes, there can be no doubt that *The Life and Times of Captain N.* is an important aesthetic event, a book of serious intellectual import and prodigious technical craftsmanship.

With the collection *16 Categories of Desire,* Glover again appears to have shifted gears slightly as "Lunar Sensitivities" presents a version of subjective diffusion that is qualitatively different from the fevered agonies of its precursors. In the story three friends—the narrator, Norris, and Kaplovsky—lay claim by turns to a common identity, as if subjectivity were transferable in a way, a communicable disease. The agoraphobic and erudite Kaplovsky appears to be ground zero of the contested identity: he has had two failed love affairs—with his teenage bride Marie-Éve and his housekeeper Angie Gosselin—is knowledgeable on atonal music and chess problems, and has written an unpublished essay on "the influence of the moon on an obscure and nearly extinct subspecies of mollusc found mainly in Long Point Bay on the north shore of Lake Erie" (130). In his last days he can barely leave the house and takes to keeping a staggering number of cats. Slowly, over the course of the story, Norris embarks on affairs with Gosselin and Marie-Éve in succession, similarly plagiarizes and ultimately publishes Kaplovsky's zoological essay, and upon Kaplovsky's death inherits the cats (which rip his face to shreds). The narrator too gradually reveals that he is implicated in the pattern of appropriated identity, as he discloses post facto his love affair with Angie Gosselin and develops an overpowering affection for Marie-Éve. He suspects (apparently rightfully) that Norris has killed Kaplovsky, and in his suspicions we intimate that he will similarly murder Norris, an act that looms gracefully and resonantly beyond the close of the text.

While subjective malleability has long been one of Glover's favored themes, here a cool, elegant, even congenial narrative surface compromises the inherent violence of the characters' duplicity or multiplicity. As the narrator puts it, in an access of self-awareness, "a facade of correctness and discipline, of tweedy civility so characteristic of Montreal's old Anglo elite, conceal[s] a passionate and wilful nature" (136). The dissonance is inspired and yields a narrative rife with paradox: at once evasive and forthright, tender and hostile, comic and tragic. The narrator describes the import of Norris's scientific work: "his famous 'Lunar Sensitivities in Certain Great Lakes Subspecies,' in which he proved decisively that a sequence of hormonal changes occurs in a rare littoral mussel through the phases of the moon, which mussel indeed apparently moves with the moon, a slow, legless dance to unheard music, an adagio perhaps, which Norris described in his conclusion as the stately back beat of existence, a rhythm of life which might yet be demonstrated to govern us all" (132). Shortly after, in observing Norris and Marie-Éve on a lunch date, he reflects:

> . . . I was able to see how all this prefigured and foreshadowed events to come, just as the present situation echoed and reiterated previous events; that we are ruled by a kind of repetition, or as Norris himself (following Kaplovsky's earlier, unpublished intuitions) wrote in "Lunar Sensitivities," by obscure and incomprehensible motivations which appear alien and random but are in fact the results of motion fused with form; that motion fused with form is a definition of life itself. (132-33)

Through these moments, the narrator subtly discloses his own plagiaristic bent, which appears to be underwritten by an irresistible cosmic force. Not exactly exculpatory, but the beauty of the cadences, as they progress from the myopically fastidious to the telescopically sublime, is considerably disarming, and we might reasonably ask the same question that the narrator himself raises in the context of Kaplovsky's murder: "Was this, finally, an act of love between the two men? Or was it just the climax in a series of violent interactions, a duel to the death?" (138) Here malice and love become almost indistinguishable.

Given the persistent echoes between the characters' libidinal treachery and the scientific disquisition (as well as their auxiliary reverberations through atonal music and chess problems), "Lunar Sensitivities" offers a compositional density that draws from its dark theme a rarely paralleled radiance. Structurally too the narrative shifts deftly between past and present events, even enfolding the past within the present action. For example, the narrator purports to describe a visit to see Norris in the story's first sentence, but veers sinuously into the past to recount, in successive loops, private episodes between Norris and Marie-Ève at a Tandoori restaurant and between himself and Kaplovsky at the narrator's apartment before divulging the import of his original meeting with Norris. The story line, in its rendering, inclines toward a quirky, loose-constructionist verisimilitude, as the narrator says of Kaplovsky's tentative visitations: "On each of his visits, I made him a lunch—sesame seed cakes, orange slices and Chartreuse in little glasses—which he barely ate but which I could see deeply touched him" (129). Yet as past events interrupt the advance of the chronology—resulting in narrative fermata that hamper without obliterating the profluential impulse—the action moves in stops and starts, one imagines much like the rhythms of Kaplovsky's celestial mollusks.

Elle

Glover's recent novel, *Elle,* could, with little fudging, be configured to synthesize all of the above structural devices, some undergoing greater permutation than others. Suffice it to say that *Elle* charts the textual territory somewhere between *Captain N.* and "La Corriveau," as it seems in some ways to hybridize these two works. But like all Glover fictions, no matter how familiar its stylistic and thematic concerns, *Elle* is very much its own thing. For the most part, the action takes place in 1542, opening shipboard in the Atlantic off the coast of Canada with the female narrator speaking tumultuously midcoitus, as she is "driven to this desperate expedient by the onset of a toothache, which, on top of the boredom, the fog and the ineffable see-sawing of the ship's deck, has lately made the voyage unendurable" (19). Unlike *Captain N.,* this story is largely a monologue, the narrator's voice strongly reminiscent of La Corriveau's (and to a lesser extent Mary Hunsacker's) acute irony; in the midst of the sex act, she remarks, "My breath is fetid with the cloves I chew for the pain. I am aware that I have been more attractive and found more salubrious places in which to make love" (20). So begins the narrative that is the inevitable complement to *Captain N.*: as the earlier novel depicts the eve of the birth of English Canada, *Elle* takes for an aesthetic subject the colonization of French Canada. And like the characters in *Captain N.*, the narrator's identity will quickly be set adrift on cross-cultural currents as she is put off the ship for her sexual indiscretion and begins her contact with the new continent. Likewise, her subjectivity will be compromised in the process, though only partly akin to the cross-pollination characteristic of the earlier novel's Anglo counterparts.

The text reveals a five-part construction, of which the narrator's Canadian experience fuels the two predominant components, occupying the vast majority of the novel's 205 pages. When the ship's commandant—a family relative referred to as the General—forcibly maroons the narrator on the Isle des Demons (an uninhabited bird rookery on the St. Lawrence), she is joined by her lover Richard, a French tennis player of some fame (with difficulty he manages to retain possession of his racket and balls), and her servant Bastienne, a debauched governess, abortionist, and apothecary healer whose skills prove ineffective in the Canadian wilds. Additionally complicating her situation, the narrator rightly suspects that she's pregnant. As the party attempts an isolated and pathetic colonization, eking out the necessities of food and shelter, by turns each of the narrator's companions dies, providing narrative benchmarks in a way: first Richard, then Bastienne. Alone and far advanced in her pregnancy, the narrator experiences her first contact with the natives, a solitary seal-hunter named Itslk on a vision quest, who arrives on the scene just as the narrator is about to be eaten by a polar bear (which instead collapses in a heap upon her, dead). The two develop a sexual affair as if submitting to a formality—antiseptic and cheerless—and from Itslk, the narrator begins to adopt the survival habits and customs of the natives. Eventually, Itslk abandons the narrator, who is coincidentally on the verge of childbirth. The infant dies too, almost immediately, bringing to a close the first part of the Canadian travelogue.

The patterned morbidity—isolated contacts ending in isolated deaths—that dominates the above extends into the second part of the narrator's colonial experience. After her infant's death, the narrator sets out across the ice bridging the St. Lawrence, leading her to yet another solitary contact as a native woman, a shaman and shapeshifter (ursanthrope or werebear, technically), attempts to nurse her back to health. She too finds her friendship with the narrator fatal, and with her death, the novel's cast begins to swell again (reviving the initial shipboard hubbub) as the narrator—ridiculously and pathetically immune to the death she disburses—endures on the periphery of a native community. Ultimately, a European whaling vessel arrives and effects her compulsory return to France. While this account of the novel's dominant action is patently linear and while the narrator herself speaks largely in the present tense, it's clear that she's narrating from a vantage point well after her ultimate return to France. Consequently, she frequently interrupts the linear movement of the island events with varied digressions, including the summation of her story's final ending place (which kicks off the second part of the Canadian narrative): back in France, married to an innkeeper named Isidore, where she writes the book we're reading (113).

These digressions signal a broader structural agenda at work in both sections: namely, the present action is striped with interpolated subnarratives, embedded stories that both disrupt and enrich the linear discursive texture. The embedded stories include the narrator's recounting of Bastienne's excessive past (53-56) and an installment-plan account of the General's doomed colonial enterprise, rendered with a surprisingly detailed accuracy: "The General can't sleep at night for the coughing, the snoring, the clandestine fornicating and the inarticulate prayers of the dying" (75). Also among them are a variety of Native American etiological myths. For example, Itslk himself recounts as purported myth the series of events that leads him to the narrator's island: a hunter pursues a bear/spirit guide that, once killed, will empower him with the ability to save his people from the European invasion (of course, the narrator, simply by force of contact, has inadvertently killed the bear). Another embedded story involves a westward-bound canoe trip in the company of the native shaman; this narrative reads as a literal event, but later is revealed to have been a dream—like the narrator's trip to Canada, a journey that is not a journey, a quest that leads nowhere. On a smaller scale, the text is similarly riddled with the shavings of the narrator's limited native vocabulary, which might be a kind of practical joke that the natives have played on Jacques Cartier, who spearheaded the colonization effort and drafted the specious lexicon. So again, in *Elle* we see Glover plying his impressive facility with fugal structural schemes.

Despite its partly linear surface and largely univocal narration, *Elle,* like *Captain N.,* adheres to a dream logic that subverts whatever linearity the text purports to offer. First, there are the myriad instances of patterned imagery, of which we might examine one particularly dense and representative case. To remedy her toothache aboard the ship, the narrator strikes upon some inventive dentistry:

she binds her tooth with a cord and attaches the other end to the collar of the General's dog, Leon, then tosses a tennis ball overboard, and when the dog scoots after it, landing in the waves, the tooth is extracted. In a pang of guilt the narrator evokes her kinship with other Glover protagonists like Pender, remarking, "He is like something of myself I have carelessly tossed away . . ." (25). Later, the dog returns in Itslk's company, having improbably made it ashore (in possession of the tennis ball no less). However, this procedure of dog abandonment recurs: once on her dream journey westward and again, irrevocably, when she boards the whaling vessel. Similarly, attempts at healing are nearly ubiquitous in the text: from the narrator's self-dentistry, to Bastienne's ineffective poultices, to the shaman's medical know-how (in traditional shamanistic practice, she sucks objects from the narrator's body, including, fittingly, a tooth). And finally, from this apparently minor tooth-extraction episode aboard the ship, the very act of tying the string around her tooth both recalls the nearly identical image of the jury-rigged penis-ring she employs to keep her seasick lover erect for their sex and resurfaces in the figure of a bear carcass strung from a tree (as well as the gallows corpses that grace the General's encampment). The result is a narrative at once fugal and centrifugal. It's as if, by the distorted logical processes of dreams, images give birth to other images, one might say even bearing the seeds of the narrative events.

This imagistic slippage also speaks to the subjective meltdown that takes place in *Elle*. Early on, when Richard's health begins to fail, the narrator dons his clothing as well as his masculinity; later, the narrator assumes the indigenous attire and tattoos her face in the manner of a friendly native with a replica of the Big Dipper (the constellation Ursa Major, the Great Bear). However, in *Elle* the subjective transformations extend further into the mythological bestiary of the natives as characters purport to shape-shift before our eyes: a talent that leads to a series of stunning revelations. The crowning example of these metamorphoses involves the shaman who can seemingly transform herself into a bear. The narrator too ostensibly develops this ability, which leaves her with elongated fingers, a pervasive hirsutism, and a torso stippled with supernumerary teats even when she's at her most womanly. When her shamanic caretaker dies while in bear form, a group of natives hangs the carcass from a tree, preparing to skin and devour it, until the narrator breaks in and completes the task herself. She takes to wearing the bear skin both to keep warm and to show her solidarity. Soon after, the European whalers arrive, and when they question her about the carcass, she concedes that "It doesn't look quite human" (164), realizing that she is wrapped not in a bearskin, but in the "old woman's skin" (164). To European eyes (the reader's eyes) the narrator has become a cannibal (perhaps this moment is a distant cousin of Glover's Dickensian discoveries). However, the narrator's bearishness isn't wholly obviated by this discovery, as we'll see. Moreover, given this revelation late in the text, readers will recall the narrator's island privations, Richard's death, and the sudden miraculous appearance of an easily butchered seal—with "almost human eyes (like Richard's)" (56); in hindsight, it becomes clear that the narrator has developed a kind of culturally loaded psychosis or epistemological blindness—her stressed apprehension substituting animal forms for human bodies—that allows her to cannibalize the corpses of her companions. In fact, given the pervasive similes by which human features are rendered edible—Bastienne's face like a "turnip" (54), Richard's like a "ham" (51)—pointed references to the Eucharist (22), and the narrator's description of her infant son, literally, as a fish (he has "appendages like fins" (102)), we might surmise that the cannibalism telescopes perhaps even beyond any definitive textual evidence, that the narrator's appetite has even more gruesome ramifications than she lets on.

In the metamorphoses from human to animal, the novel offers an exquisitely treacherous surface that can remind one favorably of *Pale Fire*. Such transformations pervade the text from its first pages. For example, in the her opening sexual congress, the narrator notices a voyeuristic rat skulking behind a bucket; quickly we learn that she has been observed by human eyes in the form of Pip, the cabin boy: a phase-shift from animal to human. As this character's name indicates, the novel does draft significantly on *Moby-Dick*—the captain of the whaling vessel has two ivory peg legs, his second set, we presume, as an identical prosthetic pair are later discovered in the belly of a beached whale (184)—and this connection suggests that the transformations extend beyond their isolated human incarnations. Of her snowed-in island encampment, the narrator remarks, "One day . . . I poke Richard's tennis racquet through the snow and perceive a sky so blue and a world so white that it assaults me with its clarity. Nothing has ever seemed this clear—and I am French, so clarity is beauty" (66-67). In the narrator's repeated evocations of the profound whiteness of the Canadian winter, it's hard not to read an analogue of Ishmael's remarks on the albino leviathan; here Canada itself is figured as a kind of white whale, the objective correlative of a quest as ambiguous and self-destructive as Ahab's. As a result, far from a simple novelistic legerdemain, these transformations and their cannibalistic import are, in every case, graphic correspondents of the text's broader thematic scope;

the colonial enterprise is itself a kind of cultural ingestion, resulting on the native side in a devouring that ends in near extinction.
What's more, as the patterned imagistic transformations fork and
multiply from level to level, from the personal to the cultural to the
cosmological, again we have a text that is prismatic and exhilarat-
ing and one that has a staggering aesthetic ax to grind as well.

The narrator's story doesn't conclude with her recovery by the
whalers, but instead she relates in a much shorter section an addendum or postscript, swiftly recounting the next twenty years of
her life in France. Some of the key images from her stint in Canada
follow her back to Europe, as doctors bleed her with leeches (more
healing) and she assumes the care of a captive bear cub, a kind of
surrogate for Leon. Highlighting this section in terms of its dramatic action are her friendship with a native girl marooned in
Canada and her final encounter with the General, among the char-
nel houses of a Parisian cemetery, where she delivers his overdue
comeuppance, revealing she can still transform herself into a bear.
With the native girl, the narrator erects a poor replica of a tribal
home, which makes the cultural cross-pollination partly palindro-
mic, providing a reduced mirror image of the North American colonization. Poignantly and, we have to admit, fittingly, the native girl
ultimately dies of consumption.

The narrator's terminal confrontation with the General is doubly
significant. First, as the narrator here recovers her bearishness—
with a single blow from her paws she lays his cheek "open to the
teeth" and slinks away from the scene of the crime in bear form
(201)—we should emphasize that, like *Captain N., Elle* seeks to
achieve a state of textual ambivalence that doesn't evaporate into
clear-cut truths. Is the narrator's shape-shifting literal? Metaphoric? Is her perceptual confusion a species of insanity? In the
dream world of the novel, it's hard to distinguish among the options,
much less resolve them; we can conclude only that the novel's instances of metamorphosis have as much claim to reality as they
ever have in Native American cultures. The text itself contains an
imagistic correspondent of this global ambiguity in the form of the
tennis court that Richard attempts to construct on the Isle de Demons. For Europeans, the sport entails a neat division between op-
ponents and yields definitive triumphs and losses. The novel offers
as a teleological rebuttal Glover's net, the network that forms along
the lines of intersection. Here a slight image renders subliminally
the dizzyingly complex process of interweaving, inversion, and con-
version that turns epistemological systems inside out.

Before proceeding to the second point of interest regarding the
General's murder, we should note that, upon her return to France,

the narrator embarks on a relationship with none other than François Rabelais, the progenitor of Pantagruel's ribald odyssey. It's likely that the occasional lists that crop up in *Elle* are a Rabelaisian inheritance. For example, the narrator catalogs the colonial party:

> Poor Canada, destined always to be on the edge of things, inimical to books and writing, plagued by insects in the summer and ice in the winter, populated by the sons and daughters of ambitious, narrow, pious, impecunious Protestants and inarticulate but lusty Catholic tennis players, not to mention the rest of the riff-raff on the expedition, drawn, by the King's order, from the prisons of Paris, Toulouse, Bordeaux, Rouen and Dijon—thieves, abortionists, frauds, panders, whores, footpads, assassins, along with the destitute and the witless, every kind of rogue except heretics, traitors and counterfeiters who were deemed unsuitable to the dignity of our pious enterprise. (43)

The Rabelaisian influence extends even more broadly. Insofar as the Canadian narrative can be said to sustain a linear continuity, at the same time it wholly dispenses with the chains of causality typical of novelistic practice (excepting perhaps Leon's stubborn endurance). The events—the deaths of Richard and Bastienne, the encounter with Itslk and the other natives, the arrival of the whalers—have an episodic feel. Similarly, the narrator's concluding altercation with the General provides a late spike in the dramatic register, but again, as the confrontation occurs after an intervening hiatus of twenty years, the encounter feels oddly dislocated and seemingly coincidental. While the narrator's incremental immersion into and subsequent withdrawal from native culture does establish a sustained developmental line, her experiences remain largely isolated, not accruing the traditional baggage of a novelistic plot. For example, Itslk never reappears to make a fuss over the narrator's living with another, rival tribe. Then again, she might have eaten him; that is, it seems as if the cannibalistic practice speaks to an aesthetic as well as a thematic dimension, the novel feeding on the corpses and/or disappearances of its cast.

Overall, the implications of such a construction are far-reaching. It's hard to miss the overtones in *Elle* of the birth of the European novel, widely held to begin with Daniel Defoe in the early eighteenth century. In the hypersexed narrator it's as if Defoe's promiscuous Moll Flanders has assumed the role of Robinson Crusoe (an allusion made explicit in the text—the English captain of the whaling vessel might have Ahab's peg legs, but he also shares Crusoe's criminally obsessive economics). And in the episodic construction, then, perhaps closer to prenovelistic writers of whom Rabelais is a chief and Melville a beneficiary, Glover has taken his impressive game straight into the creation mythology of the traditional novel and appropriated these genetic roots for his own antitraditional purpose. Again, it might be more accurate to qualify that *Elle* occupies a plane somewhere between the distorted aesthetic cosmology of Rabelais and the "realistic" pretensions ascribed to Defoe. Nevertheless, *Elle,* in this regard, amounts to a focused assault on literary tradition, an act of aesthetic aggression that, given the splendor of the text itself, turns out to be magnanimous.

Finally, *Elle* offers two remaining sections that bookend the Canadian/Franco narrative. Both exceedingly brief and italicized, the first is in the voice of the dominant narrator, relating some of her early childhood experiences in France as well as crucial information pertaining to her island experience. The last veers into third-person narration and also leaps forward into a contemporary Canadian landscape, introducing the novel's title character (the French pronoun here becomes a proper name): a writer named Elle has sex with her lover on a beach and tries to remember the story she's working on, a narrative very much like the book we've just read. The section concludes (and therefore the novel concludes) with Elle's radical dream-transformation into a bear, very close to the primary narrator's own terminal transformation.

The italicized sections also, surprisingly, appear to share a character in common: a dark-skinned man who leads children in the sculpting of sand-statuary and abducts at least one unfortunate. Additionally, he materializes in the course of the dominant colonial narrative in the figure of a native marooned on an ice floe, drifting toward France. Through an imagistic connection—a beached orca surfaces in sixteenth-century France, getting its eye jabbed out before being slaughtered; in both the French narrator's childhood sighting and Elle's sighting, the mysterious stranger wears an eye-patch (12, 203)—this ambiguous, migratory figure provides still another instance of metamorphosis, here explicitly drawing upon the myth-making of early mariners, their hallucinatory disposition by which manatees become mermaids. Further, he makes his first appearance in Canada when the narrator buries her infant son; elsewhere, the narrator corroborates the native belief that a scarecrow she constructs (to keep scavengers away from Richard's grave) is the repository of her spirit, "which Itslk hid not so long ago on the Isle of Demons" (114). Together, these two moments offer a mere taste of the widespread and tantalizing evidence regarding the stranger's identity. The text suggests, despite the logistical nightmare, that he is at once a dream effigy of the dead child as well as a correspondent—

with his transcontinental itinerary and the textual connotations of which the orca's black-and-white hulk is a minor graphic approximate—of the book to which the narrator is also giving birth.

Given this character's spatial and temporal diffusion, his boundless and factually inconceivable presence, the two slight italicized sections jostle the novel from the psychotic—the epistemological ambiguities of metamorphosis—to the metempsychotic. On the Canadian beach Elle wonders of the folk-narrative that preoccupies her, *"did the story simply inhabit the place like a ghost, letting itself nestle in the minds of receptive hosts as they came by?"* (204). The answer appears to be affirmative, the tale offered as transrationally transferable, beyond a unitary authorship and beyond the unidirectional history posited by Enlightenment rationalism, the birth of the novel, and the ongoing fluctuations of the Dow Jones (disturbingly bearish at present). The white whale the Europeans purport to hunt is instead a hopelessly mottled heap that collapses on the continental doorstep; the quest harvests, not an advantageous sum of natural resources, but an epistemological rupture, a crisis of narrative.

Clearly, *Elle* is a work of major consequence, more ambitious in scope than its slight frame indicates. However, here Glover has traded in his Nellisian war maul for a more subtle but no less devastating arsenal (a missile silo-cum-aviary, perhaps) that sustains the considerable risks inherent in such a novel. That is, in *Elle* there remains, despite the manifold horrors of the experience, a sense of the wonder immanent in the cultural collision, which is not quite the same thing that Fitzgerald famously eulogizes near the end of *The Great Gatsby*. The narrator recounts a dream of judgment day in which, "Sweet young girls with their newly printed Bibles turn ghoulish. Pious, black-clad dignitaries groan, grasp their codpieces and piss themselves. . . . Only a few healthy souls pass through the gate and venture tremulously along the path toward the château. But even these redeemed creatures have an air of regret, as if they already miss the sun, their lovers' caresses, the voice of a friend, as if, after all, there is nothing sweeter than to be alive" (123). The indictment of the European theology that underwrites the colonial enterprise is scathing—elsewhere, Richard's penis is described as "a knob of ecclesiastical purple" (21)—and make no mistake, the substance of *Elle* is more like a kick in the groin than a kiss on the cheek. Yet there remains, pervading the novel's atmosphere, a sidelong gratitude for those few consolations we have, marooned here on the earth. While being nursed by the shaman, the narrator reflects on her predicament: "This is like poetry, but it is also like madness, which is governed by the same rules of repetition and similitude" (128). If a work like

Captain N. epitomizes an aesthetic and cultural madness, *Elle*'s temperament is equally suffused with poetry, which continues to offer solace even to the damned.

In November 2003 *Elle* earned Glover the Governor General's Award in fiction (Margaret Atwood was among the other finalists). What long-term impact this honor will have on his career is difficult to foresee. Nevertheless, it offers a timely confirmation of his place among the most ambitious and skilled contemporary North American writers. In the continual recalibration and reinvention of his stylistic past, he is at the same time venturing into further, as yet uncharted, aesthetic frontiers, achieving increasingly more profound literary effects. If he should remain on the margins in his sustained campaign of aesthetic warfare, he will be out there in titanic company: a coterie including, among others, Melville, Joyce, Nabokov, and Kundera. One can hope that more North American readers will follow him into those breaches—epistemological and aesthetic—whose fault lines he continues to forge.

Works Cited

Chidley, Joe. "Rebels and Indians." Rev. of *The Life and Times of Captain N.,* by Douglas Glover. *Maclean's* 106.18 (1993): 46+.

Cowdy Crawford, Cheryl. "Becoming-Masks: *The Life and Times of Captain N.* at n – 1 Dimensions." *Henry Street* 8.1 (1999): 7-42.

Gass, William H. "The Concept of Character in Fiction." *Fiction and the Figures of Life.* New York: Knopf, 1970. 34-54.

Glover, Douglas. *Dog Attempts to Drown Man in Saskatoon.* Vancouver: Talonbooks, 1985.

—. *Elle.* Fredericton, NB: Goose Lane, 2003.

—. E-mail to the author. 24 Dec. 2002.

—. E-mail to the author. 28 Dec. 2002.

—. E-mail to the author. 12 Jan. 2003.

—. E-mail to the author. 20 Jan. 2003.

—. *A Guide to Animal Behavior.* Fredericton, NB: Goose Lane, 1991.

—. *The Life and Times of Captain N.* New York: Knopf, 1993.

—. *The Mad River and Other Stories.* Windsor, ON: Black Moss Press, 1981.

—. *Notes Home from a Prodigal Son.* Ottawa: Oberon Press, 1999.

—. *Precious.* Toronto: Seal, 1984.

—. *16 Categories of Desire.* Fredericton, NB: Goose Lane, 2000.

—. *The South Will Rise at Noon.* Markham, ON: Penguin, 1988.

Graham, Phillip. "At the Heart of the Whirlwind." Rev. of *The Life and Times of Captain N.*, by Douglas Glover. *Chicago Tribune* 28 Feb. 1993: 141.

Horton, Jerry. Rev. of *The Life and Times of Captain N.*, by Douglas Glover. *Quill & Quire* 59.3 (1993): 47.

Jackson, Lorna. "Anatomy of Desire." Rev. of *16 Categories of Desire*, by Douglas Glover. *Quill & Quire* 66.11 (2000): 29.

MacKendrick, Louis K. "The Fictions of Douglas Glover: A Preliminary Survey." *Canadian Fiction Magazine* 65 (1989): 121-32.

Malin, Irving. Rev. of *The Life and Times of Captain N.*, by Douglas Glover. *Review of Contemporary Fiction* 13.3 (1993): 231-32.

Nabokov, Vladimir. *The Real Life of Sebastian Knight.* Norfolk: New Directions, 1941.

Pellecchia, Michael. Rev. of *The South Will Rise at Noon*, by Douglas Glover. *New York Times Book Review* 19 Mar. 1989: 22.

Shklovsky, Viktor. "The Novel as Parody: Sterne's *Tristram Shandy*." *The Theory of Prose.* Trans. Benjamin Sher. Normal, IL: Dalkey Archive Press, 1990. 147-70.

Spano, Susan. Rev. of *The Life and Times of Captain N.*, by Douglas Glover. *New York Times Book Review* 2 May 1993: 18.

Sparling, Don. "Historical Fiction and Douglas Glover's *The Life and Times of Captain N.*" *Brno Studies in English* 23 (1997): 151-60.

Wilkshire, Claire. "Story and Desire." Rev. of *16 Categories of Desire*, by Douglas Glover. *Canadian Literature: A Quarterly of Criticism and Review.* Online. 12 Dec. 2002. <http://www.canlit.ca/reviews/unassigned/4_wilkshire.html>

—. "The Voices Voice Comprises: Incorporation, First-Person Narration and Gender Performance in Douglas Glover's 'Red.'" *Canadian Literature* 157 (1998): 174-79.

A Douglas Glover Checklist

The Mad River and Other Stories. Windsor, ON: Black Moss, 1981.

Precious. Toronto: Seal, 1984.

Dog Attempts to Drown Man in Saskatoon. Vancouver: Talonbooks, 1985, 1993.

The South Will Rise at Noon. Markham, ON: Penguin, 1988, 1989.

A Guide to Animal Behavior. Fredericton, NB: Goose Lane, 1991.

The Life and Times of Captain N. New York: Knopf, 1993; Fredericton, NB: Goose Lane, 2001.

Notes Home from a Prodigal Son. Ottawa: Oberon Press, 1999.

16 Categories of Desire. Fredericton, NB: Goose Lane, 2000.

Bad News of the Heart. Normal, IL: Dalkey Archive Press, 2003.

Elle. Fredericton, NB: Goose Lane, 2003.

Blaise Cendrars

Jeff Bursey

*I refuse to contribute to contemporary Parisian journals.
They are too corny, too old-fashioned. . . . I don't want to be
part of the gang. I am not behind, as you say, but ahead. . . .
I have seen a few modern foreign journals. It all belongs to
yesterday, not to today. I will be visible tomorrow. Today,
I'm working.*
—1917 letter from Cendrars to Robert Delaunay
Modernities and Other Writings xiv

Today, the Swiss-born French writer Blaise Cendrars is mostly invisible to English readers. In 1975 Martin Seymour-Smith wrote that he was "an important anti-literary writer, and one of whom a more detailed study should be made" (96). A 1992 review of the final volume of Cendrars's tetralogy begins with these words: "One might begin with a simple question: Why read 'Sky,' the fourth and concluding volume of Blaise Cendrars's memoirs? Hardly anyone remembers this man. . . . Yet, although only a few people are aware of his work, both his life and work are amazing" (Gavronsky). Three years later the respected Cendrars scholar Jay Bochner stated that he didn't know why critics had not yet compared Cendrars's *Moravagine* (1926) with Céline's *Journey to the End of the Night* (1932) and then listed the noticeable similarities between the two novels ("Blaise without War" 50). That thematic resonances between those two novels have been left unexplored in French studies is surprising; however, French scholarship on Cendrars is leagues ahead of academic and critical work in English.

Cendrars's works retain a presence in English thanks to the tireless writings of Bochner, Monique Chefdor, and a handful of translators. The French edition of his oeuvre runs to fifteen volumes. In English the first three books of his memoir tetralogy—translated as *The Astonished Man, Planus,* and *Lice*—are out of print, though the fourth, *Sky,* is still available. *Moravagine* occasionally disappears from sight. Only *Gold,* which was popular before it was transformed into the movie *Sutter's Gold,* consistently remains in print. Cendrars has not had the fortune to be translated by one consistent and sympathetic person, and some of the translations that exist date from the late 1960s and early 1970s. His daughter Miriam wrote a biography of her father, published in 1984, which remains untranslated, and there is no complete biography of Cendrars in

English. This essay, which can provide only an overview of certain aspects of Cendrars's novels and memoirs, will, I hope, initiate more interest in this neglected artist whose work spans genres, media, isms, wars, continents, and oceans.

From 1912 to 1961, hardly a year passed when Cendrars did not have something published in France and afterward throughout Europe, England, Brazil, and the English-speaking world. His poetry and prose were brought out by himself and others, his articles appeared in various avant-garde periodicals, he worked in movies, and he acted as a journalist for French and English newspapers. His first influential poem, *Easter,* appeared in book form in November 1912. (It would reappear in a 1919 collection of his work under the title "Easter in New York," by which it is more generally known.) There followed *The Prose of the Transsiberian and of Little Jehanne of France* (1913), a "simultaneous" poem printed on a single sheet of paper, two yards long, of twelve panels, and colored by Sonia Delaunay. At once, newspapers were filled with letters and opinion pieces from various individuals and groups claiming exclusive jurisdiction over the use of the word *simultaneous.* While this event has been a footnote in French art history for some time, in 1913 the poem helped establish Cendrars on the aesthetic level as a bold and exciting literary provocateur and on the mythic level as a world traveler and restless adventurer. When the First World War started, Cendrars, a Swiss citizen, joined the Foreign Legion to fight for his adopted homeland, losing his right arm (his writing arm) in September 1915. It did not take him long to resume working or traveling.

Cendrars's origins were mostly obscured by his deliberate and humorous myth-making. These legends are found in many of his books: that Cendrars escaped from his parents and ran off to Russia, where he smuggled jewels along the Transsiberian railroad, that he hunted whales, worked in Canada, juggled in a London music hall while Charlie Chaplin, "then an unknown, was the recipient of kicks on the behind" (*The Astonished Man* 146), and so on. No less exciting and interesting are the facts of his life, which were initially revealed at the beginning of the1960s. Cendrars was born Frédéric Sauser on 1 September 1887 in La Chaux de Fonds, Switzerland, the third child of Georges Sauser and Marie Dornier. His siblings were Georges and Marie. Soon after his birth, the family moved to Egypt, where Cendrars's father attempted to operate a hotel. Georges Sauser had once been a teacher of mathematics but had given that up before Cendrars's birth in favor of financial speculation and devising inventions. He instilled a love of adventure in his youngest child and unwittingly became the negative image of the grand dreamers Cendrars would be attracted to or invent: Johann August Sutter, Dan Yack, and Moravagine are larger than life, destined for greatness or extreme cruelty, and capable of organizing vast enterprises and legions of men and women. The family left Egypt after two years, and from there, in succession, Cendrars lived in England (possibly), Naples, Basel (where he met Sutter's grandson), Neuchâtel, and Germany. He learned to play piano, in all likelihood from his mother, and in Munich worked in a piano shop. Most probably through his father's influence, a Swiss watchmaker employed him in St. Petersburg from 1904 to 1907. While living there, Cendrars witnessed the 1905 revolution, which constitutes a vital part of *Moravagine*. There is speculation over whether or not he lived briefly in Beijing in 1904-1905. In 1907 he took up studies in philosophy and medicine at the University of Berne. In 1908 he was in Leipzig. There followed time in Brussels and Paris, and in 1911 he was once more in St. Petersburg. It is worth remembering that at this date Freddy Sauser was not yet Blaise Cendrars and that he was twenty-four.

The excursions Cendrars would invent, the array of characters, and the chunks of history that fill his books come from these early wanderings, his later adventures, and from the libraries he visited throughout the world. His reading of esoterica, science, pulp thrillers, philosophy, and music, to single out a few fields, is evident throughout his writing. *In Praise of the Dangerous Life* (1917; revised in 1926) indicates how much of Cendrars is made of books: "If you want to know who I am, consult a dictionary and all the encyclopedias. Don't forget bookmarks and cross-references. Leaf through. Moisten your finger. Don't skip a single page. You'll end up reading all the books in all the great libraries of the nations and you'll end up making your hole in them like a worm through pulp" (*Modernities* 18). Note that he does not say one will end up reading the canon; an established list of great works meant nothing to him. All books are valuable, from the most obscure to the most widely read.

On 21 November 1911 Cendrars sailed on the *Birma* from Libau to New York to join Féla Poznanska, a Polish woman he had met in 1909. He left the United States in June 1912 without her. Féla eventually came to France, and their first son, Odilon, was born in 1914, after which they were married. There were two more children: Rémy, their second son, born in 1916, who died in the Second World War in 1945; and Miriam, born in 1919. It seems that Féla receded fairly quickly from her husband's active life as a writer and as a soldier. She died in England in 1942. They had not divorced. (On 27 October 1949 Cendrars married an actress he had known since 1917, Raymone Duchateau.)

It was on the sea journey to New York that Freddy Sauser became Blaise Cendrart, later changed to Cendrars. The first name seems to come from *braise* (embers), the last from *cendres* (ashes), incorporating art, or *ars*. The fire imagery that recurs throughout his works, along with his fierce desire to junk outmoded styles, makes the name a fitting choice. His rebirth may have occurred during a hurricane-induced epiphany, allowing internal pressures to release in a time of certain danger during which he had to depend on the vessel's captain: "the captain declares [the storm] to be one of the three worst he has experienced in twenty-six years at sea" (qtd. in Bochner, *Blaise Cendrars* 27). It is as possible that during the sea trip the combined influence of a host of writers Cendrars devoured—Goethe, Nerval, Balzac, and especially Remy de Gourmont—helped provoke the transformation. While this is a subject of discussion without hope of a final conclusion, it can be stated that when Sauser/Cendrars arrived in New York in December 1911, he was a different man. When Cendrars left the next summer, it was with "Easter in New York" completed.

Cendrars wrote poetry from 1912 through to the late 1920s, after which he turned his back on it, in part, perhaps, because he believed he had used up the possibilities open to him in that genre. While it is not the focus of this article to discuss his poems, their role in his development is essential, and it would be remiss not to briefly set out some major titles in addition to those mentioned above, since they form a considerable portion of his career. In 1918 he released *Panama, or The Adventures of My Seven Uncles,* written over 1913-1914. John Dos Passos, an advocate of Cendrars since reading *The Prose of the Transsiberian,* translated this work into English in 1931. *Nineteen Elastic Poems* came out in 1919. The elegiac mood of "Easter in New York" was abandoned in favor of cinematic devices, collages, wordplay, and typographical experimentation. In *The War in the Luxembourg Garden* (1916) the poem appears on horizontal and vertical lines, enabling it to be read "in many directions, as if in a spiral: left to right, right to left, horizontally, diagonally, vertically" (Caws 42). *Kodak* (about which more will be said, since it illustrates Cendrars's technique of plagiarism), whose title was later changed to *Documentaries,* appeared in 1924, and the evolving *Ocean Letters* were published between 1924 and 1928. Those works are collected in *Complete Postcards from the Americas* (1976). Though their telegraphic, journalistic style may appear familiar now, their first appearance was startling. His poetry of the 1920s, despite its travelogue nature, favored the kinds of images found in films, coupled with an impersonal voice. The spare lines were displayed on the page like telegrams. As an example, here is "Publicity," from *Documentaries*:

Visit our island
It is the southernmost Japanese territory
Our country is undoubtedly too little known in Europe
It deserves attention
Animal life and plant life are most varied and
    have been hardly studied so far
All in all you will find picturesque vistas everywhere
And inland
Ruins of Buddhist temples which are sheer wonders
    of their kind (*Complete Postcards* 89)

Chefdor states that these poems "disconcerted" Cendrars's first readers, while at the same time they deepened his readers' appreciation for the well-traveled poet (Chefdor, *Blaise Cendrars* 54).

Other genres increasingly pushed poetry aside. Cendrars wrote art criticism in 1919. From 1920 to 1921 he made films, first working with Abel Gance, then at a studio in Rome. His fascination with and knowledge of the cinema can be seen in the essays and screenplays he wrote and in *Confessions of Dan Yack*. His contacts among such painters as Modigliani, Braque, Chagall, Picasso, and Picabia inspired articles that appeared primarily in 1919. (His easy camaraderie with painters and musicians extended itself to the anarchists and Russian revolutionaries he associated with prior to the First World War and with his fellow Legionnaires.) Sharing the same appreciation of what was new as the painters he admired, Cendrars brought out, through the publishing house La Sirène, an anthology of African folk tales as recounted by missionaries and explorers. *African Saga* capitalized on the growing interest in African art and culture and was issued in 1921, the same year the Pan-African Congress took place in Paris and other major centers.

One of the tales from *African Saga* would be adapted into a ballet, *La Création du monde,* with the collaboration of Fernand Léger and Darius Milhaud. It was performed by the Ballets Suédois company in 1923. Some deity characters required actors to be on stilts, and several costumes were over seven feet tall. One critic recounts, "It made the audience gasp at that time. . . . People were coming to see what they believed would be a ballet . . . and got a painting in constant motion" (Wolf). Considering the simultaneous poem *The Prose of the Transsiberian and of Little Jehanne of France,* this mingling of ballet, painting, and folk tales is a natural extension of Cendrars's search for forms that could express his aesthetic concerns. A second ballet based on a piece by Cendrars was thought up, with music by Satie and sets by Picabia, but Cendrars lost interest in the project. Bochner speculates that another foray into this newly discovered territory would be "too repetitive for him, or any lengthy collaboration too onerous" (Bochner, *Blaise Cendrars* 67). As Jean Cocteau said, Cendrars "does not follow fashion, he intersects it" (qtd. in Popkin and Popkin 263). While he would revisit the African material at the end of the decade with two more publications of tales, in 1924 his interest turned to South America.

While there is scholarly argument over how often Cendrars visited Brazil and if he did precisely what he claims to have done there, it is unnecessary to recapitulate the debate here. It is known he made the transatlantic journey in 1924, 1926, and 1927. Chefdor writes that Cendrars was put off by the "dictatorial tyranny which he thought Dada and Surrealism were exerting on poetry," and that "he grabbed the chance [to visit Brazil for the first time]" (*Blaise Cendrars* 57). Cendrars would later write, in typical telescopic fashion,

> At Tremblay-sur-Mauldre (Seine-et-Oise), the Route Nationale 10 (the N.10) passes in front of my door. . . .
> Who can know the N.10 from one end to the other? From the cathedral precincts of Notre-Dame to its terminus on the other side of the Atlantic, beyond the Ygassù, as far as the Parana river, deep in the heart of the wilderness of South America, on the frontier of Paraguay, where it gives way to swamps that my car could not get across. . . . (*The Astonished Man* 217)

He landed in Rio 6 February 1924. Bochner relates how Cendrars was stopped by immigration officials who "didn't want any one-armed labourers" (*Blaise Cendrars* 69), before being met by writers and painters. He gave lectures in São Paulo in February, May, and June. His June address to the *modernistos* was on poetry and linguistics: "This lecture proved once again how far ahead of his time he already was, for the subject of linguistics had only recently begun to claim the attention of a nonspecialized public" (Chefdor, Introduction, *Postcards* 9). The 1924 trip and subsequent visits filled his last poetical works, his fiction, and his fictionalized memoirs. For the Brazilian artists he met—including Oswaldo de Andrade, Luiz Aranha, and Paulo Prado, among others—there and in Paris, he brought the message, in Bochner's words, that "their seemingly provincial homeland was nothing to be ashamed of; quite the contrary, it was everything of importance" (*Blaise Cendrars* 69). Cendrars's reputation had preceded him. As one assessment puts it, "A word of tribute should also be given to the French poet Blaise Cendrars. . . . His free style, brilliant imagery, and fresh, ironic treatment of the modern world were all important influences on the poets of the [Brazilian] Modernist movement" (Bishop and Brasil xx). Concerning his nonartistic ventures while there, Cendrars tells this story:

This life was so beautiful [living in La Redonne, France, as he tries to finish the Dan Yack books], I wanted to enjoy my liberty right up to the last moment, before throwing myself into the battle royal that was waiting for me in Brazil, a battle with certain members of the government, a battle with the interests of certain political clans, a battle with the agents and representatives of the big petrol merchants, a press campaign against the trusts and monopolies of the United States and the leaders of the automobile industry of Detroit who, as in France, had made a business agreement with Standard Oil and the Wall Street banks to prevent any change in the manufacture of car engines destined for South America. It was a tough challenge. But I was in good form and was savouring in advance this struggle in which I would have to employ all my faculties of seduction, of diplomacy, intelligence and aggressiveness, all my sang-froid and my capacity for hard work. It promised to be more exciting than a film. (*The Astonished Man* 90)

It is amusing, and it may not be a complete fabrication.

Aesthetically restless, Cendrars chose the novel as the next genre he would explore and revitalize, turning out *Gold* (1925), *Moravagine* (1926), *Dan Yack* (1927), *Confessions of Dan Yack* (1929), and *Rhum* (1930, not translated) before abandoning the form for twenty-six years. These appeared in between his transatlantic trips to South America. The 1930s was another period of travel, this time to the United States, from which he produced newspaper copy (some that dealt with Hollywood was collected in 1936 as *Hollywood: Mecca of the Movies*). He also began writing "memoirs" (a loosely defined word when applied to his ability to fabricate), republished old articles, and spent much effort in getting the works of Al Jennings and Ferreira de Castro published. At the beginning of the Second World War, Cendrars was a journalist for the British Army, but after France was occupied, he refrained from writing for fear of persecution. In the quiet of his residence in Aix-en-Provence he kept himself out of the eye of the occupying forces. He preferred to do research in the local library. When he did resume work in 1943 it was with the same vigor as before. Following the end of the war, he issued the memoir tetralogy—or what Bochner calls "autobiographical novels" (*Blaise Cendrars* 81)—a collection of short pieces, and one last novel, and he helped adapt some of his work for radio. This extraordinary output, which embraced multiple genres and a variety of vital concerns, was finally stopped by illness, which preceded Cendrars's death in 1961.

The response to Cendrars's prose and poetry can be divided into three main streams: European, English, and Latin American. In most cases the European response quickly followed the publication of his work; the delayed translation into English of his novels and poetry—*Gold* excepted—has meant that on occasion forty years have passed between the initial publication and its notice by English-speaking reviewers. Few critics have written in English on Cendrars. Survey books on French literature of the twentieth century that are written for English readers rarely discuss him. When he is discussed, he is considered unclassifiable or else a Dadaist, a surrealist, a verbal cubist, a futurist, a Bohemian, or an antiromantic. Often his poetry is spoken of more than his prose. Since Cendrars never attached himself to a group of writers or included himself in the movements that swirled around pre- and post-First World War Europe, he is usually excluded from discussions about them. Those who rely on taxonomies can point out definite connections between Breton and Aragon, for instance: however, those writers who may be called sports are lost. Placing Cendrars proves too difficult for most critics, except in footnotes or amid a welter of other names.

The books and articles, introductions and forewords, translations and notes by both Bochner and Chefdor, who have written the most on Cendrars's life and his work for English readers, are invaluable. Other translators include Esther Allen, Alan Brown, Ron Padgett, Nina Rootes, and Garrett White. There are occasional essays on him in English, but it is an indicator of outmoded scholarship that his works continue to be left in relative obscurity.

Early on, Cendrars's poetry was admired by Richard Aldington, and Aldous Huxley, writing for the *Athenaeum* in 1920, noted that unlike Soupault, Cendrars "has something to write about" (qtd. in Pondrum 316). After classifying him as a romantic, Huxley continued, "It is just because he is prepared to cry out, without caring if he makes a fool of himself, it is just because he is not afflicted with that over-refinement and that morbid self-consciousness which prevent so many of his younger contemporaries from writing about anything serious at all, that M. Cendrars is a poet whom it is possible to read with pleasure and interest" (qtd. in Pondrum 316-17). The claim that Cendrars is a romantic is not supported by much evidence. In the postwar period, when romanticism and symbolism were discarded, when Dada and futurism were born, followed by surrealism, when reportage—at which Cendrars excelled—was beginning to take hold of literary imaginations, the hardness of his poetic lines and style and his mind capturing images like a camera attracted artists searching for new ways to express themselves. In Steve Kogan's opinion Cendrars's poetry of the 1920s has a "hard-edged precision" (255) that echoes the prose of Hemingway and Dos Passos. In fact, the reverse may be true.

Hemingway, having nothing much to say about his work, described Cendrars as "a good companion until he drank too much and, at that time, when he was lying, he was more interesting than many men telling a story truly" (81). The generally more perceptive John Dos Passos wrote on Cendrars in 1926 for the *Saturday Review of Literature* in an essay titled "Homer of the Trans-Siberian" and in 1931 translated into English *Panama, or The Adventures of My Seven Uncles* (along with "The Trans-Siberian," "Panama," and selections from two other works). He considered *Gold* "a narrative that traces the swiftest, leanest parabola of anything I've ever read, a narrative that cuts like a knife through the washy rubbish of most French writing of the present time [1926]. . . . It's over so soon you have to read it again for fear you have missed something" (197-98).

It is Henry Miller who most concisely assesses Cendrars's faults as well as his virtues. Since both arise in reviews of the novels under consideration here, it is worth presenting Miller's summation: "Many are the things which have been said against this writer . . . that his books are cinematic in style, that they are sensational, that he exaggerates and deforms à outrance, that he is prolix and verbose, that he lacks all sense of form, that he is too much the realist or else that his narratives are too incredible, and so on ad infinitum" (Miller, *The Books* 66). Here it must be said that like is calling to like, as the same charges have been laid against the author of *Tropic of Cancer.* Having exhibited the accusations, Miller supplies the defense:

> Taken altogether there is, to be sure, a grain of truth in these accusations, but let us remember—*only a grain!* They reflect the views of the paid critic, the academician, the frustrated novelist. But supposing, for a moment, we accepted them at face value. Will they hold water? Take his cinematic technique, for example. Well, are we not living in the age of the cinema? Is not this period of history more fantastic, more "incredible," than the simulacrum of it which we see unrolled on the silver screen? As for his sensationalism—have we forgotten Gilles de Rais, the Marquis de Sade, the *Memoirs* of Casanova? As for hyperbole, what of Pindar? As for prolixity and verbosity, what about Jules Romains or Marcel Proust? As for exaggeration and deformation, what of Rabelais, Swift, Céline, to mention an anomalous trinity? As for lack of form, that perennial jackass which is always kicking up its heels in the pages of literary reviews, have I not heard cultured Europeans rant about the "vegetal" aspect of Hindu temples, the façades of which are studded with a riot of human, animal and other forms? . . . [In his writing there] are detours, parentheses, asides, which are the embryonic pith and substance of books yet to come. . . . We who vaunt dear Shakespeare's madness, his elemental outbursts, are we to fear these cosmic gusts?" (*The Books* 66-67)

More recently, Kathy Acker judged Cendrars "One of the most inventive and funny writers of the early twentieth century" (qtd. in

Cendrars, *To the End of the World,* inside flyleaf). Karl Taro Greenfeld calls him "ribald, earthy, urban," and places him in the company of Miller, Charles Bukowski, and Pedro Juan Gutiérrez (Greenfeld). In contradistinction to Kogan, William Dow argues from a revisionist perspective that Dos Passos's early career may owe more to Cendrars and certain other French writers than to writers who would belong on an "Anglophone list" of influences (397). This is the opposite of how critics generally have approached Dos Passos's work. Dow quotes Marjorie Perloff, who states:

> when we ask ourselves where, on the map of modern Anglo-American poetry, we may find analogues to a Blaise Cendrars, we must look not to Cendrars's contemporaries (Pound, Yeats, Eliot, Stevens, even Williams) but to the generation that came of age in America after the Second World War, the generation of Black Mountain and the Beats, Concrete Poetry and "Naked Poetry," Ethnopoetics and Performance. To put it the other way around: what we call "postmodernism" in American poetry may be less the revolution its proponents claim it to be than an injection of French "modernism," the mode of Cendrars, of Apollinaire, later of Dada, into the native American stream that comes down to us from Emerson and Whitman. (qtd. in Dow 414, n.3)

It is possible that this opinion can help provide a way into reexamining the place of Cendrars. There remains much to be written about him, from a variety of perspectives, exploring his themes and techniques. It is the latter that this essay will focus on.

It is not too great an exaggeration to state that the First World War figures in almost every novel and in the memoirs. It is behind the scenes, either an event that the characters must participate in or encounter or the focus of the writing. With war comes death and corruption. People are killed by anonymous others, by psychopaths, through accidents and disease. In the memoirs Cendrars describes his war experiences in his own fashion, and there are several scenes of sudden and absurd deaths, as well as talk of personal vendettas that must end with a lifeless body. The narrator in these various works denigrates those in charge of any system—military, literary, and civil—while extolling Legionnaires, anarchists, Gypsies, and criminals for their stalwart natures.

Due to the combination of his medical studies and the loss of his right arm, Cendrars often inserts teratology—the study of malformations or deviations from the normal—into his novels. Any reader of U.S. Gothic will be familiar with this device. His characters can be hunchbacked, one-armed or one-legged, or sporting an unusual physical characteristic. These can be viewed as manifestations of an obsession, which may be partially true; however,

Cendrars's experience with First World War soldiers who had been trepanned or crippled (by gas, mines, and bombs) and his own lost limb allows him latitude in this area. On another level his characters of action—Sutter, Moravagine, Dan Yack, and the actress Thérèse—are psychological examples of grotesque figures, with their elaborate systems (for causing mayhem, for making money, for producing goods, for acting), oversized personalities, and boundless energy. Their activity guarantees a spectacular life filled with adventure and failure.

Noticeable in Cendrars's works is his fascination with machinery and the application of science. Raymond in *Moravagine* gives an especially detailed conception of how the present will shape the future, observing, "To modern man, the U.S.A. offers one of the finest spectacles on earth. Its busy machine world makes one think of the prodigious industriousness of prehistoric man. When one dreams within the carcass of a skyscraper or in the pullman of an American supertrain, one makes the direct acquaintance of the principle of utility" (127). It's likely William Gaddis would have sourly agreed with that sentiment. In the 1917 prose poem "Profound Today" Cendrars describes a possible present and near future: "Machines are already catching up, moving ahead. Locomotives rear and steamships whinny on the water. Never will a typewriter commit an etymological spelling error, but the man of intellect stammers, chews his words, and breaks his teeth on antique consonants. . . . Everything is artificial and very real" (*Modernities* 3-4). His regard for trains, planes, automatons, filmmaking, and radio has occasionally been used to classify Cendrars as a futurist. That was a movement with which he had little sympathy. His embracing of various media and new devices was in keeping with his art, where he looked forward to new forms with impatience and reinvented genres (for himself and for others), in tandem with his own identity.

Though enthusiastic about technical advances, Cendrars was not blind to their potential dangers. "I Have Killed" (1918) describes in detail how a soldier-narrator advances through a field to meet an enemy, supplied from boots to tobacco by the entire world: "A thousand million individuals have consecrated their day's activity, their strength, their talent, their science, their intelligence, their habits, their feelings, their hearts to me. And here I am, today, knife in hand" (*Modernities* 14). The simplest weapon possesses risks when used for such purposes as war, and everyone is connected (with some implicated) in their utilization. Thirty years later he wrote: "Belief in the benefits of science and the humanity of physicians is just as stupid, narrow-minded, and widespread among intellectuals today, in this new between-the-wars era, as it was at the end of the eighteenth century . . ." (*Sky* 167).

Cendrars's fondness for characters who could create new worlds is countered by an awareness of the destruction caused by these same people. As with his views on technology, there is a double edge to what is written, since the artist is a creator—who incidentally uses technology (the printing press, the radio, film)—out to destroy old forms. (The fire imagery in Cendrars's name comes back to mind.) In the poem "Hamac," from a 1919 collection, these lines appear about a friend of his: "Apollinaire/1900-1911/For 12 years the only poet in France" (*Selected Writings* 7). The point is clear: Cendrars returned to France in 1912, and as of that date supremacy was overthrown and the nation contained (only) two important poets. His time in Russia and the United States had introduced him to a vigorous life, diverse methods of writing, new images to incorporate into poetry, and untouched subject matter that the old guard were not able to appreciate. Seen from this perspective, Moravagine and Dan Yack come across as twins, with neither a positive commentary upon those who, through will power, invent or create something revolutionary. They are portraits of a type, though not limited to artists.

There are several less important themes that can be mentioned here. Cendrars's interest in other cultures appears in his writing and his travels. Throughout his works, cultures, customs, and languages mingle in a friendly fashion. In English criticism his novels have not been much investigated by students of postcolonial theory or multiculturalism, which seems a fertile field of study. Akin to his interest in far-off cultures is Cendrars's ability to get along with criminals, anarchists, the underworld, and those who held positions in a variety of labor-intensive occupations. In a different vein is his relationship to nature. It would be a mistake to regard his views on the environment as identical with those of Dan Yack, whose favorite gramophone recording is of a "sea-lion having its throat cut" (*Dan Yack* 36), who puts into high gear a whaling operation at Port Deception, and who shoots seals and hunts eagles. Yet an examination of Cendrars's views on ecology may result in much unexpected material.

The reading Cendrars did—of newspapers, encyclopedias, social philosophy, "mystical, visionary, and sometimes pathological" writings (Bochner, *Blaise Cendrars* 31), high and low literature—is well covered in French writing. Both Bochner and Chefdor indicate the nature and extent of his extensive reading, but a few of the most influential figures—Remy de Gourmont particularly—have dropped out of sight for English readers. It would be worthwhile reexamining their impact on his writing for an English-reading audience.

Last, through the memoirs there are metaphysical passages that ward off or defy cold analysis. While writing *Sky,* which concerns itself with levitation and contains a long section on the patron saint of aviators, St. Joseph of Copertino, Cendrars was thinking of his son Rémy, a pilot who died in the Second World War. The son bears a saint's name, and here it may be mentioned that Cendrars read throughout his life the lives of the saints. In the discussions about the novels and memoirs themselves, these and other themes will be touched on. They lie in wait for more study from English readers.

Chefdor describes Cendrars's defense of the novel:

> At a time when the traditional novel was being exposed to virulent attacks by André Breton who considered "the generous supply of novels" the result of a general stultification of the mind and reproached each novelist for adding "his personal little 'observation' to the whole," Cendrars felt that the novel alone would provide a space of sufficient magnitude for his vision and the projection of the "deep transformation of today's man." In a notice published in *Tours les livres* in April 1929, he asserted that the formula of the novel alone could develop the "active character" and the "movement" of contemporary events and people. He concluded with the confident statement that "For some five years, the French novel in the world helps to set up the new regime of human personality." (*Blaise Cendrars* 76)

There is benign braggadocio in that opinion, for as Chefdor explains, the five years refer to the five years during which Cendrars wrote novels. More to the point, his remarks indicate why he slowly withdrew from poetry. Poetry had become exhausted, dull, and restrictive. The novel had ample room for multilayered fabrication combined with reportage. In what follows the emphasis will be on the techniques Cendrars brought to the novel and the memoir. Before the techniques are discussed, the content of each novel will be summarized and a brief indication of its themes provided.

Gold

The most popular of Cendrars's works, *Gold* is likely the only novel that can attach to it the names Joseph Stalin (it was reputed to be a favorite of his) and William Faulkner (who in 1934 tried to adapt it for Howard Hawks). It is the purported history of John Augustus Sutter, from his desperate escape from Europe as Johann August

Suter to his spectacular success in California, followed by devastating failure and humiliation. The "facts" given do not match Sutter's life, which would have been learned firsthand from Sutter's grandson, whom Cendrars knew in Basel (Bochner, *Blaise Cendrars* 17, 24), and from historical texts. Cendrars emphasized Sutter to such an extent that he no longer is just a man but a giant, a symbol, and a vessel for certain concerns.

In Cendrars's telling, in 1834 Sutter leaves his family and Europe for a more profitable life in the New World. He works and saves money in New York and, when he hears of land and fortune in the west, strikes out with a convoy. The overland route is advised against due to its hardships and dangers of attack, so Sutter travels via barque to the Sandwich Islands. In Honolulu he comes up with the idea of buying slaves to help him establish his domain in California. After landing on the beaches of San Francisco in 1839, he acquires land in the Sacramento Valley from Governor Alvarado of Mexico on a ten-year concession and establishes his extensive agricultural and goods-producing garrison, New Helvetia. Sutter defends himself against the "savage tribes of the Upper Sacramento" (49), which makes him appear like a defender of Mexico, while at the same time supplying intelligence to Washington, which makes him look like a quiet ally of those who want California to be part of the Union. By the late 1840s, he owns "the largest domain in the States" (55), over twenty-two square leagues of land.

Sutter's ruin begins with the accidental discovery of gold on his land. Workmen desert him, and when news of the rich veins reach the rest of the continent and abroad, people descend on his farm. Sutter is forced to retreat from New Helvetia to the Hermitage, a refuge from the plague of avarice that occupies his former farmland. In 1850 California becomes part of the United States. Frau Sutter, contacted at some point by her husband, arrives at the Hermitage with their children, only to die soon after. A friend of Sutter's urges him to recover his strength, if only for the sake of his children, and the man of action slowly comes back to life. Slaves are retrieved from the gold mines to make the farm productive once again, but their master is engaged on the project that will consume his life and money. Using "The impotent Law" (75), Sutter lays claim to a vast extent of land, based on the concessions granted by the Mexican authorities, demanding over $225 million in reparations from individuals, the state, and Washington, all of whom had taken over his lands. When the case is decided in his favor in 1855, the citizenry, having enjoyed the freedom to settle down on Sutter's land without permission, burn down the Hermitage and kill one of his sons. His remaining family disperse or die soon after. These violent blows crush Sutter, and with the resolve of a wrecked man who has the Bible on his side, he persists in appealing directly to Washington. He dies in 1880 when a young boy mischievously lies to him that Congress has delivered a verdict in his favor.

In terms of content, little is new in this story of an immigrant's hard-won success followed by a brief period of consolidation and happiness, after which follows failure born of hubris and naïveté. These are universal characteristics found in the literatures of every culture. The style is the simplest Cendrars will ever allow. These two things may explain *Gold*'s global appeal. Sutter is the first man of action Cendrars transforms into a figure through which he can explore a host of topics: the power an individual has to create a life that satisfies one's desires and an almost inevitable (or so it is implied) rigidity of character that must be present for that life to be shaped; the greed in humankind's nature; a never resolved tension between the contemplative life and the engaged life; and the production of goods through work, using the resources of the land without care or regard for what may have existed prior to one's appearance and with little thought of any future beyond one's own.

Moravagine

The preface to *Moravagine* explains that the manuscript that makes up the bulk of the book was left in Cendrars's care: "The manuscripts are in a frightful state. They constitute the works of Moravagine. But the trunk was left with me by . . . by . . . by the Spanish prisoner, God's truth, and I must not reveal his name . . ." (9). The identity of the Spanish prisoner is soon "revealed," with some subterfuge intact, as that of a former psychiatrist, now named Raymond la Science. (Those interested in how Raymond la Science's identity was created should consult Bochner's "Blaise without War" 52-53.)

Raymond narrates that in 1900 he joined the staff of a prestigious mental-health institute, the Waldensee Sanatorium. He becomes disillusioned with treating "the too-fortunate of the earth" (22) when what he wants to study is disease: "What convention calls health is, after all, no more than this or that passing aspect of a morbid condition . . ." (17). Raymond has under his care one special patient, a regicide from the Austro-Hungarian empire named Moravagine. After hearing his story and because his scientific approach encourages him to believe the best way to examine sickness is by letting it exist in a free state, Raymond helps the "incurable" (24) break free. Moravagine jumps the wall, rips open a young girl's stomach with a knife—a pattern that will be repeated everywhere they live—and the men flee to Berlin. Three years later they join the Russian revolutionary movement in the eventful fall of 1904. Moravagine becomes an essential part of the command structure of a cell that kills officials, too-soft fellow anarchists, and innocent citizens. In 1907 Raymond and Moravagine escape to the U.S. They travel throughout the country, always fearful that police and reward-hunters are looking for them. This proves true when their guide, Lathuille, confesses he originally wanted to trap two "grand dukes" (146). He has abandoned that plan, but his fiancée has not, and Raymond and Moravagine are at risk of being captured by her family. Lathuille prevents this, and the three men make their way to a steamer that will take them to the Orinoco.

Their journey down the river in a rubberized canvas boat is described at length in language that reveals how Raymond's mind is being affected by the environment: "Through the mists and vapors all creatures and things appeared to us like opaque tattoos, blurred and faded. The sun was leprous. . . . What a dream, what an opium dream!" (156) The dying Lathuille is killed by Blue Indians (Jivaros Indians). They regard Raymond, his trance, and his medical kit with respect. Moravagine is selected to be their fertility deity. Unrestricted in his behavior for one month before his scheduled death at the hands of the priests, Moravagine binds the girls and women to him through sex and by preaching their emancipation. Sisters kill their brothers and mothers kill their children at the command of the temporary deity who will "sacrifice" almost all the women who joined him. Raymond's conscious mind has sunk under the heat, the moisture, and the events. He is brought back to himself in a canoe on the way down the Rio Negro, well away from the habitat of the Blue Indians, with Moravagine relating what happened during his stupor. The two men eventually arrive in Paris. There they meet an airplane inventor and his assistant, Blaise Cendrars. When the war breaks out, Raymond enlists in the army, only to lose his left leg. Moravagine joins the air force, and his plane is downed behind Austrian lines after he drops bombs on the Hofburg. Through chance, Raymond sees him in a neurological center where Moravagine has been hospitalized. He is mad and believes he is on Mars. The narrative concludes with details of Moravagine's death due to a tumor, followed by a brief survey of his remaining papers. A postface from 1951 concludes the novel.

This summary does no justice to the poetic prose of *Moravagine,* and a listing of the themes will similarly fail to convey the novel's richness and strangeness. Moravagine, like Augustus Sutter, is larger than life, rich, charismatic, and focused. Unlike Sutter, who was animated by a seemingly positive desire to achieve personal success and to benefit others in a patriarchal manner, Moravagine is intent on destruction. This is evident in his name (death-to-the-vagina), in his killing of women, and in his attacks on societies. The first part of the novel is titled "The Spirit of an Age," for Moravagine is a precursor to what the world will look like in 1914. He and Raymond—generally a passive, submissive spectator of the violence—in the main avoid women, except for an interlude in Russia involving Moravagine and Mascha, who dies at Moravagine's hands. Throughout the novel, philosophical disquisitions on disease, love, the Law of Utility, and the New Men of France—often brilliant pastiches of psychological and sociological thought—are offered by Raymond to explain their behavior or to provide an overview of how mankind has arrived at its current condition. The purpose of the essays is to justify for Raymond why he does what he does, as well as to sustain his stance as an objective student of world affairs and cultures. Viewed from outside the novel, as it were, the essays may, for Cendrars, serve to indict the false intellectuals and useless ascetics who, unable to withstand the corrupting influence of politicians, military enthusiasts, and other influential figures, allowed the war to happen, as well as to lay bare the tension within him of being both a contemplative and an adventurer. The war is a watermark on every page. Moravagine "would clutch my arm, demanding loudly to go back to earth," which speaks of a psychic fatigue. The homicidal maniac is tired of Mars, the god of war, yet the spirit of the age lives on in Raymond, who, after his friend's death, finally becomes a full-fledged anarchist.

The Dan Yack Novels

Dan Yack begins in St. Petersburg in September 1904, where the wealthy, eccentric Englishman Dan Yack has his heart broken by Hedwiga. She will marry a prince instead of remaining his lover. Drunk and prostrate under a table in a cabaret, he wakes to overhear part of a conversation among three artists: the poet Arkadie Goischman, the sculptor Ivan Sabakov, and the musician André Lamont. They are complaining about how underappreciated they are. Yack offers them a choice: the three men can each accept blank checks on his vast bank account or the four of them can go off for one year to a deserted spot somewhere in the world, with him paying all the expenses. In a secluded place the artists will be free from economic worries and answerable only to their muses. The men agree to this unusual proposition. On board the *Green Star,* one of Dan Yack's vessels, a globe is suspended, with each artist allowed to shoot at it once to determine where they will be deposited. Lamont shoots third, deliberately severing the string tied to the globe, which crashes to the floor. Their destination will be Antarctica. The four men are provisioned in a temporary home set up on Sturge Island. Bari, Dan Yack's dog, joins them.

"Naturally, things did not run smoothly" (42), the narrator dryly says. The syphilitic Lamont keeps himself in bed, Goischman sits and tugs at his nose, and Sabakov, in love with their patron, devises a plan for a giant ice sculpture of Dan Yack. Lamont has wrecked the careful timekeeping system that is linked to the rations, and the wind and snow aggravate their nerves. Dan Yack retains the most self-control. During one last hurricane, Lamont, maddened by illness, runs out to the ice floes, followed by Bari. Neither return. Goischman cuts off his nose, which he presents to Dan Yack. Alarmed, Dan Yack abandons him to find Ivan, only to discover his body crushed beneath the black ice statue of Dan Yack. The shelter is torn apart by the wind, and the paraffin stove's fire burns Goischman to death. Dan Yack wanders along the island until the *Green Star* returns on schedule to pick up the party.

In civilization again, specifically Chiloé and San Carlos, he revamps his family's whaling operations by entering into a partnership against the Norwegians with Hortalez, a former adversary. Soon Port Deception is in production winter and summer, day and night, slaughtering and processing whales and devising new uses and products from them. Community City is born, and Dan Yack plans to make it a Utopia. But with a seventh fishing season soon to start, his restlessness reasserts itself, for Hedwiga remains on his mind, and his own suicide occupies his thoughts. He is paralyzed: "Act, to what purpose?" (136). The novel ends with him alone in a lab making seal-liver oil tablets, plagued with questions for which he has no answers. (For English readers, the translator has added certain pages from the second volume, in the belief that "it was cruel to the hero, and frustrating to the reader, to leave Dan Yack high and dry" (*Dan Yack* 5).

In a book with many themes, only a few can be touched on here. Once again there is a resolute man of action whose business plans cause fortunes to rise and fall, but his flaws are more marked and his character less mysterious than Moravagine's. Dan Yack William, on news of his father's death, removes the William from his name and rechristens the *Old William* the *Green Star*. In conversation with Hortalez, Dan Yack talks about the chore it is to be someone's son. Yet he is haunted by something as important as Hedwiga and what she represents. On the face of the oil tablets he has created, there is the "effigy of a fat, smiling baby" (137), which makes the book come full circle. Hedwiga's parting note states, "I am sure the child I am carrying in my womb is [the Prince's]" (14), indicating that there is doubt over the paternity. Dan Yack has lost two people, but he speaks of Hedwiga alone. The absence of the child is too painful, and the simulacrum is no consolation.

When the *Green Star*'s crew sound their horns and call for the party, Dan Yack is reluctant to show himself. There is an absence here of who he was, and the replacement has not been fully integrated. Facing Captain Deene, Dan Yack "has the impression that someone has just slipped in behind him" (96). It is evident his personality has undergone a severe transformation. He doesn't realize what he is saying, he is happier alone—when this would lead to his death—and looking into a mirror on board the ship, he "doesn't recognize his own expression" (97). Near the end of the novel Dan Yack sees an iceberg melt away and wishes that one could "annihilate oneself suddenly by deliquescence" (134). The book, for all its creative energy, presents a bleak picture of a frustrated, unfulfilled, and creative man, with the coldness inside him perfectly reflected in the Antarctic landscape.

Confessions of Dan Yack is the first-person narration of fragments and episodes from Dan Yack's life, spoken hesitantly into a dictaphone over the course of January to September 1925. Dan Yack alternates between his own thoughts and what he reads from the notebooks of his dead wife, Mireille. In haphazard fashion he talks about his current life in a chalet above Chamonix—where avalanches and birds occupy his mind in a grim fashion—his soldier's career, how he met Mireille, and his last days at Port Deception, which upon the declaration of war had been taken over by the Germans. These reminiscences are interspersed with Mireille's story about her life with her father—her mother Théréson left the family for Paris, where, it will be discovered by Dan Yack, she is a madam of a prosperous brothel—her convent life, and her life as a movie actress, a career Dan Yack helped along with his wealth. It is her last movie that seemingly propels her into sickness, and in June 1924 Mireille dies from "a bizarre disease whose name I have forgotten and which I couldn't describe. . . . It was at one and the same time a mental, a mystical and a physical illness, horribly physical" (57).

The concluding pages wind down Dan Yack's affairs in Chamonix and put a stop to his rambling monologues. He has not necessarily recovered from losing Mireille. However, a new person has entered his life. In conversation with an acquaintance from St. Petersburg he learns that his former love, Hedwiga, and her husband, the Prince, were killed during the Russian Revolution. Their son Nicolas had gone missing. Dan Yack finds "an eleven-year-old boy, pale, sad, with eyes like Hedwiga's" (120) in a Paris orphanage, and

BLAISE CENDRARS / JEFF BURSEY

the two play with a rabbit in Dan Yack's new apartment: "I shall call him Dan Yack, like me" (120).

The bleakness of vision and weariness of tone in this novel seamlessly connect with the end of *Dan Yack*. The narrator is no longer a decisive man, but his life has not been without purpose since he left Port Deception. However, the eventful part of his life exists in the past, and his recapitulations of the war and the final years of the whaling operation are devoid of excitement. Dan Yack has situated himself on a mountain overlooking civilization, pained by the color of the sky ("The night is blue" recurs throughout the novel), almost delighted in the avalanches that cut off roads, yet selfishly annoyed when his favorite hotel in the town closes for the season. He was impotent in nursing Mireille, and in a mood familiar from when he shot seals in Port Deception, he plans to kill two nesting eagles when he is told Mireille has died. This scheme is ruined when he discovers that the birds are gone and that the aerie has been ransacked.

From the character of Dan Yack, it is hard to credit the statement that he has forgotten the name of the disease that kills Mireille. Toward the end of the novel Dan Yack consults a friend about his wife's illness and discloses that in the seven years he and Mireille lived together they never had sex. She was afraid to make love, Dan Yack says, and her "lesion of the heart" (57) might have played a part in this. Also important, for him she was his "little girl." The convent-taught nineteen-year-old Mireille regards Dan Yack as her "big man," "her lover," and the relationship she had with her father may have been continued with her husband. As for Dan Yack, his respect for his "little girl," who could be his daughter—he is roughly forty-five when they meet—and the failed relationship with Hedwiga may have prevented marital intimacy. That he thinks of his son early in the novel (12, 15) and scours the orphanages of Paris—the description provided of the boy mentions only Hedwiga—establishes that the boy is the missing link to a former love who will perpetuate his line. Though he wrote off his father in *Dan Yack,* he will not be erased himself.

To the End of the World

In the opening pages the seventy-nine-year-old actress Thérèse is engaged in rough sex with her twenty-year-old Legionnaire, who climaxes by vomiting, not ejaculating. She leaves Poxy unconscious and eventually makes it to rehearsal for Guy du Montauriol's play *Madame l'Arsouille,* where other characters—the director Félix Juin, a critic named Kramer who had been released from prison earlier that day after five years' incarceration, the playwright, and a Greek actress named Papayanis—are introduced. The director and the playwright are furious that Thérèse is late and have in fact conspired to replace her with Papayanis, but the two women meet and the older actress immediately disarms her naive rival. When Thérèse takes the stage in a surprise innovation, shaking off her dress, every minute of her seventy-nine years and the battering she took from the Legionnaire are exposed. The journalists' flashbulbs go off and people applaud between tears. Thérèse is not finished. She recites Villon's "La Belle heaulmière," with its opening line, "Ha, savage age, so pitiless and grim" (64), to an increasingly tearful audience. The play is an assured success before it opens. Later that night in a nearby bar, the owner, Émile, is shot by an unknown assassin. The cast and some of the crew are arrested, and for close to ninety pages the scene is restricted to a police station. Speech takes the place of action, stories are exchanged, and interrogations occur between Jean de Haulte-Chambre, the chief of police, and the suspects. When Thérèse gets out, Poxy is waiting, and they visit a man who will remove his tattoos so he can desert the Legion. There she hears more stories and one in particular about an old legless female friend whose past has always been mysterious.

The play runs for months. Each headline about the police investigation into the unsolved death adds to its allure. Juin reenacts the death of Émile just before the opening of *Madame l'Arsouille,* and Papayanis becomes the celebrity she wanted to be, married to an elderly wealthy man. Montauriol's name is made, and Juin's status increases. A scapegoat is required, and since no one stands up for Kramer, who only offers the "force of inertia . . . [and] indifference" (217), he is institutionalized in a sanatorium. He will eventually commit suicide. Haulte-Chambre, who loses his job over not finding the murderer, continues his inquiries. New York beckons, but death intervenes. Coco, the stage painter, is first to go, followed by Thérèse. Stung by a bee, she dies within two days. Poxy cleans out her bank account and is arrested after throwing an orgy for his former Legionnaires.

In the first pages of this roman à clef the reader is presented with a succinct reminder of some of Cendrars's primary themes: violence, sex, the war, teratology, and sexual energy. As Chefdor comments, "here [Cendrars] outdoes Céline and Genêt. . . . Profile upon profile of physical and moral aberrations stud the narrative to the point of parodic saturation" (*Blaise Cendrars* 136). Each story and each character deepen the mood of disgust that lies, as it were, on top of the narrative, but that never emanates from the narrative voice. According to the prefatory note, Cendrars's last novel "takes place somewhere in space, outside time, outside now" (10), and it is obvious that the exaggerations of scene and character are far removed from the reportage of his previous fictions. There are nods to the real world, as when Thérèse recalls that Mallarmé had written a poem for her (24-25), that she once saw Proust (172-73), and that she knows Blaise Cendrars (172), or when the narrator cites Henry Miller (54), but the narrative never descends into reality. Cendrars is outside the work, relishing the chance to tell more tales that stretch the bounds of credibility, while at the same time pressing in the reader's face sequences of harsh behavior that may not disgust, but that certainly require interpretation. Perhaps Chefdor is correct to conclude that *To the End of the World* is "like a storytelling carnival" (*Blaise Cendrars* 139), for it does not embrace the wider worlds present in his earlier novels. The restricted cast of types comes from close to home: Cendrars's second wife was an actress. Yet as a final novel, it displays more vigor and inventiveness than is often found in the late works of other writers.

The Tetralogy

> Every actor of genius must lead a double life so as to be imbued with the *aura* of his part; and if he unwilling to suffer this sea-change he is nothing. (*To the End of the World* 21)

Readers in English of *The Astonished Man, Lice, Planus,* and *Sky* are not presented with the full contents of the tetralogy as it appears in French. *Lice* is "partly abridged" from the French original, as the copyright page quietly indicates. The translator's note at the front of *Planus* provides a picture of what has been lost to English readers:

> In cutting the work down to the length suggested by the publishers, I have tried to omit whole sections which are self-contained in the French original. . . .
> I have reversed the sequence of two parts. . . . The latter is in the way of a digression and, in my view, less suitable as an opening section than the former. . . .
> My humble apologies to the ghost of Cendrars for tampering with his work. . . . (5)

The almost 1,000 pages that make up these four works cannot be adequately discussed here. An incomplete list of topics would include: both World Wars, Gypsies, Brazil, life in France, the writing life, Gustave Lerouge and Remy de Gourmont, the Foreign Legion and the men Cendrars served with, numerous people whose lives he invented or whom he rescued from obscurity, travels in various countries, night skies, and saints. *The Astonished Man* is the first work that broke a self-imposed silence he decided was prudent in occupied France. That these four volumes contain exaggerations and falsehoods does not undermine Cendrars's assertion that they represent his life. Henry Miller said of himself that he lied now and then in the interest of truth. The tetralogy presents aspects of Cendrar's life—imaginative, metaphysical, spiritual, and factual—that he considered most important. Like the novels, these volumes are filled with travel, humor, and scarcely credible encounters. There is a profound sense of the brutalities of the world—war, sudden death—accompanied by a delight in the beauty and absurdities that are found, or that find one, in unexpected places or that arise from the actions of people. The mix of elegy and prayer (in *Sky*), fond remembrance of fallen comrades (*Lice*), the celebration of places (especially in *Planus,* but throughout each volume), and the extravagant imagery provide a richness of detail, a broad canvas, and an exuberance that can be disconcerting to readers accustomed to a more parsimonious response in writing to life.

Cendrars adapted genres to his own needs and discarded them when they felt exhausted. He has Coco say of young people, "If they're going to make contact again with the past they have to move the ruins with modern machines . . . exploit modern life to the point of exhaustion, create it and re-create it . . . they have to envisage the day after next . . ." (*To the End of the World* 106). Coupled with Cendrars's desire to burn up old structures is a fine sense of (not just French) literary tradition and a catholic embrace of literatures from around the world. Reviewers complain that his novels wander—*Gold* being the exception—but this reveals a silent assumption that there is a nonvarying, eternally existent target at which every writer must aim. Walter Albert, a critic sympathetic to Cendrars, believed that Cendrars, "remained a little to the side of [the essay, the novel, biography, and autobiography], exploiting rather than disciplining them" (qtd. in Gunton 91). That the various genre forms need a kind of whipping implies that the novel or the poem contains just this or that kind of material packaged in specific ways. As will be seen in the following discussion of the techniques he used in novels and memoirs, like other artists, Cendrars moved throughout the republic of letters with great liberty. It would be a loss to literature if this freedom didn't exist.

Plagiarism is seldom looked on as anything other than odious. For specific purposes, Cendrars occasionally reworked the material of others. In *The Astonished Man* Cendrars writes, ". . . I was cruel enough to take Lerouge a volume of poetry and make him read, and confirm with his own eyes, some twenty original poems which I had clipped out of one of his prose works and had published under my own name!" Why? "But I had to resort to this subterfuge . . . to make him admit that . . . he too was a poet . . ." (133). In an aside Cendrars says that he won't dwell on this topic, "not wanting to start a fashion, and for the sake of the publisher, who would be mortified to learn that he had unwittingly published my poetic hoax" (133). Scholarship eventually decided to take Cendrars at his word, and as Chefdor relates, forty-one of forty-four poems in *Documentaries* were lifted and reshaped from one Lerouge book, with two other poems coming out of a 1912 travel book on the Congo (*Blaise Cendrars* 53-57).

In 1982 the children's illustrator Marcia Brown translated "Shadow," a story from Cendrars's 1929 collection *Little Black Stories for Little White Children.* That collection, for some time considered left over from the research Cendrars conducted into African folk tales, was eventually revealed to be "an adaptation of tales collected by Father H. Trilles, a nineteenth-century missionary" (Chefdor, *Blaise Cendrars* 74). An early piece, reworked several times and appearing in 1922 under the title *Moganni Nameh,* apparently contains much from Remy de Gourmont's novel *Sixtine* (Chefdor, *Blaise Cendrars* 34-35). Jay Bochner's essay on *Moravagine* describes how Cendrars used a short story by Zamuel Blazek, "in which a man committed revolutionary acts as a result of sexual perversity." Blazek is the real-life person behind the anarchist Z.Z.Z. in *Moravagine.* As Bochner notes, his presence in Cendrars's novel places Blazek inside his own fiction ("Blaise without War" 53).

This type of writing may be seen as a joke, as a slap in the face of the inattentive, as a poetic impulse to transform "raw" or found material not usually considered literature into artistic works as homage or a form of collage. It may be regarded as straight plagiarism. Readers will determine their own perspective. It is an element in Cendrars's work that he acknowledged without prompting from others.

More familiar techniques come up first in *Gold,* a novel that can be for readers (and perhaps was for Cendrars) a useful bridge between *Documentaries* and the later novels. It is also an entry point for analyzing his reportage. *Gold* is comprised of sixteen chapters contained within 128 pages. With the exception of two chapters, each is further broken down into sections, totaling seventy-four, so that one is presented with a restricted amount of information or plot in the amount of space a story in the back pages of a newspaper might take up. The sentences are long and winding, the picture panoramic, where movement, scenery, or context are concerned. When Sutter is about to head west with other travelers from Fort Independence on the banks of the Missouri, in what will be a futile attempt to reach California by land, the narrator provides this view of the bustle:

> The caravans are making ready.
> A wild confusion of animals and equipment. People are shouting at one another in every language under the sun. Germans, Frenchmen, Englishmen, Spaniards, Indians and Negroes jostle one another busily.
> People are setting off on horseback, in carriages and in long processions of covered wagons pulled by twelve pairs of oxen. Some leave on their own, others in large companies. Some are returning to the United States, others leaving them to make for the south, in the direction of Sante Fe, or for the north, towards the high pass that leads over the mountains. (25)

Here is the filmmaker's eye, presenting a description of specific details, setting out the activities people are engaged in, indirectly suggesting the noise and smells; the reportage is present in the quiet indication that there are some who are not eagerly going away but returning—with relief, in failure?—from some adventure.

On other occasions the sentences are laconic and possess a dry wit, such as during Sutter's trip to Honolulu: "On the 11th of February, masses of sargasso, or gulf-weed, are noticed around the ship" (32). In what reads like an uninspired log-book entry, Cendrars establishes the dullness that is part of travel and what occurs in the natural world, then extends it to Sutter. He is uninterested in such sights and passive when looking at the weeds. In retrospect, the entry situates the man of action in the midst of an impediment. Unless it is crafted by man's hand, the natural world leaves him cold: "On the 7th of January, nothing to report except the sighting of a sperm whale" (32). There is a subtle movement from the neutral observer to the mind of Sutter.

The terse dramatic sentences Cendrars deploys throughout the novel have the impact of poetry. Here is chapter 7 in its entirety:

> Reverie. Calm. Repose.
> It is Peace.
> No. No. No. No. No. No. No. No. No: it is GOLD!
> It is gold.
> The gold rush.
> The world is infected with gold fever.
> The great gold rush of 1848, 1849, 1850 and 1851. It will last for fifteen years.
> SAN FRANCISCO! (57)

In this passage Sutter's movement from an orderly, healthy life, through a recognition of his ruination, and to an expression of the long-lasting and debilitating sickness of greed is compressed in eight lines.

Apart from using reiteration effectively—"no" expresses disbelief, anxiety, amazement, realization, and horror—Cendrars prefers propulsive verbs. There are several passages that move at a quick pace, not because of tension, but because Cendrars has chosen specific verbs that, when linked to the present tense and implanted in longer sentences, give a tremendous rhythm to the narrative. The novel moves like a locomotive—a comparison he might have appreciated—and, as Chefdor notes, Cendrars doesn't "allow . . . for a reflective pause" (*Blaise Cendrars* 78). Lists of goods and people fill the reader with a sense of the urgency of events. Those who arrived in New York in 1834 looking for a better life include, in part, "Carbonari, the last disciples of Saint-Martin, the unknown philosopher, and Scotsmen. Generous souls and crackpots. Calabrian brigands, Hellenic patriots. Peasants from Ireland and Scandinavia. Individuals and nations, victims of the Napoleonic Wars, men sacrificed by Diplomatic Congresses. Carlists, Poles, Hungarian partisans" (16). This list transplants Sutter's story from the particular to the general—evidently there are many Sutters—and it embraces the world, just as people from every nation will descend on Sutter's land to seize his gold.

Certain features found in *Gold* reappear in his later works, but with *Moravagine* Cendrars expanded his rhetorical repertoire. In addition to the alternation between telegraphic and panoramic prose and the repetition of phrases, in his second novel there are miniessays, a thriller narrative, lengthy sentences, a colorful prose that is anything but reportage, obscure words, and dense language. Structurally, *Moravagine* is told in twenty-six chapters divided into three sections: "The Spirit of an Age"; "Life of Moravagine, an Idiot"; and "Moravagine's Manuscripts." The words belong to Raymond la Science. (Cendrars provides a preface and postface.) The A-Z structure—the alpha and omega of cruelty and horror—survives through chapter numbering in the excellent English translation by Alan Brown. Raymond's clinical interest in sickness and the pathological opens the novel, which begins in 1900:

> Hysteria, the Great Hysteria, was then much in fashion in medical circles. Following the preliminary work of the schools of Montpellier and la Salpêtrière, which had, so to speak, done no more than define and situate the object of their studies, a number of foreign men of science, particularly the Austrian, Freud, had taken up the problem, had gone into it more amply, more profoundly, had lifted it, extracted it from its purely experimental and clinical domain to make of it a kind of pataphysics of social, religious and artistic pathology, in which it was

not so much a question of coming to know the climacteric of this or that obsession born spontaneously in the farthest regions of consciousness and determining the simultaneity of the "auto-vibrism" of sensations observed in the subject, but rather of creating, of forging an entire system of sentimental (supposedly rational) symbolism of acquired or innate slips of the subconscious, a kind of key to dreams for use by psychiatrists, as codified by Freud in his works on psychoanalysis. . . . (15-16)

This is a fair distance from the straightforward sentences that make up the bulk of *Gold*. Sven Birkerts writes, "Long, telescopic sentences carry us through revolution, terror, a zone of sexual and moral nihilism" (qtd. in Gunton 97), and the at times feverish quality to the writing reveals the damaged state of the narrator. The six-page medical report near the end of the novel that relates how Moravagine died is drawn from Cendrars's medical studies.

In the narrative he provides, Raymond moves from his own thoughts to Moravagine's quite often and just as easily examines the mores and customs of other cultures. For slightly over sixty pages they are in Russia, committing acts of murder and sabotage, and within this section lie almost thirty pages from Raymond's diary. As part of one last coordinated wave of terror, he is to detonate a bomb from a safe distance before leaving Russia for good. The page-turning aspect of this part of *Moravagine* has not been sufficiently commented on and can only be gestured to here. In these pages Cendrars mimics the atmosphere of spy thrillers, with fondness and appreciation, and the control of tone and pace is remarkable. That he gave Raymond the ability to make transitions from essays to poetic writing—"A fine dust of horse-dung falls in a drizzle like the flakes of russet gold in a liqueur" (59)—is a sign of his awareness that the form of the novel need not be restricted.

Just as in *Gold* Cendrars reimagined Sutter, in this novel he summons to life historical figures and recounts recent events. The figure behind Z.Z.Z. has been mentioned above, and there is the casual reference to the Bonnot gang when Moravagine and Raymond arrive in Paris from South America (171). History books provide details of Jules Bonnot and his gang of anarchists, some of whom were tried at about the time the Paris events in *Moravagine* occur. The Blue Indians of South America, "belonged to the ancient tribe of the Jivaros" (160) of Peru, and the Jivaros exist today. Yet there is a peculiar side effect to this technique. One simply doesn't know whether or not to believe that what Cendrars has Raymond say is accurate. The historical and geographic details that underpin the novel call into question the truth of the fiction Cendrars has written, which is a result he may have expected. He did visit South

America, Russia, and the United States before this novel came out, yet there is a tendency to challenge the veracity of what has been presented. Cendrars anticipated investigation of the reportage element in his works, as the Lerouge anecdote in *The Astonished Man* suggests.

The essays represent the concerns of the times and are eye-opening pastiches of sociological thought as it existed in the period 1900-1925. The reliance on scientific discourse and the occasional odd word suits Raymond, for he is a divided figure, caught between plain speech and windy theorizing, action and observation (somewhat like Cendrars himself), high purpose and vicious behavior, until freed by Moravagine's death. Balancing essays, the adventure, travel, and thriller genres, as well as the psychological novel, is Cendrars's greatest achievement in *Moravagine*. He moved beyond examining a single anarchist to what anarchists in general foreshadowed and embodied: the forces behind the First World War, allied to the mechanical world (machines, planes, weaponry) that was becoming more and more prominent. These ideas demanded a more intricate style (occasionally verging on the purple) that was somewhat abandoned until the memoirs.

Dan Yack is told through an omniscient narrator and is structured in five parts: "Hedwiga"; "Longitude 164° 3' E (from Greenwich) Latitude 67° 5' S"; "Overwintering"; "The Sun"; "Port Deception." The prose moves freely from past to present tense. Sentences incorporate the physical setting or conditions. In one scene Dan Yack is looking at the provisions in the Antarctic hut: "The hurricane lamp he was holding lit up a row of twenty-four sugar-loaves whose white peaks emerged from thick blue wrapping-paper, like the unsuspected snowy peaks one discovers when exploring a new continent" (56). Later, the last storm of the winter is described:

> The hurricane has been raging for days now.
> The wind has just shifted. It is blowing a mixture of snow and verglas.
> A small lake, formed by the melting of the ice during the first few days of summer, has just emptied itself like an overturned cup.
> A swollen, crepuscular light.
> It is raining.
> Everything is dancing in a runnel of water.
> Everything is shaking itself out, winding itself up again.
> It is snowing. (82)

Everything is shifting about in the light and wind, and the imagery attempts to keep up with it. Events are occurring too fast for them to be depicted in more than swift strokes. As conditions deteriorate in parts 3 and 4, each character reflects on his own misery in sentences of a regular length and standard complexity, but when they try to communicate with others—with the exception of Ivan, the sculptor—they are seldom able to speak in anything but short utterances. The technique of one-word paragraphs, familiar from *Gold,* is attached to imagery that is quickly invented and then replaced to help describe a person's state or the visual field. This combination is a typographical and psychological rendering of the artists' minds. Like the ice pack at the advent of summer, their thoughts break into shards. The narrator's voice, moving in and out of each character, uses this technique also. Goischman, having cut off his nose, sits in the remains of the hut while it is being torn apart by a hurricane:

> He sees the Primus overturn and the paraffin flames run towards him, licking his legs and his chair.
> Never has Arkadie been so lucid.
> He thinks proudly: The death of a man of letters. I am dying of a plagiarism, and even this plagiarism is botched.
> In fact, Van Gogh only cut off his right ear, and, moreover, it was for a woman. Whereas I! . . .
> He despises himself, with pride.
> Futility.
> Mental lucidity.
> He burns.
> He freezes.
> He blazes. (83-84)

Dan Yack is not immune to the effects of the winter and the grisly deaths of his companions, and this is shown on the linguistic level by his own terse comments. However, he quickly recovers (on the level of the language), and the last part of the novel, "Port Deception," is filled with many long sentences as Dan Yack engages in various complex projects. Only when he thinks of suicide does the prose reduce itself to smaller units. The longer sentences indicate a whirligig of activity, unlike the frozen, circumscribed life he led on Antarctica.

Kogan considers this novel built along the lines of *The Island of Doctor Moreau* and *Heart of Darkness* (273), and this literary descent may be worth teasing out for its view of Utopia. Dan Yack's fantasy of a perfect environment, Community City, is based on whaling—i.e., deliberate and wholesale killing—the wealth of a lovelorn central character, and an absence of connection with others. To delve into the psychological motivations of his characters, Cendrars abandoned the objective stance and filtering consciousness of *Gold* and *Moravagine* respectively. In the Antarctic portion most noticeably, the thoughts of the three artists, their host, and their host's dog are relayed through interior monologues. There is a narrow depth to these investigations of motivation, and the three artists, while memorable, are by no means rounded characters. Yet this exploration of figures outside the man of action is a new device for Cendrars, and within its boundaries it is done effectively.

Again, the fidelity of certain elements in the novel are called into question. One example will be sufficient: "The current carried the schooner rapidly towards Bruni Island, which lay on their starboard bow and could be identified by a gigantic dead tree-trunk. They were now almost level with Rabbit Island, whose lighthouse sends out a beam every fifty-nine seconds" (28). An atlas will determine if these islands exist, but it is the precision of the fifty-nine seconds that causes a reader to question what is being said. Perhaps it is accurate, plucked from some book or told to Cendrars in conversation. It must also be said that "every minute" would leave the sentence unnoticeable. Cendrars's desire for a finely tuned sentence may propel a reader to examine such details independently. While *Dan Yack* is regarded in polarized fashion by critics based on its content and themes, for the purposes of an examination of his technique, it is a satisfying advancement that utilizes the strengths Cendrars exhibited in *Gold* and *Moravagine*. The length of his sentences fits snugly with the events and the characters' situations, and his language does not possess the overheated quality perfect for Raymond, but which would be disastrously off-key for Dan Yack.

Plain speech is the dominant linguistic feature of *Confessions of Dan Yack,* a brief, melancholy novel. The man of action here sits for hours reminiscing into a dictaphone about life before and with Mireille, his late wife, and reading aloud her notebooks. The nine cylinders, recorded over nine months, divide into thirteen sections. Cendrars provides this prefatory note:

This second book was not *written.*
It was *dictated* entirely into a *DICTAPHONE.*
What a pity that the printing press cannot also *record* the voice of Dan Yack, and what a pity that the pages of a book do not yet have *sound.*
But it will come.
Poor poets, let us keep working. (8)

There may be an indication here that Cendrars was experiencing a growing fatigue with or dissatisfaction over the novel form (*Rhum* (1930) will be his last novel until 1956). Yet a poor poet—not simply a novelist, it will be noted—must work with what he has. So the conceit of this novel as having been spoken by a fictional character allows Cendrars to use an episodic structure, though there are reference points that ground the work. To indicate the changes in Dan Yack, Cendrars has him halting in speech, unable to say openly what he clearly suffers from: "How can I say what I want to say, say that . . ." (10) In his next recording he says, "I want to say that . . . I should like to say . . ." (11), but he trails off. Even when he has said that Mireille is dead, he still wonders how to say that. It is not for some pages that Dan Yack finally states, "Perhaps you know, Mademoiselle, that Mireille is dead? . . . . That is what I wanted to tell you [two lines of ellipses] Yes [two lines of ellipses]" (18-19).

Readers will not be surprised to encounter the short sentences of sorrow, found in Dan Yack's voice and in Mireille's notebooks, and the longer sentences that carry with them merely the echo of life's hurly-burly. Stripped of extravagant imagery and sentence structure, the narrative is on the surface almost drab. In his instructions to the typist, Dan Yack says, ". . . I don't know how to read, still less how to read aloud. Besides, very often I started whistling so as to think of other things . . ." (18). The recording is represented in words faithful to the narrator's character, while indicating the gulfs between what is confessed and what is kept secret.

The waywardness of the narrative, which extends in time and geography from Chamonix to New Zealand, the Somme to St. Petersburg, is also new. In the wide-ranging *Moravagine* Cendrars kept things to a linear sequence, but here Dan Yack's wandering mind summons up memories in a seemingly haphazard manner, giving the reader a partial view of him, though perhaps exposing more than the narrator realizes. Cendrars's refusal to write intensively plotted books persisted, as some critics have complained. Faced with the same types of comments, Henry Miller wrote:

> There were plenty of writers who could drag a thing out to the end without letting go of the reins; what we needed was a man, like myself for instance, who didn't give a fuck what happened. . . . People have had enough of plot and character. Plot and character don't make life. Life isn't in the upper storey: life is here now, any time you say the word, any time you let rip. (*Sexus* 47-48)

Though this comes well after the release of Cendrars's major novels, it does state clearly some of Cendrars's own concerns. It is significant that after *Confessions* he returned to the reportage technique with *Rhum* and that his writing of the 1930s was largely taken up with invented histories of himself and with helping other writers get published.

To the End of the World, Cendrars's last novel, exhibits little that is new in terms of technique. This roman à clef is small in scale, restricted to the theater and to certain parts of Paris. The sentences remind one more of the memoirs than of the novels.

The tetralogy has long been noted for its style, which can strike a contemporary reader as ornate and overmuch. What will be immediately apparent is the length of the sentences, which contain facts, information, poetic turns of phrase, allusions, plot progressions, distortions of truth, and reminiscences, tumbling one after the other in clause after clause, demanding that on occasion the reader return to their beginning. Marjorie Perloff describes parts of *Sky*'s style: "The extravagantly long catalogue, whose effect depends upon intensification and hyperbole, is followed, as is so often the case, by flat, matter-of-fact assertion . . . this giving way, in its turn, to an apocalyptic note. The effect is that of a lyric poem" (4-5). The elaborate sentences can go on for eighty lines, moving in unpredictable directions, with each thought a springboard to another line. The emphasis is on associative logic rather than linear presentation. In an astute judgment, Birkerts writes, "[The reader] starts to experience the narrative with the acuity of one following a thread through a labyrinth. The time sense, the demand for sequence, are cast aside. The narrative, like the life, like any life, reveals that its true character is referential" (qtd. in Gunton 98).

Here is one typical paragraph:

> A seductive country, full of simultaneous contrasts, and highly dangerous, to judge from the unanimous discussions of the Brazilians, those feverish chatterboxes whose garrulousness masks the profound melancholy to which man is a prey in this torrid climate, feeling himself lost in the vastness of the country and utterly powerless and impotent in the face of the immensity of his task, and, in spite of the stimulus of his most exciting successes, which he knows very well to be meretricious, he tends, generation after generation, to fall back into a morbid apathy, a discouraging weariness, like his ancestor, the hardy pioneer who stretched out exhausted in his hammock and who often let himself die in the wilderness, completely disoriented, his head empty, and the rich Brazilian of today eagerly fills this emptiness with words, before falling asleep, taking his siesta in the clubs and roof gardens of the capital cities, annihilating himself with well-being, befuddling himself with self-indulgence, coddling himself with sporadic fits of melancholy and lethargy, handling immense business projects in the way that some people abuse aphrodisiacs or narcotics. (*Sky* 161)

What begins as a descriptive passage of a place moves into a judgment on the people who tried to tame the plains, jungles, and rivers of Brazil, extending back through time, then forward, and down into the psyche of contemporaries and pioneers who have been and still are discouraged and defeated, in an accumulative manner—as the sentence is itself built—by the reality that is Brazil. There are great stretches like the one just quoted, and much is packed into dense lines whose velocity is not frequently matched in the novels.

There are, as well, brief and expressive memorial notes to fallen soldiers— "GARNERO (killed at Vimy Ridge, buried the same day and rediscovered ten years later, resuscitated!)" (*Lice* 58)—and the pithy, demotic dialogue in *Lice*. Occasionally there is an aphoristic quality to the writing: "The conscience is strangled by obedience, as if it were a cord, and the will is a hanged man" (*Sky* 129). But it seems that upon breaking the self-imposed and necessary silence of the Second World War, and with the death of his son Rémy in mind, Cendrars's writing became more effusive and relaxed. From the simple speech patterns and the use of a few formal devices in *Gold* to the complex structures of the memoirs, Cendrars's use of techniques developed in sophistication, becoming more and more seamlessly integrated into the content.

The quotation at the beginning of this essay contains a line made poignant by Cendrars's obscurity: "It all belongs to yesterday, not to today. I will be visible tomorrow. Today, I'm working." He matters now in different ways from those in place from 1912 to 1961, though it is still true, as Dos Passos said, that "We need sons of Homer going about the world beating into some sort of human rhythm the shrieking hullabaloo, making us less afraid" (204). With each successive work Cendrars's prose and vision open new vistas. The novels and memoirs contain sufficient material for studies in postcolonial thought, ecocriticism, queer theory, explorations of machines and humankind, reevaluations of modernist poetry, and the history of reportage. That suggestive list, however, leaves out what a reader will value most: the wonderment experienced when immersed in Blaise Cendrars's fantastic, humor- and terror-filled worlds, where vitality and adventure cram each page, and where the expression of thought is rendered in exquisite, elastic language.

Works Cited

Bishop, Elizabeth, and Emanuel Brasil, eds. *An Anthology of Twentieth-Century Brazilian Poetry*. Middletown: Wesleyan UP, 1972.

Bochner, Jay. *Blaise Cendrars: Discovery and Re-creation*. Toronto: U of Toronto P, 1978.

—. "Blaise without War: The War on Anarchy in Blaise Cendrars's *Moravagine*." *Modernism/Modernity* 2.2 (1995): 49-62.

Caws, Mary Ann. *The Inner Theatre of Recent French Poetry*.

Princeton: Princeton UP, 1972

Cendrars, Blaise. *The Astonished Man*. Trans. Nina Rootes. London: Peter Owen, 1970.

—. *Complete Poems*. Trans. Ron Padgett. Berkeley: U of California P, 1992.

—. *Complete Postcards from the Americas: Poems of Road and Sea (Documentaries, Ocean Letters, South American Women)*. Trans. and intro. Monique Chefdor. Berkeley: U of California P, 1976.

—. *Confessions of Dan Yack*. Trans. Nina Rootes. London: Peter Owen, 1990.

—. *Dan Yack*. Trans. Nina Rootes. London: Peter Owen, 1987.

—. *Gold*. Trans. Nina Rootes. London: Peter Owen, 1982.

—. *Hollywood: Mecca of the Movies*. Trans. Garrett White. Berkeley: U of California P, 1995.

—. *Lice*. Trans. Nina Rootes. London: Peter Owen, 1973.

—. *Modernities and Other Writings*. Ed. and intro. Monique Chefdor. Trans. Esther Allen with Monique Chefdor. Lincoln: U of Nebraska P, 1992.

—. *Moravagine*. Trans. Alan Brown. London: Penguin, 1979.

—. *Planus*. Trans. Nina Rootes. London, Peter Owen, 1972.

—. *Selected Writings of Blaise Cendrars*. Ed. Walter Albert. New York: New Directions, 1966.

—. *Shadow*. Trans. Marcia Brown. New York: Scribner's, 1982.

—. *Sky*. Trans. Nina Rootes. Intro. Marjorie Perloff. New York: Paragon House, 1992.

—. *To the End of the World*. Trans. Alan Brown. London: Peter Owen/Chester Springs: Dufour Editions, 2002.

Chefdor, Monique. Introduction. *Complete Postcards from the Americas: Poems of Road and Sea (Documentaries, Ocean Letters, South American Women)*. By Blaise Cendrars. Trans. Monique Chefdor. Berkeley: U of California P, 1976. 1-44.

—. *Blaise Cendrars*. Boston: Twayne, 1980.

—. Introduction. *Modernities and Other Writings*. By Blaise Cendrars. Trans. Esther Allen with Monique Chefdor. Lincoln: U of Nebraska P, 1992. ix-xxiv.

Dos Passos, John. *Orient Express*. New York: Harper, 1927.

Dow, William. "John Dos Passos, Blaise Cendrars, and the 'Other' Modernism." *Twentieth Century Literature* 42 (1997): 396-415.

Gavronsky, Serge. "An Astonished Man." New York Times Online. 12 July 1992. 9 Jan. 1999 <http://search.nytimes.com/books.search/>

Greenfeld, Karl Taro. "Sex and the City." *New York Times Online*. 25 March 2001. 22 Oct. 2002 <http://query.nytimes.com/search/>

Gunton, Sharon R., ed. *Contemporary Literary Criticism*. Detroit: Gale Research Company, 1981.

Hemingway, Ernest. *A Moveable Feast.* New York: Scribner's, 1964.

Kogan, Steve. "The Pilgrimage of Blaise Cendrars." *Literary Imagination* 3 (2001): 254-76.

Miller, Henry. *The Books in My Life.* New York: New Directions, 1952.

—. *Sexus.* New York: Grove, 1965.

Perloff, Marjorie. Introduction. *Sky.* By Blaise Cendrars. Trans Nina Rootes. New York: Paragon House, 1992. 1-8.

Pondrom, Cyrena N. *The Road from Paris: French Influence on English Poetry 1900-1920.* Cambridge: Cambridge UP, 1974.

Popkin, Debra, and Michael Popkin, eds. *Modern French Literature.* Vol. 1. New York: Frederick Ungar, 1977.

Seymour-Smith, Martin. *Guide to Modern World Literature.* Vol. 2. London: Hodder & Stoughton, 1975.

Wolf, Matt. "A Cubist Vision of Theater as Sculpture in Motion." *New York Times Online* 13 September 1998. 22 Oct. 2002 <http://query.nytimes.com/search/>

A Blaise Cendrars Checklist

Gold (L'Or). Paris: Grasset, 1925; trans. Henry Longan Stuart. *Sutter's Gold*. New York: Harper, 1926; trans. Nina Rootes. London: Peter Owen, 2003 (U.S. dist. Dufour Editions).

Moravagine. Paris: Grasset, 1926; trans. Alan Brown. London: Peter Owen, 1970; London: Penguin, 1979; New York: Blast, 1990.

Dan Yack (Le Plan de l'Aiguille). Paris: Editions Denoël, 1927; *Antarctic Fugue*. Trans. unknown. London: Pushkin Press, 1948; trans. Nina Rootes. London: Peter Owen, 2002 (U.S. dist. Dufour Editions).

Confessions of Dan Yack (Les confessions de Dan Yack). Paris: Editions Denoël, 1929; trans. Nina Rootes. London: Peter Owen, 1990 (U.S. dist. Dufour Editions).

Hollywood: Mecca of the Movies (Hollywood, La Mecque du Cinema). Paris: Grasset, 1936; trans. Garrett White. Berkeley: U of California P, 1995.

The Astonished Man (L'Homme foudroyé). Paris: Editions Denoël, 1945; trans. Nina Rootes. London: Peter Owen, 1970.

Lice (Le Main coupée). Paris: Editions Denoël, 1946; trans. Nina Rootes. London: Peter Owen, 1973.

Planus (Bourlinguer). Paris: Editions Denoël, 1948; trans. Nina Rootes. London, Peter Owen, 1972.

Shadow. trans. Marcia Brown. New York: Scribner's, 1982.

Sky (Le Lotissement du ciel). Paris: Editions Denoël, 1949; trans. Nina Rootes. New York: Paragon House, 1992.

To the End of the World (Emmène-moi au bout du monde). Paris: Editions Denoël, 1956; trans. Alan Brown. London: Peter Owen, 1966; London: Peter Owen, 2002 (U.S. dist. Dufour Editions).

Complete Postcards from the Americas: Poems of Road and Sea (Documentaries, Ocean Letters, South American Women). Trans. and intro. Monique Chefdor. Berkeley: U of California P, 1976.

Modernities and Other Writings. Ed. and intro. Monique Chefdor Trans. Esther Allen with Monique Chefdor. Lincoln: U of Nebraska P, 1992.

Complete Poems. Trans. Ron Padgett. Berkeley: U of California P, 1992.

Severo Sarduy

Rolando Pérez

For my parents

The question as to how one should approach a difficult work of literature begs a series of questions, one of which is: What, if anything, constitutes a "difficult" work? The American composer Roger Sessions attempted to answer this question in a 1950 *New York Times* article entitled, "How a 'Difficult' Composer Gets That Way." Charged by his critics with composing "difficult music," Sessions answered that it was not that his music was difficult per se, but that people unaccustomed to listening to certain sounds found it difficult and that repeated exposure to the new sound would dispel the perceived difficulty. Severo Sarduy stated on several occasions that the label of experimental literature did not apply to his work with any degree of specificity, since all literature is by nature experimental. But, unfortunately, we live in an age that demands quick, easy answers, even when the stakes are as high as that of war. A few years ago, the Cuban writer Guillermo Cabrera Infante gave a talk at the University of Madrid where he came close to declaring the death of "difficult" or serious literature. Included in such a tragic death would undoubtedly be the works of the great writers of all epochs and nations. Clearly, Sarduy's name would be included in that sad list. He would be joined by such contemporary American writers as John Barth, Donald Barthelme, Thomas Pynchon, William T. Vollmann, and Robert Coover, whose work has been compared to Sarduy's.

Roger Sessions recalls Einstein once saying, "everything should be as simple as it can be, but not simpler" (169). Thus I want to make it clear from the outset that the purpose of this essay is not to make Sarduy simple or even simpler—an impossibility that applies not only to Sarduy but to any philosopher, writer, or artist worthy of the name. Instead, my aim is to introduce Sarduy to a monolingual English audience and to enrich—through a multiplicity of historical, ethnographic, and artistic cross-references—the reader's experience of his work. To that end, I hope that this essay proves helpful and that you join me in this wildly baroque, carnivalesque, textual adventure.

When Americans think of Latin American writers, they usually think of Carlos Fuentes, Jorge Luis Borges, Isabel Allende, and the world-renowned Gabriel García Márquez of the best-selling *One*

Hundred Years of a Solitude; it was this book that, thanks to the wonderful translation of Gregory Rabassa, put Latin American literature on the American map. The generation out of which these and other Latin American writers (like Octavio Paz, Julio Cortázar, and Mario Vargas Llosa) emerged has been called the Boom generation. It was an age of literary experimentation, and the experiments took many forms. Cortázar's *Hopscotch* liberated novelistic narrative from the traditional strictures of linearity; José Lezama Lima's *Paradiso* turned the novel into a mirror of consciousness (via the Greek eros of the banquet); and García Márquez's magic realism freed the reader from the straitjacket of the realistic novel. The three most important publications in Cuba in the late 1950s through the mid-1960s were the magazines *Orígenes* (founded by Lezama Lima), *Lunes de Revolución,* and *Ciclón.* The last two were established by dissidents of *Orígenes,* who were beginning to turn away from Lezama's poetics to redefine the essence of Cuban culture (*lo cubano*) along less traditional, nationalistic lines. One such dissident writer was Severo Sarduy, whose poetry first appeared in *Ciclón* (1956).

Sarduy was born on 25 February 1937 in the province of Camagüey to working-class parents. Camagüey, as Roberto González Echevarría has pointed out, was one of the most traditional of the Cuban provinces—ironic given Sarduy's own aggressively modern, postmodern, and antitraditionalist aesthetics (*Ruta* 15). Unlike most of his contemporaries, Sarduy did not come from a privileged background. His cultural origins were mixed: Spanish, African, and Chinese. He attended public schools throughout his life, and in 1955 he graduated from Instituto de Segunda Enseñanza de Camagüey (the equivalent of high school) with honors in arts and sciences. By the time he graduated, Sarduy had already developed an interest in literature and had published some poetry in the local newspapers. His interest in the literary life no doubt made his family uneasy. By the time he was college age, the Sarduys had, through hard work, joined the middle class, and they expected their son to choose a practical career. Convinced that he had exhausted all the educational opportunities in Camagüey, Sarudy moved to Havana, where he enrolled in medical school at the University of Havana—more likely to satisfy his parents' wishes than really to pursue a career in medicine. It was his ticket to the center of Cuban culture. In Havana he earned a living as a copy editor, writing television and radio jingles for an advertising agency. A year after his arrival in the city, Cabrera Infante published his short story "El Seguro" in the magazine *Carteles*. In the course of a year he had published several poems in *Revolución* (an anti-Batista newspaper), had established himself as editor of *Diario*

Libre, and had become a regular contributor to *Nueva Revista Cubana* and *Artes Plásticas.*

The next pivotal moment in Sarduy's life came in the fall of 1959 when he was awarded a scholarship to study art history and criticism at the Ecole du Louvre in Paris. Sarduy did not finish his art studies at the Ecole, as the director of the school died before he had even begun work on his thesis. But in Paris he met Neruda, García Márquez, Cortázar, Goytisolo, and Paz, to name but a few. By 1961 it was apparent that the revolution in Cuba had not gone as expected; the magazines that Sarduy had been involved with had disbanded, some writers had already taken flight, and the Castro regime was beginning to actively censor publications. This was the year that Sarduy decided to burn his *guayabera,* the traditional Cuban shirt, and not return to Cuba. In Paris he established connections with many of the writers associated with the progressive magazine *Tel Quel* and later collaborated with Julia Kristeva, Philippe Sollers, Roland Barthes, and other structuralist and poststructuralist writers. It is his connections with the French writers that have led many critics to accuse Sarduy of being more French than Cuban—this in spite of the fact that he never stopped writing about his native country and never stopped writing in Spanish. It was in Paris, in fact, that Sarduy wrote his first novel, *Gestos* (Gestures, 1963).

González Echevarría sees *Gestos* as Sarduy's parody of Alejo Carpentier's novella *The Chase* (1956) (*Ruta* 67). *The Chase,* which takes place in pre-Castro Cuba, has the main character run into a concert hall performance of Beethoven's Eroica Symphony to escape capture by members of the revolutionary Marxist group he has betrayed to the authorities. In *Gestos* the events take place during Batista's dictatorship, and the main character, a mulatto woman, is a singer by night, laundress by day, and a revolutionary setting bombs in public utility companies in her off hours. As a counterpoint to *The Chase,* with its references to European architecture and German classical music, the world of *Gestos* is filled with the sights and sounds of popular Cuban culture.

This brings us to the theoretical base of Sarduy's literary works: his neobaroque aesthetics, without which it is difficult to understand this original writer. Americans tend to think of Cuba either as an oppressive dictatorship (which it is) or as a country of racial equality (which it is not) with deep roots in the African continent. This neighboring country of African mythologies with its Orishas and Santeria has come to be known in recent years as the home of the Afro-Cuban sounds of Wim Wenders's film *Buena Vista Social Club.* But modern-day Cuba is also a country with roots that go back to seventeenth-century colonial Spain and to nineteenth-century China. As history has demonstrated time and again, the influence of colonial power has never been one-directional. Even when the "mission" of the colonial power was to control, manipulate, and exploit the labor and natural resources of the indigenous people, its accomplishments in this direction were always tempered by the colonized culture, whose history and mythologies stood in the way of total absorption. This process of cross-cultural pollination is often referred to as *hybridity*. As Homi K. Bhabha writes in *The Location of Culture*, "Hybridity is the sign of the productivity of colonial power, its shifting forces and fixities; it is the name for the strategic reversal of the process of domination through disavowal (that is, the production of discriminatory identities that secure the 'pure' and original identity of authority). . . . It unsettles the mimetic or narcissistic demands of colonial power but reimplicates its identifications in strategies of subversion that turn the gaze of the discriminated back upon the eye of power" (112). In short, the colonized culture reverses the process of colonization by absorbing or co-opting some of the elements of the colonial power's culture into its own. That reversal brings with it a significant transformation that determines to a great extent the identity of the new country.

Many of the Cuban writers of the early 1950s attempted to redefine Cuba's place within as well as outside of European culture in light of Cuba's African and Asian influences. From Cintio Vitier, who tried to define the Cubanness of Cuban literature in *Lo cubano en la poesia* (The Cubanness in Poetry, 1958) to Carpentier's *The Music in Cuba* (2001) to Lezama's "Images of Latin America" (1980), attempts were made to forge a unified field theory of Cuban poetics—or, more specifically, a Cuban poetics that answered to and reflected the cultural diversity of postcolonial Cuba. Luis de Gongora (1561-1627), the father of the Spanish literary baroque tradition, based his *Soledades* (Solitudes) on Ovid's Greco-mythological countryside and had little to do with the Latin American landscape. As Lezama writes, "His weddings of country girls are illuminated by the appearance of Pan in the Sicilian valleys. His poetic perspective is formed by the Greco-Latin tradition and the splendor of the baroque cornucopia of fishes and falcons" ("Image" 324). In contradistinction to the European baroque, Lezama cites *The Heroic Poem* (*Poema Heróico*) of Colombian baroque poet Hernando Domínguez Camargo (1606-1659): "I would say that to the Gongorine metaphor Domínguez opposes a very American image of space and development. . . . [I]n Domínguez's poems the decoration of the baroque cornucopia is replaced by the forest and the mountains . . ." ("Image" 324). Domínguez's baroque accurately describes the Latin American landscape because he looks at the landscape before him as *un nativo de la tierra*—a native of the land—and does not superimpose an imported image upon it.

Yet if this is so—if the European baroque failed to do justice to Latin American culture—how is the Latin American baroque different? And further, why begin with a redefinition of a national literature that drags along the baggage of a tradition that is not one's own? César Augusto Salgado's essay "Hybridity in New World Baroque Theory" can help us answer this question: "The term *baroque* was first used to designate a stylistic period of extravagant artificiality and ornamentation in post-Renaissance European art and literature and to characterize the doctrinal iconographic strategies of the Counter-Reformation. More recently it has come to describe the particular instances of Latin-American cultural alterity in the discourse of . . . New World (or for short, neo) baroque theory. Within this discourse, the baroque functions as a trope or adjective for the region's complex ethnic and artistic *mestizaje* ('racial mixture') rather than as a reference to exclusively Western cultural forms" (316). The Latin American "baroque curiosity" is part and parcel of what Lezama Lima called the American expression. It begins and it justifies its beginning with the European baroque because it needs a starting point, a history—even if that origin and that history are superseded in the process of hybridity and racial mixture. Virgil returned to mythic Troy for the founding of (mythic) Latium out of a sense of historical origins. And Sarduy's neobaroque theory is another such return, only to abandon the old land. To that end, Sarduy begins where Lezama leaves off.

Lezama Lima, Sarduy's predecessor and mentor, differentiated between the European baroque and the American baroque by equating the former with tensionless accumulation and the latter with what he called *el plutonismo,* the "Plutonism," or the explosive, disseminating nature of Latin American culture. The explosiveness is that of an "originary fire" (*fuego originario*) that fragments, disperses, and unites the various heterogeneous elements that make up Latin America. It is at this point that Sarduy's theory of the neobaroque parts ways from that of Lezama's. Sarduy the poststructuralist agrees with Lezama that the American baroque is explosive; however, the result of its explosiveness is dispersal rather than unity—in fact, dispersal and fragmentation, followed by more of the same indefinitely. Sarduy writes:

> the European baroque and the first Latin American baroque present themselves as images of a mobile and decentralized universe . . . but one which is still harmonious; they constitute themselves as bearers of a consonance: that which they have with the homogeneity and the

rhythm of the exterior logos which organizes and precedes them, even if this logos is characterized by its infinitude, by the inexhaustibility of its unfolding. . . . On the contrary, the contemporary baroque, the neobaroque, structurally reflects the disharmony, the rupture of homogeneity, of the logos as an absolute. It is this lack, which constitutes our epistemological basis. . . . Neobaroque: a necessarily pulverized reflection of a knowledge which knows that it is no longer "peacefully" closed within itself. ("Baroque" 131)

While Lezama's formulation of the Latin American baroque is grounded in art, architecture, and literature, Sarduy based his theory of the neobaroque on science or, more specifically, on contemporary theories of astronomy. Lezama's "originary fire" becomes the "Big Bang" of Sarduy's artistic and literary universe. In fact, one of his untranslated books of poetry bears the title *Bing Bang* (1974).

Thus Sarduy defined the neobaroque as the pure energy of a decentralized world:

The baroque, an overflowing cornucopia, renowned for its prodigality and dissipation—hence the *moral* resistance which it has provoked in certain cultures noted for their economy and moderation, like the French. . . . Verbiage, squandered forms, language which, because of its excessive abundance of names, can no longer designate things but only other designators of things, significants which enfold other significants in a mechanism of signification which ends by designating only itself, revealing its own grammar, the models of that grammar and its generation in the universe of words. ("Baroque" 124)

Sarduy's nonteleological conception of language, of excess, of what Georges Bataille called "expenditure without reserve," culminates in an *eros-poetics* of literature: "Play, loss, squandering, and pleasure, eroticism as an activity which is always purely playful. . . . Like baroque rhetoric, eroticism presents itself as the total rupture of the denotative, natural, direct level of language . . ." ("Baroque" 130). It is not sex as a biological function, but the eros of sex for its own pleasure—the pleasure of language that exceeds the limits of signification for its own sake—that Sarduy embraces: "Declared or not, the prejudice, sweetened by different vocabularies and adopted by successive dialectics, is the prejudice of realism. Everything about it, about its vast grammar upheld by culture, the guarantee of its ideology, assumes a *reality* outside the text, outside the literalness of writing" (*Written* 36). What the "moral," traditional bourgeoisie has never accepted is that sex may not always be for purposes of procreation—even in our so-called permissive (but nevertheless puritanical) American culture, where sex is what normal and moral, heterosexual, married people do. Similarly, what the bourgeois consumer of literature cannot accept, says Sarduy, is that language, as a fetish, may be enjoyed not for what it says, but for itself. If sex is for procreation, language is there to express and represent indubitable, concrete reality: "The one thing the bourgeoisie will not tolerate, what really drives it crazy, is the idea that *thought can think about thought,* that *language can talk about language,* that *an author does not write about something, but writes something,* as Joyce said" (*Written* 13).

Yet what if language never gets to an ultimate referent, transcendental and fixed? Why not conceive of the surface of a text as a mask—however, not as a mask that hides an actual face, but rather as a mask that merely hides another mask? Wittgenstein believed that all statements of facts refer to the particular rules of grammar a community of speakers has systemized into their own language game. Any claim, then, to certainty or doubt can be made only given the foundation and rules of the language game. In short, there is no getting beyond language. That being the case, Sarduy (who hardly ever mentions Wittgenstein) sees writing as a process of simulation that refers, not to an origin or form (in the Platonic sense), but rather to figures of simulation in a chain of relative signs, all without exception artificially constructed, either institutionally, societally, or personally. "Transvestism," writes Sarduy, "may well be the best metaphor for writing" (*Written* 37). And in his essay "Simulation" he writes, "The transvestite does not imitate woman. For him, *à la limite,* there is no woman; he knows—and paradoxically he may be the only who knows this—that *she* is just appearance, that her world and the force of her fetish conceal a defect. . . . The transvestite does not copy; he simulates . . ." (*Written* 93). "To *be* a man" or "to *be* a woman" is to *appear* as a "man" or a "woman," the result of social constructs that allow or disallow a very specific number of gestures, positions, and values within a given society. The transvestite, concludes Sarduy, knows that "woman" is a social construction—not an ontological category—and that apart from the individual *woman,* "woman" does not exist.

One highly significant point of difference between Sarduy and other Cuban writers, like Cintio Vitier, Alejo Carpentier, and Lezama, is in his rejection of his compatriots' definition of Cubanness. While Lezama and Vitier believed that one could articulate a conception of Cubanness through a return to the past, for Sarduy "Cuba" is everything that Lezama and Vitier claimed Cuba was and much more. "Cuba" is one of the many dispersed fragments that resulted from the "plutonism" of the neobaroque. Cuba is Europe, Africa, and Asia. Cuba is the Caribbean island of Columbus's

Journal, of Romeo & Julieta cigars, of Pérez Prado music, of exotic European dreams and cheap vacations. But above all, Cuba is a construction in an infinite number of language games, meaning different things to different individuals and communities. *From Cuba with A Song,* Sarduy's most difficult and experimental work, is a novel about "Cuba" as an indeterminate and irreducible text.

From Cuba with a Song (1967)

From Cuba with a Song is challenging to reader and critic alike. Having none of the formal qualities the reader of Latin American literature has come to expect from the Boom novel, *From Cuba with a Song* resists by its very nonlinear, elliptical form, a totalizing, realist reading. To speak of the "characters" and the "story" of *From Cuba with a Song* is to do the novel a great disservice—to betray in some sense its author's intentions. In this direction, few critics have been as clear and as insightfully faithful to Sarduy's literary project as González Echevarría. His masterful analysis, *La Ruta de Severo Sarduy* (Severo Sarduy's Route, 1987) is the best critical analysis of Sarduy's work.

As I indicated earlier, Sarduy's literary theory borrows much from the semiotic theory of Roland Barthes and from the structuralist, language-based psychoanalysis of Jacques Lacan (whom Sarduy also parodied). One can even detect some of the basic ideas of poststructuralism in his conceptualization of the neobaroque. As some critics have pointed out, at times Sarduy interpreted even Lezama as "as if he were a subtropical Derrida" (Pérez-Firmat, Rev. 252). Yet despite this, Sarduy is a very Cuban writer, and *From Cuba with a Song* is—regardless of the French theory behind it—a very "Cuban" novel.

De donde son los cantantes is the Spanish title of *From Cuba with a Song,* an untranslatable title that plays with the double entendre of the question and answer of Cuban identity—a sort of "who are we?" versus "where do we come from?" The Spanish phrase *de donde son los cantantes* can literally mean either of two things: *Where do the singers come from?* or *Where the singers are from. From Cuba with a Song* captures Sarduy's reference to a popular Cuban song: "de donde so los cantantes" is a line from a song entitled "Son de la loma." Written by Miguel Matamoros, a member of the Matamoros Trio, this song with its play on words was a hit in Cuba in the 1920s. Thus we see that the title of this novel is steeped in its originary culture in a way that the typical Latin American novel is not. One can read *One Hundred Years of Solitude* without having to know much about Columbian popular culture or history.

This is an interesting paradox, given that Sarduy's project is to escape the trappings of the realistic, historical novel.

At the end of *From Cuba with a Song* Sarduy included an explanatory paragraph to help the reader through the text he or she had just finished: "Three cultures, at least, have been superimposed to constitute the Cuban—Spanish, African, and Chinese—; three fictions alluding to them constitute this book" (154). The word *fictions* is perhaps Sarduy's parody of Borges's short-story collection, *Ficciones*. However, it is also an instance of Sarduy's agreement with the Argentine writer that everything is in fact *fiction*—and that "fiction" and "reality" are reversible, within and without the margins of the text/world. *From Cuba with a Song* is both a "question and an answer as to what is Cuba, and also in its own constitution, a roundabout way of saying what Cuba is, without naming it" (González Echevarría, *Ruta* 102, my translation). In short, "Cuba" *is* "Spanish," "African" and "Chinese"—all these cultures mixed together, but always within quotes—fragments of language or texts.

From Cuba with a Song is composed in four parts: "Curriculum Cubense" (as in a cube[1]); "By the River of Rose Ashes"; "Dolores Rondón"; and "The Entry of Christ into Havana." "Curriculum Cubense" sets the tone and structures the general theory of the novel in a just few pages. We are introduced to two transvestite show girls/prostitutes by the name of HELP and MERCY. Occasionally HELP and MERCY—or the Flower Girls, as they are alternately called—*hunger* for some meaning to their lives and for some fullness to their identities: "My, we're metaphysical, we must be hungry! Let's go to the Self-Service!" (15). But their arrival at the Self-Service means only that it will be up to them, and no one else, to construct their own (provisional) identities, the way one takes on a mask:

> No sooner said than done. They're off on tiptoes, pressing their tummies, slipping among the shells of rusty cars—their silky hair flows through tin scraps—stumbling, jumping over flattened and spokeless bicycle wheels, over handlebars, moss-covered horns, headlights stuffed with paper, aluminum circles with red bars. Yellow deities. . . .
>
> And off they go, the Flower Girls, the Ever-Present cross another scaffold, another avenue. There they go, under the three-leaf clover of the highways watched by helicopters. Echo tunnels. There, by the escalators, by the rails, where all the trolleys are, a second before the go signal. How speedy! (15-16).

MERCY and HELP wander through a world of neon signs, of street vendors, of mass-transit movement, of spokeless bicycles wheels left on sidewalks, endlessly turning like everything else around them, without direction. This is the Havana of Cabrera

Infante's *Three Trapped Tigers* (1971). After a Cuban-Felliniesque journey through the night, MERCY and HELP finally arrive at the Self-Service where, "The delicacies, like the plates which contain them, are made of plastic" (19).

In the second section, "By the River of Rose Ashes," we encounter Mortal Pérez, "the blond Spaniard, whose Castillian is spotless and who possesses the always uncertain attributes of power. . . . Mortal Pérez is a lecherous old general who pursues *the image* of Lotus Flower, a soprano—he thinks—at the Chinatown Opera House" (154, my italics). Lotus Flower/Empress Ming, however, is not a soprano; he/she, like MERCY and HELP, is a transvestite prostitute. The Spanish General, or "Gen." as he is also called, brings to mind two other personages of Spanish history and literature. In mistaking Lotus Flower for a Chinese soprano, Pérez echos Columbus's initial mistake of confusing the Tainos of Cuba with the people of India. And like Don Quixote, who mistakes his Dulcinea for a beautiful princess, in his own misperception Pérez falls in love with *his* Lotus Flower, "the opera singer." To his great frustration, however, the object of his desire constantly eludes him. The Flower Girls intercede and try to help Lotus Flower by acting as go-between. In the process they take advantage of the Spaniard's infatuation with the Chinese transvestite; they take his money and ransack his apartment. The General then takes revenge by sending his beloved "soprano" a lethal bracelet that will cut the veins on her wrists. From across the "Chinese Opera House"—or the seedy Shanghai Havana Burlesque"[2]—Mortal Pérez waits to see her lifeless, pale body emerge in a stretcher, as love and desire have turned to cruelty and death: "G had ended his parable, completed his parabolic cycle. From Peeping Tom to sadist. He who possesses with the eye possesses with the dagger. He would recognize her by her blood. Wound her. Pleasure is crossed with pain" (55).

It is no coincidence that the General (G, Gen., the Generator, the Origin), Mortal Pérez, is a Spaniard. Though much has been written about Cuba's African culture, the sad and shameful story of Cuba's Chinese population remains the unwritten chapter in the island's history. Sarduy's inclusion of the Chinese in "lo cubano"—or Cubanness—is a singular exception in Cuban letters. From *Gestos* to *From Cuba with a Song* and from *Cobra* to *Maitreya,* Sarduy never fails to acknowledge the impact of the Chinese on Cuba's multiethnic, multiracial identity. And Sarduy, who saw himself as a mestizo, a person of mixed race, claimed both African lineage and "a Chinese ancestor by the name of Macao"[3] (González Echevarría, *Ruta* 16).

The Chinese were brought to Cuba in the late 1840s, just as the Spanish government was beginning to realize that slavery would soon come to an end. With the abolition of slavery, the sugar- and tobacco-plantation owners would have to find ways to replace slave labor with at least some form of indentured servitude. The price of slaves had gone up so much that only the richest plantation owners could afford to import slaves from Africa. Part of the reason for this is that a great deal of pressure was put upon Spain by the British to end the slave trade. By the 1840s, one-half the population of Cuba was African slaves. Fearing slave uprisings like those of Jamaica and Haiti, the Cuban government tried to "whiten" or Europeanize the population and to find economic alternatives to slavery. In an unsuccessful experiment Irish and Spanish workers from the Canary Islands and Galicia were brought to Cuba as low-wage laborers. So in 1847 the first Chinese laborers were imported to Cuba. They were brought in as "immigrants, usually on an eight-year contract, and therefore they were not to be regarded as slaves under the treaty of 1817. But the difference was really one in name only" (Thomas 186). *The Cuban Commission Report of 1876,* an oral history of the Chinese in Cuba in the nineteenth century, graphically depicted the inhumane treatment of the Chinese "workers" brought to Cuba. Upon their arrival in Havana harbor, 70 percent of them were sent to work in the sugar plantations, while the remaining were employed as cigar makers, launderers, and tobacco plantation "laborers." Twenty years after the first 206 Chinese immigrants arrived in the island, the Chinese population had grown to over 100,000. This little known but significant element of Cubanness had, until Sarduy, been ignored in Cuban history.

The third part of *From Cuba with a Song* features one of Sarduy's most memorable "characters," Dolores Rondón. Dolores, a mulatto woman—singer, poet, courtesan—is the embodiment of exactly one third of Cuban culture. Oscar Montero traces Sarduy's Dolores Rondón to Gertrudis Gomez de Avellaneda's character of the same name (104). Whether such a person really existed is open to question, but it's precisely the textual indeterminateness that makes for the richness of the legend. The undecidability between "reality" and "fiction" is clearly what attracted Sarduy to the Dolores lore. The name *Dolores,* which in Spanish means *pain,* is, as Montero remarks, "bombastic" and melodramatic (105). Dolores, curvaceous, sensuous, with a full "round behind," is an Americano's fantasy of the racially mixed Caribbean woman. Sarduy's Dolores marries Mortal Pérez—a character having the same name as the General from "By the River of Rose Ashes." But is he the same character? It is certainly the same linguistic sign, which, like any name, may refer to a specific object or not. The major similarity between the Mortal Pérez of section 2 and the Mortal Pérez of section 3 is that they're both white.

Dolores, a poor singer, "legitimate daughter of Ochun, queen of the river and the sky" (60),[4] moves to Camagüey, where she meets Mortal Pérez, a corrupt local politician with high ambitions. In a bitter parody of the violently possessive institution of marriage, the Spaniard asks for Dolores's "hand" in matrimony, which the narrator/apologist says is not to be interpreted to mean that the Spaniard literally wants to cut off her hand, as in the old colonial practice of cutting off the hands of "delinquent slaves," in any case, "as far as we know" (69). After Dolores and Pérez marry, they move (as did the young Sarduy) from Camagüey to Havana. There Pérez becomes a senator, and in a short time the newlyweds come to enjoy the opulent decadence that comes with a political career. And though there are no direct references to a particular government, it is safe to assume that Sarduy had the Batista dictatorship in mind.

At the height of his political career, Pérez provides his prime minister with a "Hawaiian" dancer for his pleasures. But when the prime minister discovers that the "Hawaiian" dancer is not Hawaiian at all, but a mulatto dancer from Camagüey, he accuses Pérez of malevolent deception, of trafficking in white slavery, drug smuggling, and "an attempt against public morality" (80). In the end Pérez is ousted from public office and declared persona non grata. The prime minister, like all politicians, demands realism—that there be, even if no one really believes in it, a fixed relation between a sign or a word and its referent or object. There is no room for simulation in the State. Stripped of power, influence, wealth, and property, Dolores returns to her initial condition of poverty. Dolores and her now barefoot and sore husband conclude that their past failure to honor the Afro-Cuban deities (of Santeria) had led to their downfall. The deities "are like dogs": if you ignore them "they go away" (86).

"Dolores Rondón" begins with the ten-line poem inscribed on Dolores's tombstone. In other words, it begins at the end:

> Dolores Rondón did here
> reach the end of her career . . . (56)

And from beginning to end it is death that mediates the story: Sarduy 's Narrator One and Narrator Two "present the life of Dolores Rondón" (57), while MERCY, HELP, and CLEMENCY later join the narration as oracles of the end predestined in the beginning:

HELP (*realizing the evil he has done*): All must perish!
MERCY (*and he sprays himself from head to toe with an atomizer*):
We are nothing!
CLEMENCY: (*and he combs his hair*): From dust to dust! (62)

Through her marriage to Mortal Pérez, Dolores attempts to get, as she says, "out of her hole" (59), to escape the conditions of provincial poverty. But in her marriage to Pérez lies her death, her *mortality*. Mortal Pérez, the Spaniard, the white senator, is a harbinger of death. Even if he is not the same Pérez of the second section, his first name and his family name—representative of colonial Spain—will bring about the death of the Chinese "Lotus Flower" and the African Dolores Rondón. *In his name* the death of these two oppressed cultures is foretold.

The fourth and final section, "The Entry of Christ into Havana," is in some ways the reversal of the Mortal Pérez story in the preceding two sections. Here Mortal Pérez is not the desiring subject, but the absent object of desire. This section begins in southern, Moorish Spain with HELP and MERCY in search of a Christ-like Mortal Pérez, and it ends, as with all such mystical journeys, in a union with the nothingness of death: "Help and Mercy bend down to listen: nothing, not even the birds have remained. So do the Veiled and Vigilant spend day and night at the ruins, waiting. 'Waiting is to become nothing . . .'" (94-95). In their search for Mortal Pérez, HELP and MERCY leave Cadiz for Cuba. They arrive in Santiago de Cuba, where in the cathedral they come across a large wooden Christ. Like true believers, they immediately see in the wooden cross a Mortal Pérez/Christ image. In a pilgrimage from one end of the island to the other, they carry the wooden Christ from Santiago to Havana, by way of Camagüey, where the procession is confused with one of Senator Mortal Pérez's political meetings (as state and church processions are often difficult to distinguish from one other). HELP and MERCY's savior is the Christ of Hollywood movies and kitsch iconography—blond, blue-eyed, and sexy: "His picture was everywhere, endlessly repeated, to the point of ridicule or simply boredom: pasted up, ripped off, pulled apart, nailed on every door, pasted around every pole, decorated with mustaches, with pricks dripping into His mouth, even in colors—oh so blond and beautiful, just like Greta Garbo—not to mention the stained-glass reproductions in the Galiano subway. Wherever you look, He looks back" (142).

Christ, an object of consumption like any other object in consumer, capitalist society, is voraciously consumed like candy by the masses: "His name was in all the shop windows. They ate Him in mint candies. They dressed up like Him, wearing little crowns of thorns (their faces white with rice powder) and small blood flowers.

It was all so pretty" (143). And as they carry the wooden Christ to Havana, his body—consumed by his fans—deteriorates into nothingness. People from everywhere come to touch him, to worship him, and consequently they have worn down "the wood of His feet with kisses" (131). By the time he arrives in Havana, "Christ" has pretty much disintegrated: "He saw himself crumble. He fell into pieces, with a moan. Wood falling in water. His bald, leprous head split in two. The empty holes of the eyes, the white, perforated lips, the nose in its bone, the ears plugged with two black clots" (152). The entry of Christ into Havana is also the entry of Christ into death. The procession that has carried the crumbling Christ to the capital arrives in the middle of a snowfall that covers everything in white. Sarduy's Christ dies in the snow (a climatic impossibility in Cuba, but certainly not a textual or symbolic one): "the forehead, the cold globes of the eyes, the trunk . . . sank into the snow as if looking for something buried. And further up, the curve of the back. The legs in pieces; the snow buried them" (152).

There are several striking elements in this last section. As some critics have pointed out, Christ's entry into Havana may be read as an allusion to Fidel Castro and his troops' entry into Havana in 1959 after the popular overthrow of the Batista dictatorship. It should be noted that although Castro later denied ever having any religious beliefs, one of the reasons for his popularity is that throughout his campaign against Batista he wore a crucifix around his neck, leading people to see him as a Christ-like figure, a liberator of the oppressed masses.[5] In addition, that our Mortal Pérez/Christ/Castro enters Havana during a snowstorm is not inconsequential. White is the color of death in Santeria. Moreover, "the white, or European, component in Cuban culture is the historical one, leading up to violence and nothingness . . ." (González Echevarría, "Severo Sarduy" 1440). This violence and death, along with the more positive aspects of the mixing of Chinese, African, and Spanish culture, are what makes for Cuba's undecidable, multifaceted national identity. For Sarduy, the Cubanness of Cuba is not to be pinned down. The "essence" of Cuban nationhood, elliptical as it is, is precisely its lack of essence. Sarduy's conclusion is the end result of the lessons of the twentieth century—a significant mark of his modernism. Time and again we have been witness to the bloodiness of essentialism—from the gulags to the death camps and everything else in between.

Cobra (1972)

Cobra can be interpreted as continuation of From Cuba with a Song. If Cuba is nothing other than a sign that may stand for different things to different people and there is no "real" Cuba outside of language, then the same thing can be said of other countries. In *Cobra* it is not Cuba that is at the center of the text, but India. These two very diverse countries do have something in common: when Columbus arrived in the Caribbean, he confused the indigenous peoples with the people of India. As González Echevarría writes, "The Orient is for Sarduy . . . Columbus's first mistake" (*Ruta* 167, my translation). *Cobra* is a novel of such mistakes, disfigurements, and transformations, a novel of transsexuality and transvestism as metaphors of the plasticity and artificiality of identity.

Cobra begins in the "Lyrical Theater of Dolls"—the theater of writing where characters and events can be brought onto the stage or made to disappear with equal ease. When Madam declares that "literature still needs themes" (12), narrator says, " 'Shut up or I'll take you out of the chapter'—this narrative cannot continue" (12). But the narrative does continue, except not as a traditional, linear narrative. The body of *Cobra*'s text is a patchwork.

The mistress of ceremony at the Lyrical Theater of Dolls—a sideshow of identity—is Madam, whose favorite dancing "doll," the transvestite Cobra, complains that "her" feet are too big and that men run away from her at the sight of her feet: "Cobra was her greatest accomplishment, her 'rabbit-foot.' Despite her feet and shadow . . . she preferred her to all the other dolls, finished or in process" (5). But Cobra, her creation, is still not happy with "her" condition. It is not enough for her to be the "favorite" doll; she wants to be completely perfect, or else what is the point of being queen of the theater? "What good is it to be queen of the Lyrical Theater of Dolls, and to have the best collection of mechanical toys, if at the sight of my feet men run away and cats start climbing on them?" (3).

In order to rescue Cobra from her "orthopedic determinism," the Madam concocts a strong potion to shrink Cobra's feet. However, the drug is so strong that it also shrinks all of Cobra and the Madam herself. In the process Cobra acquires a double—a (white) dwarf, "Pup" ("abbreviated from La Poupée to La Pupa and to the tenuous explosion of Pup"[6] (27)). But Cobra, still dissatisfied with her transformation, wants to become a total woman. Cadillac, her rival, tells Cobra of Doctor Ktazob,[7] who transformed her by giving her a large male member. When Cobra tells her that she wants Ktazob to make "her" into a woman, Madam (who believes in the linearity of narrative and the order of realism) tries to warn her against it: "You're going to Ktazob, my dear, as easy as if you were going to a dentist. . . . Get off that cloud: after the butchery and if you can stand it, what awaits you is a rainfall of punctures, tweezings and scrapings, wax in your breasts, crystal in your veins, mushroom vapors in your nose and green yeast by mouth. Cover your eyes with grapes. Your ears with plugs. A yellow dog will lick your feet" (57).

Cobra disregards the warning and journeys to Tangier, where she goes under Ktazob's knife, in one of the most graphic, bloodiest sex-change operations in all of literature. Ktazob's operating room—if one can call it that—is like the dolls' stage, a theater of (psychic) cruelty. To prepare her for what is to come, Ktazob tells Cobra that she must, like a Sufi, transfer her pain to her double, Pup: "The Sufistic martyrs were invulnerable: their disciples suffered for them" (59). What follows is the surgery, with Ktazob assisted by the Alterer, Cobra's Instructor, and Pup's Instructor.

> COBRA'S INSTRUCTOR—"Think of a very hot sun. . . ."
> The Master gets ready.

> Pup screams. Splashes. Big drops of thick ink flee toward the edges of Cobra's body. Lighting. Rupture. Red branches that descend, forking rapidly along the sides of a triangle—the vertex torn out–over the white skin of the thighs, along the nickel surface, following the contours of the hips, between the trunk and the arms, forming puddles in the armpits, thin speeding threads over the shoulders, matting the hair: two streams of blood, down to the floor. (64-65)

Cut to: Cobra in the red-light district in Amsterdam, but is it the same Cobra? Cobra in Amsterdam is a young man who has answered some personal ads from leather, S&M, dominant men. He walks through the streets of Amsterdam, looking at the prostitutes sitting behind the window displays and walking into the bar where he has come to meet his masters. "We were waiting for you," says one of them, who "wore his name on his back, tattooed in the leather, dull black upon the shiny black of the hide" (77). These are the men who will initiate him, who will put him through a rite of passage—from that of a slave or submissive to that of a master. One of them says, "It's a good thing you came. Today's the day. Because to be a leader you have to pass through submission, to gain power you have to lose it, to command you have to first lower yourself as far as we want: to the point of nausea" (77). The names of the "masters" are Scorpion, Tundra, Tiger, and Totem. Tundra tells Cobra that he will have to be given an animal name, and together they decide on Cobra, because, as Totem says, "Cobra: so that he will poison. So that he will strangle. So that he will curl around his victims and suffocate them. So that his breath will hypnotize, and his eyes will shine in the night, monstrous, golden" (87).

Cobra becomes "Cobra," then, through an identity that is grafted upon him. As Kushigian writes, "*Cobra*'s constitution is always complex, because it is transmutable, from reptile to person, from singular to plural, back again" ("Gender" 54). A tabula rasa before meeting the five gurus, Cobra becomes what they want him to become. In the process the initiation goes too far and Cobra ends up dead. The passage from "ignorance" to the fixity of a univocal identity (or knowledge), as traditionally mediated through violence, has the potential to culminate in the mutilation or death of its subject.

The cultures of the ancient and the modern world, of East and West, meet in *Cobra* as consumer objects. And the difference between Tibetan monks and S&M practitioners is negligible. Since everything is a surface, everything *appears* on the same plane. Buddhist monks seated at the feet of a statue of Buddha share their space with a movie poster of Marlon Brando in *The Wild One*. And why not? Movie stars have become objects of veneration and worship on the same plane as Buddhist deities. The religious fetish and the media fetish are one, both erotically charged and destined for the same place—Sarduy's "empty center." When Tiger asks the Guru what is the quickest way to liberation, the Guru responds, "Don't think about it" (102). Later when Totem asks Rosa, "What should I do to keep it hard while I'm putting it in?" Rosa, echoing the Guru, responds, "Don't think about it" (118).

Truth is arbitrary, an artifact of history. "Writing is the art of re-creating reality," writes Sarduy (*Cobra* 7), and the "Indian Journal" section of *Cobra* is exemplary of this conception of writing. In the end there is no difference for Sarduy between the "Himalayan artificer" who arrives in Tibet wearing a silk tie with an "Eiffel tower and a naked woman lying on the *Folies Chéries* caption" (7) and the Christopher Columbus who arrived in the Americas five hundred years ago, bringing with him all the baggage of Western European culture. Note Sarduy's parody of Columbus's diary: "All young, as I have said, and all of a good height, a very fine people: their hair is not curly, but straight and as coarse as horse hair, and all have very broad brows and heads, broader than those of any people I have seen before, and their eyes are very fine and not small, and they are not at all black, but the color of Canary Islanders. A most tame people" (134). This is what Lezama had criticized in the peninsular sensibility and particularly in Columbus's European-colored vision of the Americas. Lezama clearly captured Columbus's superimposition of European mythology and culture onto the Latin American landscapes, making references to sirens, dolphins, and other animals that had nothing to do with the Latin American jungle or sea. But Sarduy takes Lezama's acute conclusion one step further when he makes us realize that nothing has changed, that we are as guilty as Columbus of superimposing Western, bourgeois, consumerist values on the rest of the world. Reality is made of transvestism, simulation, and theater, and there is no getting behind the facade of representation, the stage scenery where real "reality" awaits our discovery. The "Indian" only exists as a simulation of an "Indian" (of "Latin America" or "India"). " 'Tonight,' the doorman announces, 'on this stage, a real god' " (134). And later, "With a red circle between their eyes, four thick girls are smiling—golden dentures—dancing a Beckoning to Dawn on the proscenium; in the background, on a luminous float which climbs among celluloid clouds, the Sun God appears with a slicked mustache and golden circles on his cheekbones; at his feet, blinking spotlights of all colors, the throne of the maharajah, his favorite" (134). Crucifixes of Christ (as in *From Cuba with a Song*) or statuettes of the various Buddhist deities, it's all the same. The sacred emptied out by capitalism does not discriminate among religions. There is no economic system as tolerant as capitalism. Its only enemy is stasis; i.e., that tragic moment, constantly deferred, when capital would cease to flow: "Outside, at the foot of the mosque, peddler stands, statue bazaars are crowded together: dealers auction off miniatures, tankas painted over with the wrong gods, coarse ivory deities, torn Tibetan banners" (142).

The monstrosity of capitalism lies in that anything can be grafted onto anything else, since everything is exchangeable, including death. *Cobra,* like *From Cuba with a Song,* ends with a snowy landscape, the Afro-Cuban whiteness of death, except that in *Cobra,* and for that matter in Buddhism, death is not an end. Death is merely a spin in the wheel of eternal return; albeit reincarnation (e.g., in the wrong kind of animal) is what the Buddhist seeks to escape: "between the peaks, maybe the wind will make the prayer wheels spin, aligned upon the walls of the abandoned monasteries, upon the alters buried by the snow" (148). The World/Text is a mandala, which, after being painstakingly built, is dismantled in a sacred ritual of desecration. "At dawn we shall start out again . . ." (149) to build another mandala in search for the elliptical, "empty center." The Spanish infinitive *cobrar* means *to collect, to charge,* but there is no payoff in *Cobra.* It begins where it ends and it ends where it begins, like the cobra snake of India that bites its own tale.

Maitreya (1978)

Sarduy's fourth novel bears the same name as the fourth and future Buddha.[8] Contrary to the opinion of some critics that *Cobra* is a novel about Cuban identity, *Cobra* is in fact about the impossibility of identity per se. *Maitreya,* contrary to common critical opinion, is not a novel of exile, but instead a novel of nomadism, free of the nostalgic yearning for the old land. To be in exile is to be outside one's land, outside of one's center. But if, as Sarduy claims, there is nothing in the center, then the yearning for an (empty) center makes no sense. At most, such a yearning is a remnant of the age before the death of God—when there was a still a horizon to guide us back home. "Woe," writes Nietzsche, "when you feel homesick for the land as if it had offered more freedom—and there is no longer any 'land'" (180-81). All geographies will be new geographies, mappings of our own making as we traverse the new, empty spaces. "Wither are we moving? Away from all suns? Are we not plunging continually? Backward, sideward, in all directions? Is there still any up or down? Are we not straying as through an infinite nothing? Do we not feel the breath of empty space?" (Nietzsche 181). That Sarduy bases his theory of the neobaroque on astronomy is no coincidence. The baroque worldview begins with Galileo's decentering of the earth, and it ends in the ellipsis of the neobaroque, where there is no center—or perhaps more accurately, where the center is absence, "the ghost limb" of the old world. In Juan Goytisolo's *Juan the Landless* (1977) Sarduy finds the nomadic movement that characterizes the modern world. In a passage reminiscent of Nietzsche, Sarduy writes, "To flee. Where? Not toward *utopia,* the imaginary, regressive, or false place, but rather toward a *distopia*: the no place, *wandering,* the attribute—and not the ambiance—of he who is without a land" ("Deterritorialization" 104-05). Sarduy situates Goytisolo's work as one of periphery, nomadism, and the ex-centric discourse of postmodernity.

> *Periphery, nomadism*: Goytisolo's work, his extraordinary centrifugal force, are inscribed in the resonance of these two words, in the lines of tension they magnetically extend; always toward the exterior, toward the outside that beckons, far from the sedentary group and its codes, far from the despot and his administrative machine. It's the power of the *ex-centric* discourse, a runaway, the opposite of instituted law, in complicity with someone waiting across the border, the destruction of the city under siege. ("Deterritorialization" 104)

Sarduy's interpretation of Goytisolo's work mirrors his own worldview as reflected in *Maitreya*. The title "Deterritorialization" is a term borrowed from Deleuze and Guattari's *Anti-Oedipus* (1977). For Deleuze and Guattari, the concept of deterritoralization and nomadism refers first to the liberating ungrounding of desire, and second to the nonsegmented, elliptical movement that finds expression in a novel such as *Maitreya*: "'Hurry,' the visitor prodded him: 'he's about to give the wheel a quarter turn'" (156). This line

marks the beginning of *Maitreya*—a first reference to the movement of time that will usher in the fourth Buddha. Hence, the
"quarter turn," the fourth text. As the master lama lies dying, Tibetan monks attend to his needs, kiss his feet in devotion, and turn
the prayer wheels: "Secretive, huddled together like Chinese animals on the eve of an earthquake, the four monks entered the next
room, where the master was dying. . . . One of the larger prayer
wheels rotated. Someone was sobbing" (157). The famous monas-
tery, snuggled deep in the snows of the Himalayas at an altitude of
13,000 feet—the "Roof of the World," as it is also referred to—hangs
over a precipice in Sarduy's text, as its inhabitants await the death
of their master, while outside Mao Tse-tung's revolutionary Red
Army plans the invasion and destruction of the "opiate" within its
walls. González Echevarría writes, "The snow that covers Havana
at the end of the last story in *De donde son los cantantes* (1967)
[*From Cuba with a Song*] anticipates the Tibetan snow that closes
Cobra (1972) and opens *Maitreya* (1978). Whiteness is death, absence, the empty page . . ." (*Celestina's Brood* 212). Where there is
snow there is death. The snow that covers Lhasa in *Maitreya* can be
read as a symbolic marker of the Chinese communist revolution of
1949. Both the Chinese and the Cuban revolutions have been responsible for the wholesale destruction of thousands of citizens, the
elimination of basic human freedoms, and dictatorships that have
survived the collapse of the Soviet Union: "From the high monas-
tery—were they officiating at off-hours, celebrating sleepless divinities, meowing guardians of the temple?—brief explosions were
heard, first dispersed, sifted by the wind, as if from beyond the
jungle, but then clearer, planks falling, tree trunks rolling down the
slope. No: the newcomer recognized them immediately: gunshots
from Chinese rifles" (161).

   In October 1950 the Chinese Red Army invaded Tibet with
40,000 troops, destroying temples and homes and killing over 4,000
Tibetans who opposed them. "But Buddhism will continue to live in
the reincarnation of the fourth Buddha," declares the master, prior
to the invasion, before he dies: ". . . I will be reborn . . . .You will find
me in the water, with my eyes closed. I will be the Instructor. A rain-
bow of wide stripes will encircle my feet" (158). And indeed, in India
the late master's prophecy comes true. A group of traveling Tibetan
monks one day comes across the person whom they believe to be the
fourth Buddha foretold by their master. The Leng sisters, who of
course appear in the text without introduction, are washing a little
boy in a plastic wash basin when suddenly the monks enter: "In a
large plastic basin—seven flourescent colors—purposely splashing
the figures, they were bathing a little boy who squeezed his eyes

shut so that soap wouldn't get in" (164). He does not close his eyes in meditation, but, as Sarduy irreverently tells us, the little boy squeezes his eyes so that the soap will not get in. Yet the monks interpret the little boy's "closed eyes" as a sign that he is in fact Maitreya, the One whose coming they have been anticipating. Soon thereafter, the monks begin to make plans for the new lama, but the Leng sisters, who don't see themselves as anyone's servants, poison the monks with "strychnine-sprinkled Alicante nougats" (168) and take the train through Pakistan, all the while gulping down "greasy bags of fried plantains and open cans of hot beer" (169).

In Ceylon the Leng sisters open a vegetarian hotel. There the little boy becomes a successful celebrity guru who, eventually bored with his role as Instructor, begins to respond despondently to every question asked of him:

> He responded to every koan with a belch, a hoot or the easy aphorism "Samsara is nirvana."
> When the elders, who in his absence had began to charge entrance fees, to diminish the rations of chicken, to give preference to curious aristocrats or influential people and fill the vacillating trays with boiled flour and avocados—they were contriving, besides, an order that "would take his message to the west"—became aware that he was beginning to take his mission lightly and was drinking double martinis in the kitchen, without caring a fig about dharmas, they turned sour and grumpy. (180)

The Instructor, himself a product (like any other product) of Western orientalism, reaches the pinnacle of occidental enlightenment through an attitude of absolute indifference. But in response to the Instructor's "bad attitude," the Leng sisters take the young, indifferent, lethargic lama aside and give him a piece of their mind: "you're going to learn English on records so that everybody can understand you" (181). The Instructor, in other words, is going to be an "oriental" guru whether he likes it or not. For orientalism, the exoticism of the East sells. English will only widen his "message" or, what is the same, his marketability in the global economy. The Leng sisters—oriental subjects themselves—are not about to see their successful business venture go under. They need cash to keep the business going: "Where are we going to find the cash to maintain the sliding waves and to protect from moths the bamboo tablets on which the few statements you make are engraved?" (181).

However, the Leng sisters' niece, Illuminated, sees that their financial enterprise is about to collapse, so she leaves for Cuba with her friend Honey Boy. When Honey Boy arrives in Havana, the first thing he is told is to remove his skirt (presumably his Tibetan monk's garb) because Cuban men don't wear skirts (186). Meanwhile, back in Ceylon, the Instructor announces his own death: "This very night, once the football scores are out, I will enter nirvana forever" (190). Thus death and nirvana are parodied and emptied of all their meaning by a Western event that has assumed greater importance than death and religion. As one critic notes, "As many of the previous examples demonstrate, one of Sarduy's effective ironic mechanisms is his recourse to the incongruous, the banal and the scatological. Sarduy's most carefully elaborated effort to debase the Tibetan Buddhist religion which serves as the only thematic constant in the novel appropriately concerns the well-known quest for a reincarnated lama" (Pellón 10). Upon the death of the Instructor, the Leng sisters cremate him and perform a series of rituals in memoriam, reminiscent of the rites performed for the master at the beginning of the book—though "nothing," we are told, remains of him (199). And precisely because "life is nothing" (193), the Leng sisters are able to console themselves with hot chocolate and "churros" (the Spanish-type crullers) (194).

Alternating in part 2 are four sections entitled "The Double" and "The Fist." The death of the Instructor is followed in part 2 with the birth of the double—the twin sisters Tremendous and Divine. They "were born together," Sarduy informs us (203). Born from whom? We don't know. The twins are brought into the world by a Chinese midwife, who recites Afro-Cuban prayers throughout the delivery. And (eight lines) later, as in a literary fast-forward, the prepubescent twins come to discover that they possess special powers of healing and divination: "One day, by pure chance—they were playing ring-around-a-rosy—they discovered that if they passed their hand or jumped three times over a cripple or a person in pain, the paralysis or shooting pain would instantly disappear" (203-04). Success makes the gluttonous Tremendous and Divine become as obese as the personages of Botero's paintings and sculptures, of Diego Velázquez's *Las Meninas,* and of Juan Carreño's *Dressed Monsters*: "The more strides the twins made as healers, the more prosperous and plump, in their sugary gluttony, they became" (204).

Then the day comes when the twins have "their first menstruation suddenly and in unison," and on that day they "lost all their powers" (206).[9] Despite all kinds of prayers to the orishas, their powers fail to return, and for a time the twins end up having to return everything that they had purchased on credit and become launderers. What saves them is the discovery that they have operatic singing voices. So in mock-bourgeois, religious optimism, Sarduy writes, "A lost gift implies the emergence of another, or rather: what disappears in the symbolic order reappears in the real to hallucinate us: soon the needy twins discovered that their voices, sustained by the puffy expansion of their diaphragms, and by the substantial calories of sugarcane juice, reached powerful soprano tessituras" (207). The twins become a hit singing in Chinese operas. Admired by many for their "sumptuous fannies and lascivious faces," the Fatties, come to be "forever" known as Ladies Divine and Tremendous (208).

One of their admirers is Louis Leng, "who came to congratulate them one evening, euphoric after observing the rotundities of Solidarity" (208). Sarduy transports the character of Louis Leng, the master chef from Lezama Lima's *Paradiso* (1974), to *Maitreya*. The wealthy Cemí family of *Paradiso* (direct descendants of Spaniards) employ a black chef by the name of Juan Izquierdo, who by his own account was a student of the great Chinese chef Louis Leng. In justification of his culinary choices he reports, "I learned my art from that proud Chinaman Louis Leng, who added the mastery of confection to his ancient and refined cooking while he loafed around the Cuban Embassy in Paris. Later he worked in North Carolina, with lots of pastry and young turkey breasts, and I am the continuation of that tradition . . ." (*Paradiso* 13). Juan Izquierdo, who is implicitly brought into the narrative of *Maitreya* through Louis Leng, shares with the Chinese character a history of Spanish colonial oppression, in the employ of the rich Cemí family. Sarduy's Louis Leng, seducer of the twins, is the son of Honey Boy and Illuminated (208).

The action shifts from Cuba to Miami when Lady Tremendous dives into a swimming pool in Sagua la Grande and reemerges in the surf off of Miami among dolphins who receive her "with indignant cries" (211). Lady Tremendous is accompanied by Louis Leng and a dwarf named "Slippery Slice" by the Miami Cubans: "Because of his tenacious hold on Cuban customs and the pleated guayabera he wore to debutante balls, the frozen generations of southwest Miami would later call him a 'Slice of Cuba'" (211-12). This is obviously an instance of Sarduy poking fun at the stereotypical Cuban American exiles of Miami—a generation, in Sarduy's assessment, frozen in time. While in Miami, Louis Leng services the sexually insatiable Lady Tremendous and the dwarf, who because of his size has to perform with a plastic phallus. To the chagrin of Lady Tremendous, who has grown used to Leng's sexual services, out of nowhere, "smashing through the art-nouveau roof of the pergola, wrecking the delicate, vegetal, iridescent crystal and iron structures—a misfired bomb—fell Lady Divine" (215). Lady Tremendous receives her twin sister "with indignant cries" (215).

The action then switches to New York, where Leng has opened a restaurant and where Lady Tremendous, high on drugs, roller-skates to the fountain in Washington Square Park: "She reached Washington Square. The aluminized warm mist blurred the forms of the square. She kept losing speed as if sand were blowing against her wheels. She stopped beside the fountain" (237). Out of the fountain, Venus-like, emerges a man, "fresh as a cucumber, with an aloof lilt that didn't suit the situation at all" (238). The first words out of the man's mouth are: "I'm Iranian," followed by, "Profession . . . Chauffeur" (238). The Iranian utters words typically exchanged by Americans when meeting each other for the first time.

Jump to Iran: Lady Tremendous, the "divine macho" Iranian, and the dwarf have opened a brothel that caters to petro-dollar sheiks. The dwarf, a member of the F.A.A. (Fist Fuckers of America) and a master of the sadomasochistic art of "fist fucking," runs into trouble one day when a "potentate from Oman" (252) takes umbrage with the dwarf's favorite act, jumps off the table in anger, and threatens him: "In less time than it takes for a monkey to scratch his eye, you're going to disappear from this shady establishment, from the city . . . and off the face of the earth. You have abused caliphal toler-ance, allowing yourself backroom backhanded handlings, violating the annals of the Empire. Now you're going to hear the wind raising sand" (254). Next, the narrator tells us, "They all resurfaced at the Grand Hôtel de France," in what is possibly Morocco. Here the Ira-nian penetrates Lady Tremendous from behind, and from the act Lady Tremendous gives anal birth to an oversized baby, born with webbed fingers and toes: "His earlobes, three times longer than nor-mal. Forty solid, even teeth protected a long, pointy tongue: excel-lent sense of taste. Strong jaw. Delicate, golden skin. A body both flexible and firm like an arum stalk; wide torso, the chest of a bull, rounded shoulders, full thighs, the legs of a gazelle. His arms, hang-ing, touched his knees. A thin membrane joined his toes and fin-gers" (269). Some time later in pre-Soviet-occupied Afghanistan, the dwarf and Lady Tremendous's "anal son" lie buried in the desert, "like Koranic saints joined together . . . between oil wells" (272), while Lady Tremendous has become a figure of worship for Afghani men and women.

Maitreya is a "novel of exile" if by that we mean a novel about the myth of exile. For the very idea of a missing center, an origin, and the consequent nostalgia of exile is practically nonexistent in *Maitreya*. It is a mistake not to take Sarduy's burning of his *guayabera* in Paris seriously. Doubtless, there was something of the symbolic in it, and Sarduy himself admits to it in a satirical associa-tion with Hernán Cortés's act of burning his ships after his arrival in Mexico. But especially significant is the fact that Sarduy related this story in French, his second language, and not in Spanish. In Sarduy's burning of his *guayabera* there is conscious affirmation of the condition of being landless and homeless. Sarduy's characters are all landless. In philosophical terms they are exemplars of the idea that existence precedes essence or perhaps more accurately that existence preempts essence. "The Orient in Sarduy is a false, chimerical origin" (González Echevarría, "Narrative" 156), but so is everything else related to the idea of a fixed identity. Dispersion and not the originary unity of the Spanish baroque characterizes the Sarduyan novel. As Pellón writes, "there is interculturalism, plurality, osmosis: a universe in miniature. . . . Society is linked to the idea of space, but culture—like the individual—is mobile, drifting like wind" (38). The *monstrous* is the hybrid (*mestizaje*)—an aspect of excess, e.g., the celestial body known as a "white dwarf," which possesses one of the densest forms of matter in the universe. The dissolution of "white" culture that Goytisolo writes about is the dissolution of a "white dwarf" in space and the dispersal of its energy as its center begins to die off. Expenditure of energy without reserve, dispersal, ejection, evacuation, transvestism, simulation, the nomadism of cultures, the deterritorialization of desire, and the explosion (*plutonism*) of the elliptical neobaroque are what moves in the prayer wheels in *Maitreya*. In short, by Sarduy's own definition, *Maitreya* is the neobaroque text par excellence.

For Voice (1977)

For Voice collects Sarduy's radio plays written between the mid-1960s and the mid-1970s. Despite the amount of critical writing devoted to Sarduy's essays, novels, and poetry, *For Voice* remains undeservedly ignored by readers, directors, and critics. Written at a time when Robbe-Grillet's theory of the new novel was in vogue, the dialogue in these dramatic works is presented as a surface that is not the upper layer of a fathomable or unfathomable psychological depth, but instead is the surface of a sign without a signified. The Japanese haiku, for instance, operates in this fashion, free of the moralistic intrusiveness of individual consciousness.[10] The actants, as Sarduy calls them, are not the characters of realist drama. Words and actants are interchangeable in such a way that one cannot claim such and such of X and follow X in Aristotelian fashion through to the end, where at last time, place, plot, and character come neatly together in a final exposition of textual meaning. Few writers outside of Sarduy have written dramatic works for radio as masterfully: "Besides Beckett's contributions to the genre, such as *All That Fall, Words and Music,* or *Cascando,* it is difficult to cite other examples of the same caliber" (Barnard 10). Sarduy's radio plays have been produced in France, Germany, Spain, and England.

The Beach, the first play in the collection and the most successful of the radio plays, has received various radio productions over the years in several languages. The language of *The Beach,* stripped down to its bare essentials, is as naked as its bodies. Naked bodies=naked language. The actants are M1, M2, M3 and W1, W2, W3: textures, surfaces, and gestures without proper names. The play acknowledges from the start the potential dangers to which the surface of the naked body/language on the beach/page is susceptible. The six actants, Europeans and Americans enjoying the beach at Cannes and the sounds of bossa nova, have the money to play in one of the most exclusive playgrounds in Europe. M3, who in sequence 5 is a porn star, awaits the arrival of residuals from his latest movie, "Opium and Flagellation in the Dock Districts" (26). In sequence 12, M3 turns out to be an unsuspecting trick of W3, who is now a call girl; the object of desire (gigolo, porno star) becomes the consumer of sex. At a certain point in the play the actants interchangeably perceive the bodies of a couple and the body of a woman lying on the beach. In sequence 10 the dead body of a young woman has washed ashore; in sequence 14 the body of the girl on the beach—reminiscent of "the woman turned to gold in Goldfinger" (44)—is a scene in "Opium and Flagellation in the Dock Districts," an underground film. Sequence 16, on the other hand, has a couple (W1 and M1?) lying on the beach in a sort of dispassionate version of *From Here to Eternity.* And when "she [W3?] moved away . . . We drew closer," says M1. W2 responds: *"You and me"* (47). The "you and me" is half-empty to the extent that the "you" of the phrase is at all times interchangeable for another you, as occurs in sequence 13 where the female actants (W1, W2, and W3) of the play fall in love with each other.

The sequences in *The Beach* are like footprints on the sand: erased by the ebb and flow of the sea: "In each band or 'beach' (*playa*) the sequence is restructured and one of its details varied or transformed into its opposite. In each band the narrative begins from zero; it erases, retracts, and denies what has been written previously, and imposes a new version. There is no final outcome, for the different versions have equivalent values" (*For Voice* 15). Therefore, *"the same text"* (*For Voice* 55). From the Arab who rents the beach umbrellas (Camus's Arab, who in Sarduy's play is not murdered), to the advertising plane, to the João Gilberto music continually playing in the background, to the naked bodies of men and women, the beach as a series of triangles contains the browns, the reds, and the greens of Miró, the blues and flesh tones of Hockney, and the obesely baroque family of Botero, all in a whirl of the pleasure of the writerly, painterly, musical, and epidermal text.

Fall: Barroco Funerario is, as the subtitle suggests, a funerary baroque piece. Its movement is downward: to catacombs and sarcophagi. "*Fall* is the reverse side of *The Beach,*" writes Sarduy in the introductory note to the play, "instead of the body apotheosized and eroticism, the body degraded and death" (60). *Fall* is made up of six sequences or galleries, as in the Italian sense of the word, *galleria,* meaning "a covered passage, catacomb, place where paintings are exhibited, tunnel, etc." (60). And just as there are six sequences, there are also six voices. Voices 1, 3, and 5 are male; voices 2, 4, and 6 are female. In what seems to be a backhanded homage (or parody) of Pirandello's *Six Characters in Search of an Author,* one of the passages refers to the voices as "six characters" (66). The difference between Pirandello's and Sarduy's aesthetics is that *Fall* is a play written literally after the "fall" or death of the Author/God, as declared by Roland Barthes. And Sarduy makes clear that there are no "characters" in his radio plays: instead there are voices, by no means in search of an author. Moreover, it is precisely because there are no characters that the actors are free to do with the "play" whatever they wish. Sarduy writes,

> The actors may, if they wish, replace the cited sentence with another drawn from the same text. They may also exclude the citation, or add a sentence of their own invention, summarizing, clarifying, judging, commentating on or parodying the "dramatic situation." Or finally, while retaining the citation proposed by the author, they may add another of their own invention. In brief, in an attempt to eliminate the passive notion of actor-interpreter, the actor must pass through the "other" side of the work, to participate in or challenge it as he re-emerges at the moment of its genesis. (59-60)

The first death in *Fall,* then, is the author's. The author dies so that the actor, the reader, and the listener may be born; the author is reincarnated, if you will, in all three.

Re-Cite: Combine Hearing follows *Fall* because it is a play about the death of the author and the work and the birth of the text. In opposition to the authorial/authoritarian voice of the Author/God—the originator of a decipherable message—Sarduy re-cites William S. Burroughs's model of the Sender as Virus transmitter, *Naked Lunch*'s many references to biocontrol experiments, and "the principle behind the Mayan codices," where the priests of the

community—"about one percent of the population" (95)—sent tele-
pathic signals to the workers about what to feel and when:
"Shortly after birth, a surgeon could install connections in the
brain. A miniature radio receiver could be plugged in and the subject controlled from the SS, that is the STATE-CONTROLLED
SENDERS" (95). The initials *SS,* which stand for STATE-CON-
TROLLED SENDERS, also and obviously stand for the SS of Nazi
Germany, but more personally to Severo Sarduy himself as an Au-
thor/God—a position that he clearly rejects. The Speaker, address-
ing his audience in *Re-Cite,* says that the position of the Sender is
supreme and that to include messages besides the Sender's would
mean that somebody else besides the Sender "has feelings of his
own, which could louse up the Sender's continuity" (95). The idea
that someone other than the Sender could participate in a process
of communication undermines the privileged position of the autho-
rial/authority figure.

Following Barthes's definition of a text as a tissue (or patchwork)
of quotations, Sarduy begins *Re-Cite* with an epigram from Robert
Rauschenberg: " 'I call what I make combine-paintings,' that is combined works, combinations. I want to avoid categories this way"
(85). All of Sarduy's work can be viewed as *combine-writing*—a kind
of writing that frees itself from the restrictions of canonical genre
distinctions. *Re-Cite* blurs all genre categories by being music,
voice, literature, and poetry, in one; it is also, as Barthes says, "a tissue of quotations drawn from the innumerable centres of [Eastern
and Western] culture" (146). The music selected for the play is a
Dionne Warwick record and a musical anthology of the Orient fea-
turing Tibetan music. "With the participation," writes Sarduy, of the
following: "the classified page of the *Justice Weekly,* the scientific
page of the daily *Le Monde,* the text of Lichtenstein's canvas,
Hopeles, 1963, a page from William Seward Burrough's *Naked
Lunch,* a description by Giancarlo Marmori in *Ceremony of a Body,*
a description by Chen fou in *Tales of a Floating Life,*" and lastly
"several passages from *Cobra*" (88). In fact, *Cobra* the Text (Sir/
Señor Text(o)—as opposed to the Sir Baroque of Lezama) displaces
Severo Sarduy, the Author. But that's alright, says Sarduy, authorial power is illusory: "It can never be a means to anything more
than control and more slavery . . . junk" (96). The day comes, however, when the receivers get tired of the Sender and replace him
with another Sender. What remains then is the white surface (of the
page) on which another body/text will be inscribed—re-incarnated,
repeated, as something other. In the "end"—at the place where we
start from—the voices from *Cobra* re-cite the fourfold truths: White,
White, White, White.

The Ant-killers is Sarduy's political play—a historical piece, with the kind of political and social commentary unusual for Sarduy. The play, as Sarduy writes, "is a text on decolonization: of territories and of bodies. Of territories: Portugal restores liberty to its colonies" (*For Voice* 113). Everything in the play is there to displace through all kinds of ways and by all kinds of means both state and individual fascism—i.e., the fascism referred to by Michel Foucault as microfascism. As Sarduy well knows, both forms of fascism flow into each other. The decolonization (or deterritorialization) of nations brings with it the decolonization of bodies and vice versa (*For Voice* 113). To cut up, to decenter, is to launch an attack against the central colonizing powers of society, which aim to take over and maintain control over everything outside their periphery.

"This takes place in Portugal," writes Sarduy in mockery of traditional realist literature: "So this takes place in Portugal, on a solid blue background, bright acrylic. Overexposed, pasted, cut-up, with a close-up's clarity, a striped, colored fabric is unfolding slowly, opening like a flower, in slow motion. Plain geometries, blood red, chlorophyll green" (116). So this is the Portugal written about, spoken of: the Portugal of flat surfaces, of canvasses, of overexposed photographs, of cut-ups, of souvenir T-shirts, of plain geometries of red and green stripes. And because it is the Portugal of *representation,* it is the Portugal of colonization—the country to the west of Spain that had control over Guinea, Mozambique, and Angola until 1974, colonies deprived of their own national and cultural identities, colonies *represented* by the Portuguese flag.

The historical moment is not experienced directly, but is represented or mediated by the press for consumption. There is no history outside of the text. "What we call history is the history of the word," writes Burroughs. "In the beginning of *that* history was the word" (*Ticket* 50). And *the Word* for Burroughs constitutes the most devastating virus the world has ever known. In the play, one French tourist says, "we heard the first reports of the April Revolution in Portugal, and decided *to go and see* the new regime, as if it were a matter of a three-star hotel, or something really quaint. *We wanted to photograph everything* in a few days" (117, my italics). Portugal, Angola, Guinea, and Mozambique as surfaces for consumption are no different from "porcelain plates" or "embroidered napkins" (117). All we know from the passage above is that the French tourists have gone "to see the new regime"; what we don't know is which regime. Objects of consumption, regimes, nations, cultures, and religions are all equally exchangeable with one another. There are two sets of tourists in *The Ant-killers.* One set is enjoying the beach in Almancil, outside Lisbon (a center of power), and the other set is visiting the savanna in Angola. If the center is the colonizing power, whatever is outside of it is its colony/subject and/or its opposition. Rebellion takes place from the outside, from the margins. The tourists staying in the Angolan savanna are also the ant-killers of the title, who resort to killing the ants that have "invaded" their encampment: "They'd even squandered their last *escudos* on an insect bomb" (120). The Portuguese central power saw its subjects as mere ants to be gotten rid off at the first sign of insurrection: "They had organized their defense in concentric circles. An outer circle, or no-man's land, where enemy movements were tolerated, but closely observed as an alert was sounded. An intermediate circle, where dissuasion was attempted with an accidental rockslide. An inner circle, where they resorted to heavy manoeuvers: sand and fire" (122). But who is the "they" of the sentence—the Portuguese or the revolutionaries? I believe Sarduy has left it ambiguous because a concentric model of power—and all power is concentric—is indeed relative, relational, and exchangeable. At the end of the passage we don't know if it is an ant colony or a Portugese colony whose extermination is being planned. A bridge named after the Portuguese dictator Oliveira Salazar is renamed "William Burroughs" (122) after the revolution of '74, and soon what was at the margins becomes a canonical inscription—the monument of a new tradition and power base.

Burroughs's concept of the Word as a virus that contaminates every aspect of life is taken to its ultimate conclusion in Sarduy's play: as sign (of radicalness) "William Burroughs" replaces the equally and arbitrarily exchangeable sign (of state power), "Salazar." This is why in 1974 the Portuguese authorities announced that it was their hope that "*the brotherhood of the Portuguese language*" (128, my italics) would continue to be the glue that kept the ex-colonies united. But ultimately the music of Angola, Mozambique, and the Republic of Guinea-Bissau push out—decenter—the dominant culture. Young white students end up wearing, dancing to, and absorbing the African cultures that were once dominated by Western Europe: "Around the radio, a few, naked and brightly painted, with branches plaited around their heads, mimed a primitive dance, laughing: a feigned ritual" (123). The radio as an instrument that transmits sound waves through the air can be both an instrument of power and an instrument of liberation. In effect, a radio projects a series of concentric wavefronts that can be likened to the ripples caused by the throwing of a pebble into a body of water, where the concentric waves go out from the center, until the center ceases to be important, with the dissipation of its influence. Fortunately, with the drop of every pebble comes the ripple effects of spreading concentric wavefronts that push out the elements of the dominant central power "toward the edge" (113) of the historical text, where the explosive and dispersive heterogeneity of the neobaroque deconstructs itself like galaxies in a continual process of expansion and contraction. The *Ant-killers* aims at a decolonization of the voice, of the work, the text, the author, of all political discourse, be it of the left or the right, and of bodies, Western and non-Western alike. For all his refusal to be connected with a politics of *engagement* (113), *The Ant-killers* is Sarduy's most politically engaged text.

Christ on the Rue Jacob (1994)

Christ on the Rue Jacob is one of Sarduy's later books and, like all his other works, a text that escapes facile genre categorization. The most general thing one can say about it is that it is a work of prose. By Sarduy's own assessment, "These are neither articles nor essays, nor commentaries on images or painting: their genre is ambiguous . . ." (*Christ* viii). *Christ* is Sarduy's most accessible text and a wonderful introduction to his work. It is, to borrow Akira Kurosawa's title phrase, *something like an autobiography*. Written in what Sarduy called "epiphanies" for an age "starved for religion" (*Christ* vii), the text is a retracing of life's bodily (scars) and mnemonic inscriptions, i.e., of the inscriptions that make us who we are: "By surveying these scars from my head down to my feet, I have sketched a possible autobiography, summarized in an archeology of the skin. The only thing that matters in one's personal story is whatever has been ciphered on the body and thus continues to talk, to narrate, to stimulate the incident responsible for its inscription" (*Christ* vii).

Christ on the Rue Jacob is composed of two parts: a reading or retracing of the "body's scars," what Sarduy calls "a personal archeology" (*Christ* viii), and "an inventory of marks, not physical but mnemonic. . . . Images—of a city, of a painting—incidents, events, *deaths*" (*Christ* viii, my italics). The word *death* is important here because Sarduy wrote so much about it throughout his career as a writer. In the last years of his life he wrote quite extensively about his own imminent death from AIDS and about the death of his friends, who had meant to so much to him. In June 1993 Sarduy died at the age of fifty-two in Paris. With the exception of *Christ on the Rue Jacob,* his last five works, *Colibrí* (Hummingbird, 1984), *Cocuyo* (Firefly, 1990), *Un testigo fugaz y disfrazado* (A Witness Fleeing and Disguised, 1993), the posthumously published *Pájaros de la playa* (Beach Birds, 1993) and *Epitafios* (Epitaphs, 1994), remain untranslated.

Pájaros de la playa takes place on a tropical island, probably Cuba. Located near the beach is a hospital/sanatorium where the elderly and gay, suffering from the ravages of the AIDS virus, are interned. What the elderly and the gay men suffering from AIDS— or the "malady," as Sarduy refers to it—have in common is a fight against death, against the humiliating decomposition of their in- continent, oozing bodies. One character, ironically named Siempreviva (Alwaysalive), resorts to all kinds of nontraditional curative methods in her hope for a restored youth. Evident in *Pájaros de la playa*[11] is the enforced isolation of the characters from the rest of the world. Their "internment" recalls the inhumane quarantine of homosexuals with AIDS by Castro's regime—a quar- antine that lasted until the late 1980s—and the subject of Nestor Almendro's award winning documentary *Improper Conduct* (1984). In *Pájaros de la playa* "the body continues to corrode on its unremit- ting path to putrefaction. A slow kind of leprosy scorches it until the narrator turns into an 'organic wreck' " (Prieto, *Body* 137). The body in all of Sarduy's texts, to use Beckett's word, *oozes* from its orifices, quartered, mutilated, tortured, tattooed, inscribed in ink, blood, and semen. The primary colors for gay men dying of AIDS, says Sarduy, are red (for blood) and white (for semen).

Though Sarduy himself never made this connection, the writer who represents the virus of inscription and the inscription of the virus on the body is William Burroughs, whom he never tired of cit- ing. Burroughs once wrote, "My general theory since 1971 has been that the Word is literally a virus, and that it has not been recognized as such because it has achieved a state of relatively stable symbiosis with its human hosts; that is to say, the Word Virus (the Other Half) has established itself so firmly as an accepted part of the human or- ganism that it can now sneer at gangster viruses like smallpox and turn them in to the Pasteur Institute. But the Word clearly bears the single identifying feature of virus: it is an organism with no in- ternal function other than to replicate itself" (*Adding Machine* 48). Written a decade before the discovery of AIDS, Burroughs's analogi- cal conception of language as virus coincides with Sarduy's formula- tion of the reproductive/repetitive function of language. For Sarduy, the will to write is an irrepressible drive "based on the repetition of a gesture . . . which involves the repetition of a preparatory ritual— words, rhythms, sometimes whole phrases or paragraphs . . ." (*Christ* 85). Sarduy continued to write to the very end of his life, in an effort to turn the (AIDS) virus into a text: to make the blood marks on his body confluent with the ink marks on the page. As Sarduy puts it, "literature is an art of tattooing; within the amor- phous mass of informational language it inscribes, encodes the true signs of signification. But this inscription is not possible without wounding, without loss" (*Written* 41). Writing, he adds, is "the art of proliferation."

Christ on the Rue Jacob is the embodiment (in praxis) of Sarduy's earlier theoretical work *Written on a Body*. The title itself, tongue-in-cheek, refers to a number of events in Sarduy's life, the first of which is a childhood accident: "As I ran, I passed under the orange tree. I felt nothing when the thorn embedded itself into my skull" (*Christ* 6). What is amusing here is Sarduy's anecdote in connection with the image of Christ's crown of thorns. He didn't even feel it, admits Sarduy. The title also alludes to James Ensor's painting *The Entry of Christ into Brussels in 1889* and to an unnamed painting that Sarduy saw being delivered to a church or the nearby Louvre Museum at the intersection of Rue Jacob and Bonaparte in Paris: "Suddenly traffic stopped to make way for a large open truck. It was delivering a painting as large as a house to some church or the nearby Louvre. The painting was rounded at the top, as if it were going to be hung in a specific place, between two columns and under an arch. It portrayed the scourging of Christ, who was contemplating the Rue Jacob, the bar, *perhaps even my ice-cold beer*" (26-27, my italics). Sarduy leaves out the title of the painting and refers to it as "a painting" either because he in fact did not recognize it, which is hard to believe given his extensive knowledge of art history, or because he knew the painting, but was more interested in presenting it as a generic example of Christian iconography than in citing it. In either case, as Sarduy informs the reader at the beginning of the book, the gaze of his archeology of the body travels from the head (as in Christ's/Sarduy's embedded thorn(s)) down to his feet (Christ's feet nailed to the cross/Sarduy's wart). This wart, reports Sarduy, had grown on the sole of his foot. This wart, the first mark of Sarduy's AIDS, is the text/flesh that announces the beginning of the end. During the medical procedure, the doctor asks Sarduy if he feels anything; Sarduy says no, but he smells "something burning outside . . . like burnt rubber" (35). To this, the doctor replies, "It's not outside . . . and it's not rubber. I've already removed the wart and now I'm cauterizing your skin. What you smell is singed human flesh. . . . We Jews . . . are very familiar with this smell" (35).

In Sarduy's inimitable way, the Jewish Holocaust and the AIDS holocaust are brought together through a history of the flesh. Moreover, in Nazi Germany homosexuality was punishable first by either sterilization or castration and then, finally, by death. While the Jews in concentration camps were made to wear the two overlapping yellow triangles, symbol of the Star of David, homosexuals

were made to wear an inverted pink triangle. The inverted pink triangle became a symbol for the gay liberation movement of the
1970s, and then in the 1980s it was adopted by the gay organization
ACT-UP (AIDS Coalition to Unleash Power) in its fight against
AIDS. Because nothing is innocent in his work, Sarduy, I am convinced, was well aware of all these associations. The Sarduyean
world is contiguous, analogical, connected through myth, religion,
the flesh, and the text. The four cardinal points are part of the same
web, and separation is what no one can bear. What every individual
seeks is unity within one's self and with the world, albeit with a
world of veils and illusions where unity can be only a goal: "At that
time we were very close, my mother and I: we were *literally almost*
the same person" (5, my italics). The word *literally* is often used as a
synonym for the word *exactly*. But Sarduy cleverly qualifies "literally" by placing the word "almost" next to it, thereby undermining
the sense of exactness. Furthermore, one may interpret "literally" to
mean "by the letter," in which case, "almost" becomes a rhetorical,
linguistic sign without a referent in the world, since things either
are or they are not. When Sarduy feels the pain of the surgeon's
scalpel on his head, he realizes that pain is one thing that can't be
shared. The pain is his and no one else's. Not even his mother can
feel his pain: "The icy feel of the anesthetic as it touched my head
plunged me into myself. The pain was mine. This was not my
mother's body that suffered . . ." (6-7). The first scar is the scar of our
separation or, as François Wahl put it, the scar of "umbilical exci-
sion" (qtd. in *Christ* 29). This invisible scar we carry with us
throughout our lives. After our initial separation from the mother
come so many other such separations—deaths—physical and spiritual from family members, friends, and lovers.

Most of the second part of *Christ on the Rue Jacob* deals with the
death of Sarduy's friends: Lezama, Roland Barthes, Witold
Gombrowicz, Virgilio Piñera, Italo Calvino, Calvert Casey, and
Emir Rodríguez Monegal, to name only a few. In the event that is
death, in its stark finality, writing can only remain silent. In an
epiphany of *Christ on the Rue Jacob* that bears the same title as a
book by Beckett, *Texts for Nothing,* Sarduy writes: "Writing is useless. It does nothing to rescue those who are swept away by a sea of
lava, who lie already beneath that stone" (93). Death is what every
writer confronts. Even though the journalist and the media mogul
deal with the same raw material as the writer—that is to say, the
Word—it is only the writer/artist who confronts death in his work
without fear, without looking away: "I mean a real writer, like
Beckett, Genet, Joyce, Hemingway, Conrad, Fitzgerald, Kafka . . .
right away we have a distinction, can you imagine a writer or an

artist who would be afraid to hear the word DEATH? I sure can't. Any writer who cannot hear that word is not a writer" (Burroughs, *Adding Machine* 50), and any writer who can't face death head-on is not a writer either. Sarduy places it at the very center of everything he wrote.

In telling the story of the time he fell and broke his lower lip horsing around with a friend at Princeton University, Sarduy describes the scene at the hospital waiting to get his lip stitched thus: "That Sunday morning, a dozen doctors and nurses, red-eyed like sleepwalkers, were dealing with their patients in total exhaustion. They pulled Coke after Coke from a soda machine. . . . I could hear through the dirty transparency of the curtain: 'I wonder if she'll die.' Someone, without the least formality, the way you request a piece of information, was inquiring about death" (24-25). Beautiful and poignant, Sarduy's anecdote of his experience at the Princeton hospital is told in a manner that can be described only as one of outraged understanding. The lights of Lezama, Virgilio Piñera, Calvert Casey, Italo Calvino, Severo Sarduy, et al.—these bright stars who once illuminated the dark, night sky disappear one day in an instant, like white dwarfs. "The white dwarf state," says the English astronomer Fred Hoyle, "is the graveyard all stars will ultimately reach" (248). Fortunately for us, because they are so distant, their light will continue to reach us for a long time to come. In the eternally recurrent spin of the prayer wheels, "this farewell is a warm introduction" (Moore 243) to a writer and an artist deserving of the same or greater admiration and respect that other Latin American writers of his literary generation have enjoyed.

"Translating" Sarduy

Given the relative difficulty of his writing, Sarduy was fortunate to have such wonderful English translators as Carol Maier and Suzanne Jill Levine. And by the same token, Levine and Maier were fortunate to work with a writer as supportive as Sarduy. Levine's translation of Sarduy's work began with *From Cuba with a Song,* originally published along with *Hell Has No Limits* (1966) by José Donoso and *Holy Place* (1962) by Carlos Fuentes, under the title *Triple Cross* (1972).

As previously noted, *From Cuba with a Song* is a translation of *De donde son los cantantes,* a title that can be interpreted as both a question and a statement—a play on words that is lost in the English rendition. Faced with the difficult task of translating an untranslatable title, Levine attempted in a number of ways to capture in English—even if only minimally—the multivoicedness of the original until finally settling on *From Cuba with a Song.* What is interesting in her account of the difficulties she faced in translating Sarduy's second novel—something that Sarduy himself warned her about—is his openness to her experiments. At one point, Levine proposed entitling the novel "From Cuba with Love," as a misquote of the movie *From Russia with Love,* and Sarduy, a fan of James Bond movies, was quite amused and even agreeable to it. Levine writes, "Sarduy's playful response to 'From Cuba with Love' was prefaced by praise of the baroque extravagance of another Bond film, *Diamonds Are Forever,* whose plot is almost impossible to disentangle" (150), as is the "plot," of course, of *From Cuba with a Song.* In a letter to Levine, Sarduy wrote, "Now I don't feel so cheated by not having been the author of *Diamonds Are Forever* which . . . is divine for its heavy ornamentality, its baroque transvestism, its conceptual labyrinth. Of all the the titles you propose I prefer From Cuba with Love . . . because it evokes the supermacho CIA agent. Now that Cuban journalism insists upon my filiation with that benevolent institution, nothing could be more opportune" (qtd. in Levine 150).

Although Levine seems to have proposed the James Bond-sounding title half in jest, she had legitimate reasons for doing so. *From Cuba with a Song* is peppered with countless references to American pop culture. HELP and MERCY appear dressed as "motorcycle molls, their helmets adorned with Fifties iconography" (Levine 150) of Elvis Presley, James Dean, Paul Anka, Tab Hunter, Pat Boone, and Rock Hudson. In the end, however, Levine decided on the title that would capture the novel's playful, irreverent, treatment of Cubannes:

> *From Cuba with Love* made its way to *From Cuba with a Song* to signal more clearly the text's poetic function as a song, and its Cubanity, making explicit what was implied in the original title. Though not a grammatical ellipsis like the original, this title could also be an incomplete answer to a suspended question, a fragment of a sentence that in this case might be "They came from Cuba with a song." It completes the original half-sentence: "The singers are from . . . Cuba with a song" not in a linear but in a circular way, *from* the syntactic link both posing and responding to the enigma of origin. (151)

The question of origin is one that haunts every translator in the quest to render his/her translation as faithful to the original text as possible. It is what translators agonize over in the course of their thankless work. But Sarduy, who was never "faithful" to the original sources of his citations, did not expect faithfulness from his translators. If anything, he gave them ample freedom to play, even to misquote him, as he misquoted so many authors in his own texts. In the translators' afterword to *Christ on the Rue Jacob,* Levine and Maier discuss their elusive search for the original passage from Burroughs's *Naked Lunch* to accurately insert it in the English translation. They write, "When one searches through Burroughs's novel for the passage Sarduy cites, so as to insert the 'original' English into the translation, it becomes evident that, although the bulk of the paragraph does indeed correspond to an identifiable passage, some sentences have been taken from other sections of the book, and there is one sentence that Sarduy has apparently added himself" (Levine 164). Turning the religious concept of a "faithful" translation on its head, Sarduy instead put into play the exquisite joys of textual infidelity. He "translated" authors and cultures (as in the Latin *traslatio*) by transposing them. "Like Flaubert *in Salambô,* Sarduy 'translates' the non-Occidental experience" (Levine 173). In fact, he saw his own life in Paris as that of a translated Cuban into French and vice versa. He denied "the dichotomy between exile and home" and "between translation and original" (Levine 151). There is no home (*nostos*) to feel nostalgic about.

In *Cobra,* for instance, the question of the twins' origins never comes up. They are not from the plains; they are not from the mountains. They emerge out of Woman's womb as if out of nothing. But then as González Echevarría acutely notes, one rarely encounters conventional familial groups in Sarduy's narratives ("Severo Sarduy" 1442). The question of origins is either an ontological or a historical one, and history in this instance has been denied the twins from the outset (as it happened with the Africans and Chinese in Cuba). Also, the history of the world is a history of texts, and here as elsewhere, the non-Western matrix has been denied a place in the Western canon. The history of colonialism and slavery is the story of the West assuming the role of cultural midwife while denying the Other any claim to a history prior to the conquest. The twins (African and Chinese) are delivered by a Chinese African midwife, herself the subject of colonial *mestizaje,* most likely lacking any knowledge of her past. The same thing has occurred in this country with African Americans. It is a very small minority of African Americans who can trace their origins back either to a specific family or even to a general geographical location in Africa. The history of the Americas is the story of a translated people. Any attempt at finding the original source is likely to terminate in a experience similar to that of Levine and Maier's with respect to the Burroughs quote, where some of the original lines of the text may still be intact, while others may have been either altered or added to create another story.

To the question of whether the Americas have a common history/literature (*historia*), the answer, as Gustavo Pérez-Firmat says, is twofold. The Americas, or the geography that serves as the referent for the sign "America," is complex and manifold. Although the cultures and histories of the different countries of the Americas cannot be funneled into one, except perhaps in the most superficial way, "the Americas' cultural indebtedness to Europe is but one feature that the literatures of the New World have in common" ("Introduction" 2). The history of Cuba, for one, is connected by many factors to the history of the United States and Europe. Yet certain critics have argued—and I include myself among them—that there is little in Sarduy that could really be considered Cuban and that in fact Sarduy is more French in literary and cultural sensibility than he is Cuban (see my *Severo Sarduy and the Religion of Text*). González Echevarría's long-standing defense of Sarduy against such "accusations" from critics like me, Roberto Fernández Retamar, and others postulates a Sarduy whose Cubanness (*lo cubano*) is implicitly inscribed in every single one of his texts with the blood of *la patria*. On further consideration I believe that both González Echevarría and my camp are wrong and wrong for the same reason. If Sarduy was a French writer cross-dressed as a Cuban, he was also a Cuban cross-dressed as French writer. The failure to take Sarduy's opposition to nationhood seriously is perhaps the worst form of betrayal. If there was anything that Sarduy refused to endorse, it was the outworn romanticism of nationhood. It is not that Sarduy was a cross-dresser of Cuban culture; it is more that as a Cuban living most of his life outside of his native country, Sarduy saw Cuba as the Cuba of texts—an object of transvestism and simulation no different from Paris. Sarduy knew Cuba, loved Cuba, wrote about Cuba with all the gusto of the transvestite who, having put on his/her mascara, proudly goes out for the night. What the transvestite knows, said Sarduy, is that *a woman is just appearance,* and by extension so is a *country*—signifiers in the order of simulacra. Starving for an identity? Join MERCY and HELP at the Self-Service. The twenty-two-year-old Sarduy "stayed in Paris because, at that stage of his career, his commitment to art, to writing, and to his own growth concerned him far more than making a statement of political allegiance. The truth of the matter is that for Sarduy . . . writing *is* the revolution" (Prieto, "In-Fringe" 267).

Prieto's assessment of Sarduy's decision to stay in Paris after his scholarship ran out rings true at least to this critic. But what was at first the self-chosen life of an expatriate became some years later a life of exile. In the late 1970s, at the height of the cold war, Sarduy—

along with other Cuban writers living in and outside of Cuba—was accused of working for the CIA and denounced as a traitor to the revolution by the Castro regime. Refusing to take the accusations seriously or to heed the ultimatum of being in (with the regime) or out (against it), Sarduy opted for neither and in response took up the arms of a revolutionary, nonteleological literature of concentricity, mockingly deconstructive of power.

One of Sarduy's weapons of choice was the Cuban *choteo*. More devastating than irony or parody—the latter of which begins by respectfully citing the source and then transforming it for its own ends—*choteo* doesn't take the source or anything else seriously. Pérez-Firmat writes, "The contrast with the subtlety and refinement of irony, which finds fertile soil in old and tradition-laden nations like England could not be sharper" ("Riddles" 72). According to Cuban cultural critic Jorge Mañach, *choteo* was everything that was wrong with postcolonial Cuba. He attributed "the prevalence of *choteo* in Cuba to the youth of the Republic" (Pérez-Firmat, "Riddles" 72). If you asked anyone on the street, he said, to define *choteo,* they would all agree that it consists in making fun of everything. In his 1940 essay "Indagación del choteo" (Investigation into Choteo), Mañach charged that *choteo* appeals to the basest and lowest common denominator of Cuban society. Jocular, mocking, and scatological, *choteo* reduces, levels, and lowers everything with which it comes in contact. In this sense, says Pérez-Firmat, "choteo is doubly low: it is 'low' humor that 'lowers' its victims" ("Riddles" 72-73). Further and more important with respect to Sarduy's use of it, it holds absolutely nothing sacred. The sacred, in fact, may just be its favorite subject of attack. Anarchic in nature, dismissive of class and social distinctions, it laughs at all traditions by making light of them. "Everything is carnival, everything is parody, everything is laughter" (Kushigian, *"Dialogue"* 76, my translation), says Sarduy as he laughs at the myth of Maitreya by placing the Instructor inside a plastic wash basin. And so, "we witness the superimposition of the Cuban culture or specifically, the *choteo* onto Oriental philosophy" (Kushigian, *"Dialogue"* 76). But it's not just the Orient that suffers the slings and arrows of Sarduy's *choteo*—so does the West. The severity of Sarduy's *choteo* lies in the fact that it is not only rhetorical but also, and perhaps of even greater importance, formal—a mockery of the prudish bourgeois expectation that writing should always be about something, with an identifiable referent outside of language. The Bahktinian carnivalesque aspect of *choteo,* with its affront to all kinds of social hierarchies and middle-class hypocrisy, is potentially liberating. Taken too far, however, *choteo* can end up in the kind of nihilism that Nietzsche warned could result from a reevaluation of values. If, as

Pérez-Firmat claims, Mañach overlooked the *culo* (ass) in "lo vernáculo" (the vernacular) ("Riddles" 72), Sarduy certainly did not. The dung heap of Western civilization lay nearby in the horizon. How one transformed the dung heap into something else, into something positive, was another matter—the material of art. Ana Maria Barrenechea is right on target when she says that Sarduy's Cuba— in all its religious, ethnic, and racial multiplicity—is a metaphor for a world the gods (Yoruba and Judeo-Christian) have abandoned (234). In the absence of gods, we are left with the dangerous freedom of the Self-Service. And yet to look back will no longer offer comfort, for we are also the age that knows that the "greatness" of the past was steeped in human blood. "Barbarism," writes Sarduy, "thy name is the Western World" (*For Voice* 101).

In the years following World War II, the French asked themselves whether anything could be said to be socially redeeming in de Sade. Why not burn de Sade? Such a question could only make someone like Sarduy cringe in horror and rightly so. However, one could ask the same question about Sarduy with respect to the North American context. The answer, I believe, would be a positive one. For Sarduy's challenge to the traditional notion of identity raises questions that remain problematically unanswered in American society. America's history of racism is the end result of the way we as a society have constructed, distributed, and economically propagated a certain conception of national identity. The obsession with placing people in religious, racial, and ethnic boxes has to do with a desperate attempt at filling what is experienced as an empty center with an artificially constructed identity that has yet to utter its "true" name. "Laughter, mockery as the mask of nothingness, *choteo* as a challenge to emptiness," is tantamount to "identity as a negation of identity" (González Echevarría, *Ruta* 130, my translation). The secret, if we ever allow Pandora to let it fly out of her box, is: no, we are not number one; there isn't and there never was a number one in the elliptical and concentric circles that make our world.

Notes

[1] Sarduy associated the word *cube* with cubism as well as with the glass cubes of West Coast sculptor Larry Bell, of which he writes, "Larry Bell's art . . . destroys the notion of art as a reference to something other than its own physique: the support, the armature, is precisely what constitutes the work" (*Written* 82).

[2] The Shanghai Theater of Sarduy's novel is pure kitsch, as kitschy as a Pedro Almodóvar tableau. Varderi points out the connection between Sarduy's narratives and Almodóvar's films.

[3] Either Sarduy's claim was a fiction—in his way of thinking, a simulation of reality—or he did in fact have a Chinese ancestor who was named Macao on his arrival in Cuba.

[4] Cuba's patron saint, Our Lady of Charity, is also the Santeria deity Ochun, goddess of the rivers and eros.

[5] The title "The Entry of Christ into Havana" is also an allusion to James Ensor's (1860-1949) carnivalesque painting *The Entry of Christ into Brussels in 1889*. Ensor, among other things, was a painter of masks, and the mask as a trope of simulation is central to Sarduy. The title of Sarduy's third novel, *Cobra,* is a reference to the artistic group from Copenhagen, Brussels, and Amsterdam known as COBRA, of which Ensor was a member.

[6] Sarduy was highly influenced by the work of the German artist Hans Bellmer (1902-1975). He is best known for a series of disturbing photographs of two dolls he constructed in the 1930s. The dolls are disassembled torsos in various sexual positions: tied to trees, spread-eagled, or quartered. These doll photos do much to clarify Sarduy's vision of the Lyrical Theater of the Dolls, especially in that Bellmer's dolls were double and that parts of one were often interchanged with parts of the other. Bellmer wrote a book entitled *Die Puppe* (1934) in which his dolls were characters in a theater of cruelty.

[7] The name *Ktazob,* as Prieto has discovered, combines the Arabic word *zob,* meaning *penis,* with Sarduy's contraction of the Spanish word *quitar, to remove,* with the root consonants *kt.* In short, *Ktazob* stands for "the penis remover" (*Body* 265, n5).

[8] Maitreya "resides in Tushita heaven and is expected to appear on earth in human form four thousand years after the disappearance of Gautama Buddha" (Coulter and Turner 303).

[9] This idea also appears in Sarduy's radio play *Fall.* The association of the twins' first period with the loss of their power of divination and healing goes back to the Nepalese Buddhist belief in the Devi or Goddess Durga. Her three sexual aspects are Kumari (prepubesence), Lakshmi (sexual maturity), and Mahakali (seasoned detachment). As part of a religious ceremony a prepubescent girl is chosen to represent the goddess, and she remains a Kumari Devi until the day of her first menstruation, after which the search for a new Kumari Devi begins all over again.

[10] This connection was not lost on Sarduy. In 1981 he wrote a radio play titled *Tanka,* after the classic form of Japanese poetry. The *tanka* is composed of five lines with five, seven, five, seven, and seven syllables.

[11] In the Cuban argot the word *pájaro* (bird) is pejorative, equivalent of the English word *fag.* Hence Sarduy's reference to a "colibrí," or a hummingbird, and to "pájaros de la playa," or beach birds, could be translated as "beach queers." In *Colibrí* his father says to Sarduy, "You are part of a long line of Sarduy men, and until now there have never been any fags (*pájaros*) in this family. I don't want anyone pointing the finger at me on the street. So you are now going to burn those *four pieces of shit*" (129, my italics, my translation). Clearly, the four pieces of shit are Sarduy's first four novels.

Works Cited

Barnard, Philip. Preface. *For Voice*. By Severo Sarduy. Pittsburgh: Latin American Literary Review Press, 1985. 9-11.

Barrenechea, Ana Maria. "Severo Sarduy o la Aventura Textual." *Textos Hispanoamericanos De Sarmiento a Sarduy*. Caracas: Monte Avila Editores, 1978. 221-34.

Barthes, Roland. "The Death of the Author." *Image, Music, Text*. Trans. Stephen Heath. New York: Hill & Wang, 1977. 142-48.

Beckett, Samuel. *Cascando and Other Short Dramatic Pieces*. New York: Grove, 1968.

Bhabha, Homi K. *The Location of Culture*. London: Routledge, 1994.

Bowker, John, ed. *The Oxford Dictionary of World Religions*. Oxford: Oxford UP, 1997.

Burroughs, William. *The Adding Machine: Selected Essays*. New York: Seaver, 1986.

—. *Naked Lunch*. New York: Grove, 1959.

—. *The Ticket that Exploded*. New York: Grove, 1987.

Carpentier, Alejo. *The Chase*. Trans. Alfred Mac Adam. New York: Farrar, Straus & Giroux, 1989.

Coulter, Charles Russel, and Patricia Turner. *Encyclopedia of Ancient Deities*. Jefferson: McFarland, 2000.

González Echevarría, Roberto. *Celestina's Brood: Continuities of the Baroque in Spanish and Latin American Literatures*. Durham: Duke UP, 1993.

—. "La nación desde *De donde son los cantantes a Pájaros de la Playa*." *Cuadernos Hispanoamericanos* 563 (May 1997): 55-67.

—. "Narrative and Prophecy in the Post-Modern Novel: Sarduy's *Maitreya*." *World Affairs* 150.2. (1987): 147-62.

—. *La Ruta de Severo Sarduy*. Hanover: Ediciones del Norte, 1987.

—. "Severo Sarduy." *Latin American Writers*. Vol. 2. Ed. Carlos A. Solé and Maria Isabel Abreu. New York: Scribner's, 1989.

Goytisolo, Juan. *Juan the Landless*. Trans. Helen R. Lane. New York: Viking, 1977.

Hoyle, Fred. *Astronomy*. New York: Doubleday, 1962.

Kushigian, Julia. "*Dialogue and Displacement*: The Orchestration of Sarduy." *Orientalism in the Hispanic Literary Tradition: In Dialogue With Borges, Paz, and Sarduy*. Albuquerque: U of New Mexico P, 1991. 71-101.

—. "Gender and Culture Reconsidered: The Transformation of *Cobra* into *Bildungsroman*." *Between the Self and the Void: Essays in Honor of Severo Sarduy*. Ed. Alicia Rivero-Potter. Boulder: Society of Spanish and Spanish-American Studies, 1998. 49-64.

Levine, Suzanne Jill. *The Subversive Scribe: Translating Latin American Fiction.* Saint Paul: Graywolf, 1991.

Lezama Lima, José. "Image of Latin America." *Latin America in Its Literature.* Trans. Mary G. Berg. Ed. Ivan A. Schulman. New York: Holmes & Meir, 1980. 321-27.

—. *Paradiso.* Trans. Gregory Rabassa. New York: Farrar, Straus & Giroux, 1974.

Montero, Oscar. *The Name Game: Writing / Fading Writer in De Donde Son Los Cantantes.* Chapel Hill: North Carolina Studies in the Romance Languages and Literatures–U.N.C. Department of Romance Languages, 1988.

Moore, Steven. Rev. of *Christ on the Rue Jacob,* by Severo Sarduy. *Review of Contemporary Fiction* 15.3 (1995): 242-43.

Nietzsche, Friedrich. *The Gay Science.* Trans. Walter Kaufmann. New York: Vintage, 1974.

Pellón, Gustavo. "Severo Sarduy's Strategy of Irony: Paradigmatic Indecision in *Cobra* and *Maitreya.*" *Latin American Literary Review* 23 (Fall-Winter 1983): 7-13.

Pérez, Rolando. *Severo Sarduy and the Religion of the Text.* Lanham: UP of America, 1988.

Pérez-Firmat, Gustavo. "Introduction: Cheek to Cheek." *Do the Americas Have a Common Literature?* Ed. Gustavo Pérez-Firmat. Durham: Duke UP, 1990. 1-5.

—.Rev. of *José Lezama Lima's Joyful Vision: A Study of "Paradiso" and Other Prose Works,* by Gustavo Pellón. *Hispanic Review* 59.2. (1991): 252-54.

—. "Riddles of the Sphincter." *Literature and Liminality: Festive Readings in the Hispanic Tradition.* Durham: Duke UP, 1986. 53-74.

Prieto, René. *Body of Writing: Figuring Desire in Spanish American Literature.* Durham: Duke UP, 2000.

—. "In-Fringe: The Role of French Criticism in the Fiction of Nicole Brossard and Severo Sarduy." *Do the Americas Have a Common Literature?* Ed. Gustavo Pérez-Firmat. Durham: Duke UP, 1990. 266-81.

Salgado, César Augusto. "Hybridity in New World Baroque Theory." *Journal of American Folklore* 112.445 (Summer 1999): 316-31.

Sarduy, Severo. "The Baroque and the Neobaroque." *Latin America in Its Literature.* Trans. Mary G. Berg. Ed. Ivan A. Schulman. New York: Holmes & Meir, 1980. 115-32.

—. *Christ on the Rue Jacob.* Trans. Suzanne Jill Levine and Carol Maier. San Francisco: Mercury House, 1995.

—. *"Cobra" and "Maitreya."* Trans. Suzanne Jill Levine. Intro. James McCourt. Normal: Dalkey Archive Press, 1995.

—. *Colibarí.* Barcelona: Argos Vergara, 1984.

—. "Deterritorialization." Trans. Naomi Lindstrom. *Review of Contemporary Fiction* 4.2 (1984): 104-09.

—. *For Voice (The Beach, Fall, Re-cite, The Ant-killers).* Trans. Phillip Barnard. Pittsburgh: Latin American Literary Review Press, 1985.

—. *From Cuba with a Song.* Trans. Suzanne Jill Levine. Los Angeles: Sun & Moon, 1994.

—. *Written on a Body.* Trans. Carol Meir. New York: Lumen, 1989.

Sessions, Roger. *Roger Sessions on Music: Collected Essays.* Ed. Edward T. Cone. Princeton: Princeton UP, 1979.

Thomas, Hugh. *Cuba, or, The Pursuit of Freedom.* New York: Da Capo, 1998.

Varderi, Alejandro. *Severo Sarduy y Pedro Almodóvar: del barroco al kitsch en la narrativa y el cine posmodernos.* Madrid: Editorial Pliegos, 1996.

A Severo Sarduy Checklist

From Cuba with a Song. 1967. Trans. Suzanne Jill Levine. Los Angeles: Sun & Moon, 1994.

"Cobra" and "Maitreya." 1972/1978. Trans. Suzanne Jill Levine. Intro. James McCourt. Normal: Dalkey Archive Press, 1995.

For Voice (The Beach, Fall, Re-cite, The Ant-Killers). 1977. Trans. Phillip Barnard. Pittsburgh: Latin American Literary Review Press, 1985.

Christ on the Rue Jacob. 1994. Trans. Suzanne Jill Levine and Carol Maier. San Francisco: Mercury House, 1995.

Book Reviews

Yuri Druzhnikov. *Angels on the Head of a Pin*. Trans. Thomas Moore. Peter Owen/Dufour, 2003. 566 pp. $34.95.

This stunning work of genius led to Druzhnikov's being blacklisted for his mocking depiction of the return of the cult of personality to the Soviet Union after Khrushchev, revealing in its twisted logic the bleakly intimidating spectacle of hyperbolic doublethink. The author skillfully interweaves and plays off the pathetically self-serving shenanigans of a legion of personalities, whose sometimes considerably attenuated links to the editor of *Trudovaya Pravda* attract narrative interest. After a heart attack on his way to a meeting of the Central Committee, editor Makartsev's subsequent stay in hospital leaves his formerly tight ship at the paper without ballast, as in turn each of several figures on the staff, joined by co-workers, relatives, and friends, displays a singular propensity to lurch and founder in the service of ambition, love, or fleeting security in the heavy wake of the 1968 incursion into Czechoslovakia. Yagubov, the new deputy, capitalizes on an unexpected opportunity to supplant his boss. Senior writer Rappoport, a wily gulag veteran, steers clear of yet another change in political fortune while ghosting the paper's campaigns in behalf of the new orthodoxy, as well as all the letters to the editor and speeches delivered by the entire spectrum of party apparatchiks. This conniving constellation of writers, colleagues, minor functionaries, their (sometimes highly placed) comrades and foes offers ample evidence of the degree to which petty intrigue and mindless brutality consumed everyone, from "Big Eyebrows" to the editor's feckless son. As the noose tightens around a junior writer whose latest samizdat mysteriously appears on Makartsev's desk, driving him to distraction while contributing to the distressing turn of affairs at the paper, Druzhnikov's clowns, rogues, vamps, and ingenues play an antic round of confidence, self-deception, and betrayal to a rhythm as scathingly funny as it is unrelentingly deadly. [Michael Pinker]

Han Shaogong. *A Dictionary of Maqiao*. Trans. Julia Lovell. Columbia Univ. Press, 2003. 322 pp. $27.95.

The premise of this "dictionary" is that the local peculiarities of language usage reveal the outlook and way of life of a tiny remote village in southern China. This fascinating novel also presents itself as an ethnographic work whose compiler, explicitly identified as the author himself, was among the millions of youths "sent down" to the countryside during the Cultural Revolution to learn from the peasants. The loose dictionary format allows considerable flexibility in assembling diverse local narratives, augmented by research and speculative commentary to construct a complex portrait of Maqiao, primarily during the communist era. While we meet a gallery of colorful characters, none are allowed more than momentary prominence, and the focus is on a sympathetic but unsentimental portrayal of the harsh, often brutal, but not infrequently humorous life in the Chinese country-side. Han is well known for his interest in the residual elements of tradition and the deep structure of Chinese culture, so the disruptions of the communist regime are mostly experienced as passing epiphenomenona against the larger rhythms of peasant existence and history. Yet the roots of culture as examined through language prove to be anything but immutable and unambiguous, and as Julia Lovell points out in her preface, this living sense of language offers an implied critique of the abstract rigidities of Mao-speak. While on the one hand this novel details the uniqueness and exotic alienness of a specific place, on the other the educated urban re-corder draws out the implications for Chinese society and culture in general. In its formal inventiveness, its nuanced depiction of Chinese peasant life, and its speculative explorations into the Chinese cultural psyche, this is one of the finest novels of the post-Mao era to so far make its way into English. [Jeffrey Twitchell-Waas]

Leslie Scalapino. *Dahlia's Iris: Secret Autobiography and Fiction*. FC2, 2003. 213 pp. Paper: $13.95; *Zither & Autobiography*. Wesleyan Univ. Press, 2003. 110 pp. $30.00; paper: $14.95.

Leslie Scalapino has long wrestled with the implications (indeed, the illusion) of the moment. Her avant-garde work—poetry, dramas, essays, visual arts, fiction—is restlessly intent on shattering the apparent coherency of the immediate and exposing the durable layers that lurk unsuspected in the time and the space we dismiss as familiar and banal. Drawing from a suggestive legacy in Buddhist traditions that upend tidy Western notions of linearity and causality, Scalapino's writings routinely, audaciously transgress genres, uneasing, then upsetting, and finally gracefully illuminating. Her audience has come to expect startling language that freely devises a sonic system that sustains a fetching, hypnotic, hallucinatory experience, at once deeply emotional and yet serenely detached, the reading itself becoming an event in which the unfolding text is an organic, shifting proposal about how we are finally to describe, contain, and understand the self lodged fitfully in the moment.

How perfect, then, for Scalapino to interrogate the murder-mystery genre: *Dahlia's Iris* is, at foundation level, an old-fashioned police drama (in the not-too-distant future, somebody is killing Hispanic boys brought to San Francisco as a cheap labor source) in which a phalanx of police detectives must search through a matrix of sinister possibilities in an effort to achieve clarity and solution—not surprisingly, Scalapino is far more interested in the search and its implications. The detective-story grounding becomes splendidly suggestive, dreamlike, symbolic. Indeed, the search for mystery comes to privilege a countertext that evolves with elegant subversion:

based on an esoteric Tibetan genre, a spiritual autobiography is an exercise not in the traditional Western autobiography that assembles a person's life-events, sensations and actions and memories, into reassuring plot, but rather an exercise in exploring a life's spiritual intensities in which identity and memory as narrow and personal give way to a broader understanding of a visionary self, a poetic sort of endeavor conceding that truth is finally elusive and that the self is a deception and a distraction. Scalapino further splices into this unfolding text allusions to a clutch of science-fiction cult films that expose the fragility of the human form and the deception of its solidity (*Invasion of the Body Snatchers, Terminator 2,* and *Blade Runner*) and thus transforms the reading into an authentic experience, an engaging preoccupation with adjusting to a subtle voice determined to unsettle time into a free-motion now.

Zither & Autobiography is a splendid complementary text. In the opening work Scalapino sets aside her signature symbolic, elusive prose-line to draw a vivid and specific narrative of her own upbringing (particularly her extensive experiences in the East) and, more critically, her long fascination with and deep artistic debt to Zen. As a memory text *Autobiography* not surprisingly insists on decentering the notion of past and creating instead a fluid and recursive sense of how memories find their way into a vibrant nontime that defies reassuring configurings of past, present, and future. Throughout the narrative, as we move through exotic locales, we are given generous moments of Scalapino's unerring eye for detail, the lyric strike of her poetic ear, which renders such geographies vivid and clean. In the accompanying text, *Zither,* Scalapino investigates the familiar parameters of *King Lear* to produce an anarchic, translucent reimagining of that staid text into an accumulating, hypnotic read, ongoing and interactive, that necessarily redefines itself upon repeated readings, that counters expectations of viable form by revealing fluidity itself as structure. Scrutiny becomes plot, language becomes suspense, reader becomes character, and mystery ultimately becomes solution. [Joseph Dewey]

Marcel Bénabou. *L'Appentis revisité.* Berg International, Paris, 2003. 93 pp. €9.00.

Marcel Bénabou's latest book is a collection of short pieces, nine of them in all. Readers who have come under the heady sway of his longer works will not be disappointed here, for despite their brevity, each of these texts is vintage Bénabou. That is to say, they are tortured and pungent; they are written in a mode that questions the most fundamental terms of writing; and they play ironically on their own impossibly ironical stance. The piece that lends its title to the collection as a whole was first conceived, Bénabou tells us, when he found that a chapter was "missing" from Georges Perec's *Life A User's Manual*. Bénabou's original intent was to supply that missing chapter, but the project evolved into something else, a cabinet of wonders, constructed with borrowings from Perec's works and animated by its own logic. The French word *appentis* denotes a kind of storage space contiguous to a larger and more central space, a lean-to, an outbuilding, a shed. That is the kind of space that Bénabou invites his reader to "revisit" here, and it is a space structured by a variety of trompe l'oeil effects, on the level of both theme and technique. Other paths in Bénabou's garden are equally forking. There is, for instance, a letter sent by an author to his editor, accompanying a finished book manuscript. It's his first piece of writing after years of silence, and although his friends now refer to him as a "new Lazarus," he frets that, as Lichtenberg suggested, the last and best touch one can give to a manuscript is to burn it. There is another letter in this collection, addressed to an eminent counterfeiter of letters by one of his disciples. The master had forged—and sold handsomely—holograph letters from Aeschylus to Pythagoras and Alexander to Aristotle, among many others. All of them are in French, serving to demonstrate (not incidentally) that French was indeed the original language. In another piece Bénabou offers a handy set of directions for writers wishing to begin a new book. Followed closely, those directions result in a text where each gesture turns back upon the one that precedes, where each step forward revisits what has gone before, where every word the writer puts into play takes its place as a pawn in a broader play on words. Clearly, any book produced according to that recipe will be an agile, slippery, delightfully quirky piece of work—and one that might just as well be signed "Marcel Bénabou." [Warren Motte]

———————

Alexandra Papaditsas and Kent Johnson. *The Miseries of Poetry: Traductions from the Greek*. Skanky Possum (www.skankypossum.com), 2003. 56 pp. Paper: $7.00.

Deep in the dark wilds of unlikely Culver City, CA, hides the Museum of Jurassic Technology, wherein fantasy and half-learned history commingle to reveal that either we know nothing or we can know nothing. With *The Miseries of Poetry* Kent Johnson and Alexandra Papaditsas have created, orangely, a paperbook-adaptation of the Culver City museum; for in each way that the MJT is an examination of curios and collections, *The Miseries* is a rollick through translation and what we know of Greek poetry. We know that they were dirty buggers, so here we read, "our pretty helmsman will grow light-headed from / pressing tight, in fear, the cheeks of his succulent ass." We know that they were philosophers, and so we have a Greek Buddhism in "All opposition is seamlessly interconnected by atomic joints." And we know that lacunae clutter the manuscripts, so we get gaps—dare I say aporiae?—infiltrating the texts, but here the missing parts compete with the words, creating an antipalimpsest. But this book of poetry is a fiction. Kent Johnson has admitted as much in an interview: "Only four out of the twenty poems . . . have any recognizable relationship to an original text. Most of the poems are pure inventions, ascribed in the book to both real and invented poets." These are not translations: they are traductions, though we are not traduced. This is Kent Johnson, turning the author into a hole in the papyrus: "*[Here there is an oblong hole, as if burned by laser rays shot out from gauze covered eyes.]*" Complete with paratextual blurbs by forty-two contemporary authors, plus a "Vestibulum" by Slavoj Zizek, this slim book is a boggling beauty, where we learn to "chorus our dead to the music / of the humming strings." [Lucas Klein]

––––––––––––––

Jorge Amado. *Tent of Miracles*. Trans. Barbara Shelby Merello. Intro. Ilan Stavans. Univ. of Wisconsin Press, 2003. 380 pp. Paper: $16.95; *Tieta*. Trans. Barbara Shelby Merello. Intro. Moacyr Scliar. Univ. of Wisconsin Press, 2003. 671 pp. Paper: $18.95. (Reprints)

Timed as a memorial to Jorge Amado's death in 2001, these two novels are new English editions of *Tent of Miracles* and *Tieta*. The novels were written in 1969 and 1977 respectively, and they represent the second phase of Amado's literary career, the phase of *Dona Flor and Her Two Husbands,* when he shifted from more overtly political narrative to writing that was full of excess, sensual delight, and the richness of everyday life.

Tent of Miracles will resonate well with readers who have recently come to rethink the relationship between U.S. academic interests and Latin America and the way that it is only after a Latin American writer or scholar gains fame in the U.S. and/or Europe that they are valued at home. The novel's center, since protagonist is not quite the appropriate term, is Pedro Archanjo, a self-taught Afro-Brazilian scholar who has published on miscegenation, Afro-Brazilian culture, and Bahian cooking. Archanjo's death sets a series of narrative threads into motion. First, we have the arrival of James D. Levenson, a professor at Columbia University and a Nobel Prize winner, who considers Archanjo a giant in the field of ethnology and folklore and wants to conduct research on his work. Levenson is an instant celebrity with myriad Bahians vying for his attention. Levenson's interest in the work of Archanjo sets in motion two other threads. In the process of his research the reader receives an extraordinary biography of Archanjo, of his struggles to get his work published, of his avid interest in Afro-Brazilian culture and Bahian life, and of his complicated personal life. Parallel to the unraveling of the dead ethnologist's life, Amado tells the story of Bahia as it endeavors to capitalize on the centennial of Archanjo's death by throwing a huge celebration. The plans for the party, the commotion around Levenson, and the memories of those who knew Archanjo reveal larger concerns about Brazilian society and the nation's problems with cultural identity.

Even though these two novels signal the second phase of Amado's work, they continue his undying concern for the future of Brazil, and many of the social insights in *Tent of Miracles* are central to *Tieta* as well. *Tieta* also centers on a figure with a marginal and complicated relationship to her community. Also, while Tieta is ostensibly the protagonist of this novel, Amado once again fills the text with a variety of characters (not the least of which is the author himself), who take on key roles in the narrative. Another multilayered story, *Tieta* is about the return of a woman who had been cast out of her family and her community as a young girl. She returns after years in Sao Paulo as a prostitute to spend time with her family. Over the years she has sent money to her family, and they have come to believe that she went to the city and married a wealthy man. Her wealth and success draw attention and admiration. Tieta embodies two of Amado's central concerns—sensuality and social activism—and these twin interests are artfully intertwined throughout the novel and across the characters. In Tieta's case they come to a head in her passionate affair with her virgin nephew, who had planned to become a priest, and her involvement in trying to stop a multinational, famous for excessive pollution, from setting up a plant on the coast of her small town. Rich in narrative structure and remarkable in the description of Brazilian plenitude, these novels are smart, witty, and fun. [Sophia A. McClennen]

Wilson Harris. *The Mask of the Beggar*. Faber & Faber, 2003. 172 pp. £16.99.

The Mask of the Beggar, Wilson Harris's twenty-fourth novel, can be read as a recapitulation of what he has been voicing (in that peculiarly personal rhythm of his prose) in all of his work, immersing the reader in dimensions of time and space that are dreamlike, unsettling, and yet profoundly real. A summation of his ideas and obsessions, the new novel contains passages germane to Harris's enduring fascination with Amerindian myths and his belief in "visionary Time" and statements defining the peculiar aesthetics of his art with its cross-cultural references. Harris states in a prefatory note that "*The Mask of the Beggar* is based on the disguise Odysseus adopts on returning to his kingdom in Ithaca" and that "Well-nigh forgotten, ancient pre-Columbian imageries are explored"—a declaration of his method in all of his work and an important key to understanding any of it. Harris's great achievement has been that he created, then sustained in his entire work, a singular form, a prose with unfamiliar stresses and curious juxtapositions of ancient and modern images, making the reader hear the heartbeat of the Guyanese interior, which is his image for the eternal soul of the universe.

The world witnessed by Harris has many dimensions. A seemingly serene landscape is alive with past presences; long-forgotten mythic symbols burst out of the land that seems suddenly fissured by the internal pressure of its own particular history; it is a world in which even the fossils are murmuring a Jungian message. There are no named characters, except what Harris calls "solid ghosts," in *The Mask of the Beggar*; the narrator in the first four chapters is the statue of a sculptor's mother, and in the remaining three the sculptor himself; the "solid ghosts" include Odysseus, Lazarus, Montezuma, Cortés, and the symbolically important mythological figure of Quetzalcoatl. What is narrated is not a story—unless it is *the* story of the human race—but rather a discussion of ideas related to the imaginative content of all of Harris's work. There is no plot or action, only intellectual design that advances the ideas; where the earlier novels painted vivid landscapes of the Americas, *The Mask of the Beggar* barely contains a sketch.

From the very first sentence of the prefatory note—"In *The Mask of the Beggar* a nameless artist seeks mutualities between cultures"—to long statements in the final chapter, Harris expresses his ideas directly rather than, as in much of his previous work, expecting the reader to engage in literary archeology. In this sense *The Mask of the Beggar* is his most personal novel, and the nameless artist is perhaps named Wilson Harris; some twenty pages from the end, the sculptor-narrator declares in emphatic italics, "*I am largely an intuitive writer,*" and proceeds to recite a credo that, coming in the final pages of his last novel, functions as a retrospective elucidation of all of Wilson Harris's work. [Zulfikar Ghose]

Lyn Hejinian. *The Fatalist.* Omnidawn, 2003. 84 pp. Paper: $12.95.

The Fatalist belongs to a category of Lyn Hejinian's book-length collage poems—along with works such as *Happiness* and *Slowly*—that take as their title a one-word concept and proceed to use this concept not so much as the determinate focus of the work but rather as a loose theme around which to organize a huge range of materials. The melding of aphorisms, pieces of lit theory, fragments of anecdote, and colloquial remarks within these books amounts less to a meditation on a theme than to a meditation away from it. In this latest book, "fate" plays many roles and is always falling into adjacent ideas and images, disappearing and reappearing throughout the text. We "regard uncertainty (fate) / as potentially a purveyor of pain," then learn that pain has "enormous decontextualizing power." Fate is "occurrence," but is also "what has happened to one, not what is going to happen." It is "not all that will happen / except in retrospect." Elsewhere, "Positions are always changing / things for us," which presumably includes "in retrospect." In all instances, "fate" connects to other concepts, either new or recurring, each concept like one color on a giant Rubik's Cube called "The Fatalist" that is forever twisting and recombining before us. Some of the resulting juxtapositions are more fruitful than others; one of the more interesting for me is to see fate in terms of literary closure. With Diderot's *Jacques the Fatalist* always in the background, and with Diderot himself regularly in the foreground—"one of my own particular heroes" (mine, too)—of a book by the author of the excellent essay "The Rejection of Closure," it is hard not to consider fate (or the traditional understanding of fate satirized by Diderot) and closure as sharing some ground: they are determinate, prescribed; they are everything that, as Diderot's Jacques says, "is written up above." Hejinian has placed Diderot in her book because he "subverted all possibility of [closure]," but his presence also underscores several of *The Fatalist*'s other values, including the pleasures of digression and the subversive nature of limitless play. [Martin Riker]

Jeff VanderMeer and Mark Roberts, eds. *The Thackery T. Lambshead Pocket Guide to Eccentric & Discredited Diseases.* Night Shade, 2003. 297 pp. $24.00.

Composing a work of fiction within the vocabulary and form of a nonfiction genre can be a powerful way to fuse the exploratory nature of imaginative writing with the concerns of the world outside the book. It's not surprising, then, to see novels written as travel guides, recipes, or even in-flight safety instructions. Simultaneously blurring and highlighting the disjunction between the fictive and the real, satire is automatic; when practiced with a more encompassing consciousness it becomes metafiction, or even meta-nonfiction, not only taking up its own subject matter, e.g., the medical profession, not only doing all the things we expect of literature, but also dissecting the assumptions of an appropriated nonfictive skin. *The Thackery T. Lambshead Pocket Guide to Eccentric & Discredited Diseases* is one such work: a collection of short fictions that often mimic the prudishness, guesswork, cultural and scientific myopia, and Latinate stuffiness of medical taxonomies from the nineteenth century. Abundantly illustrated, containing descriptions of over seventy-five invented diseases, from "Internalized Tattooing" to "Hsing's Spontaneous Self-Flaying Sarcoma," as well as other ancillary biographies and news reports, the *Pocket Guide* is encyclopedic in content and effect. Given this range—over fifty authors with speculative, experimental, and surreal leanings are represented—some unevenness isn't surprising. Still, diseases like "The Fellatio of Language: CNN and the Etiology of Lewinsky Fever" have a strong pull, as do the guide's many revealing medical observations, e.g., "the hangman's noose provides an instant tourniquet (though perhaps not 'cure') for a condemned prisoner with a nosebleed"; consider also the invitation to wonder why the intestinal tract of a woman in the Appalachians would develop an ornate and internal calligraphy that spells out, over and over, the words "Kill Me." Many of the diseases try to get at our humanity through culture, as does the description for Ebercitas, "the doleful condition of *trying too hard* to impress a woman," which results in "appalling poetry, music, art" as well as "good poetry, music, art." Others do so through our technology or basic human conditions like isolation or, as the guide describes it, Fungal Disenchantment, which can be brought on through "hearsay, rumor, and speculation." That is, at its best the disease guide is a reflection of our attempts to understand ourselves or our society, especially when something goes wrong, especially something that has no name. [Steve Tomasula]

Peter Carey. *My Life as a Fake.* Knopf, 2003. 266 pp. $24.00.

The title alerts us to the art of fakery (or the fakery of art). When the narrator, Sarah Wode-Douglass, tries to find material for her literary magazine, the *Modern Review,* she becomes obsessed with the poetry of "McCorkle"; she believes that it will save her magazine, that it is the work of genius. But at the same time, she recognizes that "McCorkle" may not exist, that he may be a clever hoax, a creation of Christopher Chubb, the poor, suffering poet living not in her rational England, but in the sordid streets of Kuala Lumpur. Carey underlines Wode-Douglass's possible madness, her longing to see validity and meaning, even if she claims that she has clear judgment. The opening pages seem to assault her beliefs. She tells us that she is "drawn to [John Slater] and repulsed by him." She trusts Slater, a mediocre poet, who admires publicity, gossip, celebrity. As Sarah moves from Slater to Chubb to McCorkle, she reveals that she is on edge, not in command of her critical faculties. She wants to see Slater and Chubb and McCorkle as distinct persons, but at times they become dangerously out of control—that is, *her* control. We are not really surprised that she admits to a breakdown. The various reversals and transformations warn us not to accept all of her narration. The exoticism of Malaysia seems to be an objective correlative. It is a land of poverty, brutality, and ripe beauty. At one point she tells us: "And that was how I became a fake myself, pretending that I would 'write him up.'" The winding thoughts of Sarah can't be fully trusted. Is she true to herself and to the three writers she describes? Or is she a delusional creator? Carey's astonishing novel is more than an epistemological thriller, a dream romance; it is an inquiry into the sources of true art. Henry James was fascinated by the "madness of art." So is Carey, who in this grim comedy of (t)errors explores the sources of great poetry, the art that, as Picasso claimed, results in the monstrous mating of "lie like truth." [Irving Malin]

Angélica Gorodischer. *Kalpa Imperial: The Greatest Empire that Never Was*. Trans. Ursula K. Le Guin. Small Beer, 2003. 246 pp. Paper: $16.00.

In *Kalpa Imperial* an imaginary world is described through a series of short stories told by a "storyteller." This nameless narrator is the one constant force through the book, occasionally lapsing into personal asides but mostly presenting the stories with a fablelike authority. This storytelling tradition is at the core of the novel, Gorodischer's first to be translated into English, and it adheres to the fundamentals of oral legends. It's easy to compare Gorodischer to Borges, for both are Argentinean writers who gravitate toward the fantastic. And like Borges's most memorable works, Gorodischer works in short narratives that are thematically related without focusing on a single thread. But *Kalpa Imperial* actually reminds me of the more light-hearted writings of Stanislaw Lem, such as his *Cyberiad*—conveying stories with a gentle approach to drama and a lackadaisical, almost whimsical spirit. Her fables are infused with humor, yet they never become outright silly. Creating a mythology of kings, queens, nobles, peasants, and soldiers, Gorodischer never gets bogged down in the trappings of fantasy writing. Her imagination conjures mysterious alchemists, generals and beggars who trade places, and princes who think that they are ferrets. While some of this imagery may be familiar to fantasy readers, Gorodischer avoids tepid dramatic tendencies and cookie-cutter plots. There's a very modern undercurrent to the Kalpa empire, with tales focusing on power (in a political sense) rather than generic moral lessons. Her mythology is consistent—wide in scope, yet not overwhelming. The myriad names of places and people can be confusing, almost Tolkeinesque in their linguistic originality. But the stories constantly move and keep the book from becoming overwhelming. Gorodischer has a sizeable body of work to be discovered, with eighteen books yet to reach English readers, and this is an impressive introduction. [John W. Fail]

Gerald Vizenor. *Hiroshima Bugi: Atomu 57.* Univ. of Nebraska Press, 2003. 208 pp. $26.95.

Gerald Vizenor contributes to Nebraska's Native Storiers series a novel that challenges conventional notions of ethnic, cultural, and stylistic purity. The title means, roughly, "Hiroshima boogie-woogie, in the fifty-seventh year after the dropping of the atomic bomb." This bugi consists of a sequence of semiautobiographical and fantastical stories written by Ronin Ainoko Browne, an orphan in search of his hybrid heritage. Ronin's father was an Anishinaabe soldier who translated for General MacArthur during the occupation of Japan, while his mother was a nationalist Japanese bugi dancer. Initially, Ronin's elliptic and allusive stories are confusing, to say the least. But Vizenor supplies them with explanatory commentaries written by another Anishinaabe veteran of WWII, Ronin's father's best friend during the final months of his life at the Hotel Manidoo in Nogales, Arizona. Several years after their encounter, Ronin assigns his "Manidoo Envoy" the task of compiling, editing, and annotating his stories. These stories follow Ronin through several misadventures with a diverse band of outcasts, who join him in staging a series of kabuki-style, guerrilla-theater protests against the hypocrisies and false promises of commemorative sites like the Atomic Bomb Dome in Hiroshima and the Yasukuni Jinja Shrine to the war dead in Tokyo. As the Manidoo Envoy explains, "Ronin was at war with traditions and simulations of peace, and in a mighty theater pose he advanced the outrageous idea of more nuclear weapons for peace and called for a supranational soldiery to enforce a nuclear peace." While Ronin's adventures are initially difficult to wade into, this collection of stories and commentaries is a fascinatingly eclectic pastiche, full of references to historical and cultural studies of Japan, retellings of tales from kabuki theater and international cinema, allusions to Anishinaabe and Ainu folk tales, and homages to such figures as the actor Toshiro Mifune, the adventurer Ranald MacDonald, and the writer Lafcadio Hearn. In this requiem for the atomic age's forgotten victims, Vizenor offers us another sophisticated, alternately sensitive and ironic meditation on the importance of cultural cross-fertilization and remembrance. [Thomas Hove]

Q Synopsis. *Johnny Werd: The Fire Continues.* Spineless, 2003. 124 pp. $19.95; paper: $9.95.

Every generation reinvents Holden Caulfield, the misfit resisting the onset of complacency and banality, the lost cause locked on pause, shadowed too early by the absurdity of inevitable mortality. Johnny Werd, unable to commit to his education, haunted by a sister's suicide, intrigued by the energy of setting things aflame, is a post-Gen-X Holden, the generation nurtured by television and sugared cereal, their myths drawn from *Star Wars* and their humor from *The Simpsons,* their childhood defined by *Sesame Street,* their adolescence by the cool lure of recreational narcotics—each channeled by Johnny's "voice," itself an unsettling ventriloquism that splinters point of view into points of views. Although this slender experiment riotously spoofs traditional narrative, it is nonetheless unsettling. Holden at his loneliest had the refuge of his own narrative, the comfort of an unfolding plot, the reassuring stability of his narrating voice, the block of chapters and the rhythm of sentences, and always a sympathetic reader. Not so here. Johnny Werd is left without a real-world environment—he thrives within the fuselage-world of his own language constructions in a "narrative" itself dismissive of storytelling. And, in the end, he is left lonelier than Holden ever could be: the isolate comforted by the kinetic tapping of his own keyboard. We eavesdrop, we read—although our invitation is presumptive, our presence intrusive. This is finally an exorcise/exercise of words, a desperate/exuberant, private act of revisiting form. Plot collapses into paragraph premises, characters are word-chords, sentences implode into Joycean sonic events, sinuous patterns of exotic diction and unrestricted syntax. But there lurks a strained uneasiness over the performance, a terror over a depthless world that has justified such audacious refuge. A narrative so given to the pyrotechnics of language closes with a most unsettling concession: "Give me some text with silences in it." [Joseph Dewey]

Christine Schutt. *Florida*. TriQuarterly Books, 2003. 152 pp. $22.95.

Florida is Christine Schutt's second book (the first being the astounding story-collection *Nightwork*) and her first novel. At the heart of the book is Alice Fivey, left fatherless at a young age and raised by relatives when her mother is institutionalized. The narrative, told by Alice herself, is about her relationship to her aunts and uncles, to the chauffeur Arthur, to her mother, and to others around her as she grows up a semi-orphan, always on the verge of being shuttled to the next place. Told as Alice herself is trying to become a writer, *Florida* (it becomes obvious late in the book) is a novel about an artist's development and the Dedalusian reintegration of that development into the artwork. The Florida of the title is less an actual place than Alice's mother's imagined ideal, a place where one can be free of distress, and the implication at the end of the book is that this is a place, as her mother approaches her own Florida through death, that Alice herself has finally begun to find. *Florida* has many of the strengths that made *Nightwork* such an interesting collection. Schutt's language is careful and musical, often elliptical. She has a knack for startling but apt descriptions, and one gets the sense that she has been careful about every word. The novel itself is told in short bursts, with some chapters being no more than a few sentences long and most no more than a few pages. But the narrative's length is also in tension with its ellipticality, and the story threatens to feel almost too revealed, threatens to lose some of its mystery and to give way to a relatively simple tale of a woman's growth. Narrative thus has a different importance (and more primacy) here than in Schutt's stories. However, Schutt manages nonetheless to walk a very delicate line, giving us most of the satisfactions of her earlier narratives even as she begins to allow her fiction to open into something new. *Florida* is a promising and multifaceted book suggesting that Schutt's art is expanding. [Brian Evenson]

Laird Hunt. *Indiana, Indiana*. Coffee House, 2003. 204 pp. $20.00.

At first glance Laird Hunt's second novel seems very different from his debut, *The Impossibly*. Whereas the first was set in various unnamed European cities, this novel takes place in the American rural Midwest; while the first featured labyrinthine sentences of contradiction, retractions, and qualifications, the sentences here are lyrical, liquid, natural, and evocative; where *The Impossibly* portrayed sophisticated shadow figures engaged in obscure Spy vs. Spy machinations, *Indiana, Indiana* tells the story of an older farmer, his family, his visions, and his love. Still, both books demonstrate Hunt's unique talent for the individual detail, as well as his extraordinary ability to completely imagine and construct entire fictive worlds. *Indiana, Indiana* is composed of minute, intimate, and memorable details: a windowsill littered with flies, the stump of a saw player's missing finger, the red feather of a cardinal against blackened trees. Hunt possesses a poet's eye for the evocative image, and it's tempting to luxuriate in his descriptive prose. Although his images can stop time, it's a wonderful feeling when you begin to realize the momentum sneaking up on you, when you begin to feel the subterranean connections and see the veiled linkages, when you recognize the narrative beneath the stillness. Hunt also knows, more than any American writer I've read recently, what to leave out. Or more precisely, he understands that creating a complete fictive world is dependent on creating absence and void as well as presence: "For every piece of their lives that is still visible, said Virgil, there are thousands of pieces that are not." Hunt is a master of those invisible pieces. *Indiana, Indiana* is a subtle, elegant, and haunting novel. [Jeffrey DeShell]

Lara Stapleton and Veronica Gonzalez, eds. *Juncture: 25 Very Good Stories and 12 Excellent Drawings*. Soft Skull, 2003. 280 pp. Paper: $18.95.

Teachers of creative writing on the lookout for an anthology that assembles experimental work by pioneering writers in that field will be excited by *Juncture*. Concentrating on authors who have rejected the traditional forms of fiction (or decided to pursue those forms in a highly experimental fashion), *Juncture* seeks to establish new trajectories, presenting a collection unified by its postmodern acceptance of and comfort with disunity. Here readers will find such writers as Ben Marcus, Shelley Jackson, Jonathan Lethem, and Colson Whitehead—writers for whom the telling is often more important than the tale. In each story, language itself becomes a character, so much so that one is sometimes encouraged to rethink ideas of narrative, of what, precisely, constitutes *story*. These tales seem to argue that narrative tension exists in the fundamental relationships of well-crafted language, that it is an inevitable by-product of signification. Also of interest is the way in which many of the fictional pieces address notions of the body: Marcus's story, "The New Female Head," and Jackson's piece, "Bone," in particular deal with new ways of viewing human anatomy: as site of cultural contestation, as pop iconography, as hyperreal setting and backdrop. Any yet the body is only one of many notions that *Juncture* causes us to reevaluate. As Jonathan Lethem tells us in "The Dystopianist, Thinking of His Rival, Is Interrupted by a Knock on the Door": "The Dystopianist destroyed the world again that morning . . . destroyed it by cabbages." Lethem's piece can be read as an absurdist annihilation of fiction-as-dream, but, like many of the stories in *Juncture,* it performs a perfect act of deconstruction. As so often happens in the work of Jorge Luis Borges and Vladimir Nabokov (writers often evoked in this collection), it rebuilds its fictive world even while taking it apart. [Aaron Gwyn]

Renee Gladman. *The Activist*. Krupskaya, 2003. 145 pp. Paper: $11.00.

A haunting and hilarious mix of dreams, news reports, confessions, and internal monologues, Renee Gladman's latest book is an absurdist political satire and a poetic consideration of points of contact among people, people and society, people and cities, and also, perhaps most captivatingly, between a person's sense of self in opposition to her sense of the Other or sense of herself as the Other. At the heart of the story is the J. Gifford Bridge, reputed by the government to have been blown up by activists. However, a group of scientists declare that the bridge has not been blown up and contend that it may never have existed as "a crossing point" at all, commuters protest their inability to use the bridge, and the activists themselves will "not admit to 'living a life among people.' " In response to the activists' refusal to communicate in codified terms, one government agent complains, " 'Instead of a hunger strike . . . it's as though they are issuing a logic one'—but then immediately added that he didn't know what he meant by that." Crossing points of all kinds are threatened, language continually fails to connect people as they unknowingly spew nonsense at one another, or have trouble saying what they mean, or aren't sure they know what they want to say, can't remember if what they said was what they meant, or if they said it out loud, or to themselves, or in a dream. In addition, maps go blank and the infrastructure of the city is attacked or perhaps never existed. Given these circumstances, everyone is afraid. The activists end one meeting because, "Each feeling himself so separate from the others began to grow tired, to grow heavy with that unassailable exhaustion—fear." And the primary fear is to be alone—physically, politically, psychologically. So characters cling to political movements or familiar-if-meaningless slogans in hopes of being swept up in the patriotic or rebellious fervor of belonging, as if this will solidify a watery reality or reconnect what may have once been workable crossing points. It seems unlikely that anything can mend the rift. The reader (along with the characters) is engrossed but dazed by the book's structure and style. And yet Gladman's prose is precise, and her book is strangely optimistic. [Danielle Dutton]

Jincy Willett. *Winner of the National Book Award.* Dunne/St. Martin's, 2003. 323 pp. $23.95.

Bookish Dorcas, middle-aged, with a lifelong disinterest in the carnal, weathers a Rhode Island hurricane in the library where she works by drinking spiked coffee and reading *In the Driver's Seat: The Abigail Mather Story,* a true-crime thing about an abused woman's justifiable homicide of her total bastard of a husband, Conrad Lowe. Dorcas is both amused and embittered by the book, which is understandable, given that Abigail is Dorcas's fraternal twin and everything Dorcas isn't: "Mother favored Abigail in character, and me in sympathy. Mother *admired* me. That was nice." Dorcas, narrating her own version of the events depicted in her sister's book, details Abigail's voracious sexual appetites and her ability to ensnare pretty much anyone she chooses (as well as, in one ugly but oddly transcendent scene, a group of men who choose her). All of this ceases when the sisters encounter the anguine Conrad, a dashingly sleazy writer who initially seems to take a strong interest in Dorcas, much to both sisters' confusion. Abigail's eventual marriage to Conrad is indeed a horror, but Dorcas's take on it is far more revealing than Abigail's. As with most novels whose endings are revealed at the outset, *Winner* isn't about its story so much as its telling, and Willett tells it very well, a little like a gentile (and gentler) Elkin in her reach, her poignant cynicism, and her contrast between high and low registers. There's surprisingly little direct interplay between Abigail's and Dorcas's narratives, to Willett's credit: the book-within-a-book is an easy means to set up Dorcas's ruminations and evoke emotion—sort of a straw device—but Willett excerpts *In the Driver's Seat* sparingly, to droll, very funny effect. *Winner,* in fact, is hilarious despite its themes—some might opine that the phrase "funny as hell" was coined to describe novels like this. [Tim Feeney]

Aaron Zimmerman. *By the Time You Finish This Book You Might Be Dead: Changing and Improving Your Life through CUTLAS by Eliot Greebee.* Spuyten Duyvil, 2003. 250 pp. Paper: $13.00.

"Under normal circumstances, I have no doubt that my ability to consume anything far exceeds that of anyone else I encounter. After all, I've built my entire life's work around such practices." So claims Eliot Greebee, protagonist of Aaron Zimmerman's novel and obese creator of CUTLAS (Cost/ Benefit Unit-Based Transactional Life Analysis System). Throughout *BtTYFTBYMBD* we watch Eliot, femme fatale Justine, and her girlfriend Giselle wallow in their own crapulence: tossing empty beer-bottles off a Manhattan high-rise rooftop, taunting and assaulting freak-show midgets, riding Coney Island's Wonder Wheel on psychoactive drugs, and reveling in posh sex clubs. Interspersed between these narrative chapters are excerpts from Eliot's self-help book expounding CUTLAS, a stripped-down, consumer-oriented existentialism. French philosophy forms a conceptual undercurrent for the book: the sophistic arguments of this super-sized Sartre harken back to the perverse enlightenment logic of Sade, and Zimmerman's prose sparkles when he engages Batialleian religious imagery (e.g., the "porcine holocaust," or Eliot Greebee's meditations on death while floating drugged and naked upon the Atlantic). Zimmerman draws a charmingly puerile Eliot, unable to wait for a moment, philosophically unable to delay gratification, physically unable to resist consuming any potable on his person, whether candy, drugs, or alcohol. Eliot is completely determined by consumer culture and dreams in "richer colors, deep green the color of Astroturf, purple like grape Bubble-Yum, orange like Orange Crush, red like Hawaiian Punch." [Matthew L. McAlpin]

João de Melo. *My World Is Not of This Kingdom.* Trans. Gregory Rabassa. Aliform, 2003. 248 pp. Paper: $15.95.

The Azores may "exist to most Americans only as mid-Atlantic flecks on a map," as Katherine Vaz puts it in her introduction to *My World Is Not of This Kingdom,* but the tiny islands speak with a loud voice through their representative, João de Melo. His 1980s novel has been newly translated for an anglophone audience that will be pleased to add the archipelago to a literary atlas that includes García Márquez's Macondo and Fuentes's Mexico. *My World* is in effect a founding myth for the Azores, and it has an appropriately primal tone, with language marked by power and portent. Its characters are outsized, notably Mayor Guilherme Jose Bento, "better known by the name of 'Goraz,' elephant fish, because of his bulging red eyes," who kills a horse with a single blow, successfully battles nine knife-wielding assailants, and terrorizes his townspeople. His oppression is just one of many thumbs under which most of de Melo's figures squirm; they must answer to political and ecclesiastical forces from far away whose authority is vaguely understood and whose whims seem as arbitrary as nature. At one point the animals of the islands weep in apparent despair, which phenomenon is explained as follows: "Just like us, they sense that they're the property of this land and the prisoners, perhaps, of the sea, the water, and the salt." The islands and the book are built by the human struggle against all these constraints, and both are ultimately as rude and beautiful as the paintings in the caves at Lascaux. [James Crossley]

Andrew Lewis Conn. *P.* Soft Skull, 2003. 365 pp. Paper: $15.00.

Often, first-time novelists are encumbered by extravagant praise that doesn't allow room for them to grow or to make errors. Similarly, readers' expectations are dictated by selective blurbs. So ignore the gush on the cover and simply enjoy *P,* a romance novel set in the pornography industry. Conn's adaptation of Aristotelian unities allows a stream-of-consciousness identifiable with *Ulysses,* the headlines of *U.S.A.,* a cartoon screenplay, a semispiritual catechism, and the type of realism founded on pop culture to nuzzle each other, if at times uneasily. *P* is not as profound in its content or as adventurous in its use of elements as its billing proclaims, and the writing is at times too jokey and uneven, but Conn presents a good show, which is not pornographic (fair warning to those who buy it with the aim of self-arousal). Like a porn film, *P* offers an unreal setting, but one that is more appropriate to the search for romance than to sexual satisfaction. Benjamin Seymour, the lead character, is a filmmaker and a quirky individual who, at a fundamental level, is out of place in his chosen profession. While it is a tired device to have him the same age as Christ, with everything that follows from that, his sadness and history are rendered believably, and the tact and sympathy shown toward him indicate Conn's potential. Finn, the other major character, is not a credible portrayal of a regular ten-year-old runaway girl, but again, this is a romance, a seemingly improbable one, not a naturalistic novel. *P* is a diverting read that is cautiously experimental, and it nostalgically depicts New York in 1996. This first novel shows talent that deserves to be encouraged, not smothered under the hype of copywriting. [Jeff Bursey]

Gustaw Herling. *The Noonday Cemetery and Other Stories*. Trans. Bill Johnston. New Directions, 2003. 281 pp. $25.95.

In his last collection of stories Gustaw Herling speaks in the voice of a Polish writer like himself, resident in Naples after World War II, unfolding signal events in the lives of friends, acquaintances, strangers, even historical figures like Carlo Gesualdo, prince of Venosa. This patient, selfless narrator, whose witness to the transformations wrought by deeply felt experience invites us to share his wonder, proves a wonderfully transparent medium. In "The Noonday Cemetery: An Open Story" he probes the apparent murder-suicide of a woman, once married to a Wehrmacht officer, and the gravedigger of an old cemetery perched atop a cliff near Albino, beneath which, in a rude cabin at its base, their bodies were found. "A Hot Breath from the Desert" explores the misfortunes of two expatriate English archaeologists, man and wife, when the wife unaccountably loses her mind, as recalled in conversation by the investigating magistrate at the husband's trial for her mercy killing. In "Ashes: The Fall of the House of Loris" a malign curse reminiscent of Poe's lurking menace inhabits an island near Sicily, harassing its victim, a close friend of the writer, to what seems his ineluctable doom. "The Notebook of William Moulding, Pensioner," the only story not set in Italy, presents the final days of England's last state executioner, attesting as well to Herling's fascination with tales of a learned, introspective nature purportedly informed by historical inquiry. In this vein the Russian musicologist in "A Madrigal of Mourning" becomes so enchanted by her work on Gesualdo, the Renaissance composer of sublime vocal harmonies and murderer of his wife and her lover, that she falls in love with his romantic legend. Dispassionate yet intimate, Herling's moral tales of blighted destinies present the last word of a poetic sensibility whose legacy remains as affecting as it is convincing. [Michael Pinker]

Glen Duncan. *I, Lucifer*. Grove, 2003. 262 pp. Paper: $13.00.

In *I, Lucifer* Satan has been given one last chance for forgiveness. After spending a month in corporeal form, the Prince of Darkness will be given the choice to exit the body and return to hell or to continue in the body and live out its life (with the corresponding chance of ascending to heaven). The body God provides is that of Declan Gunn, a writer in the throes of despair who is taking a bath with a packet of razor blades. As the Old Serpent gets into the swing of corporeal living, he decides to write a novel to "set the record straight"; the Fallen Angel, it seems, believes that he has been misrepresented throughout history. Though willing to admit to periodic nudging, the corporeal Father of Lies insists that, for the most part, man needs little or no encouragement; he also rejects brutality: "Brutality is to evil what a Big Mac is to hunger: it gets a job done, it accomplishes *something*—but utterly without beauty." Glen Duncan's novel is playful and fluid as it delves into life and theology; *I, Lucifer* is also metafictional, overtly exploring the business of novel-writing. Penelope, Gunn's girlfriend, recounts a conversation she had with the pre-Satanized Gunn: "I remember that conversation we had about how much you thought it was bogus, all that talk about starting with a theme and then grafting a story onto it. You said it was pretentious revisionism, and that any writer being honest would admit that you start with a character, or a situation." One situation central to the story is that of Stanley Milgram's obedience experiment, in which subjects were asked to administer shocks to others. Only one person, Ron Ridenhour, refused to administer even the first shock. Ron Ridenhour was also the man responsible for bringing to light the My Lai massacre in Vietnam. While the novel's themes periodically bog down, Glen Duncan is to be commended for continuing Milton's tradition of rendering Satan as, well, an engaging personality. [Alan Tinkler]

Knut Hamsun. *The Last Joy*. Trans. Sverre Lyngstad. Green Integer, 2003. 279 pp. Paper: $12.95.

In Sverre Lyngstad's new translation of Knut Hamsun's 1912 novel, a fiftyish narrator leaves the isolation of his idyllic forest retreat for an alpine tourist resort, where he meets Miss Ingeborg Torsen, an educated and attractive young schoolteacher. A world-weary traveler, the narrator observes, "Nothing escapes me yet, though everything passes me by." With "no tasks, no aspirations, no ambitions," he remains sanguine about his lost youth and vitality, frequently arguing that life exists for the young and lamenting that he is too old. Nevertheless, he follows Miss Torsen from the resort to the city and develops a voyeuristic preoccupation with her sexual life, ultimately endorsing her marriage to a simple farmer because he imagines it will allow her to escape her sordid fate as a career woman for the more traditional roles of wife and mother. In his scornful criticism of modern Norwegian society, Hamsun's narrator reserves his harshest words for the modern woman, depicted as "an eternal schoolgirl" unfit for marriage, and for a tourist economy obsessed with "making Norway still more eye-catching to those Anglo-Saxons." Throughout the novel Hamsun and his narrator excoriate the banal mediocrity of city life and dismiss artistic and intellectual activity that alienates the individual from the glorious intimacies of rural life. [Trey Strecker]

Harry Mulisch. *Siegfried*. Trans. Paul Vincent. Viking, 2003. 180 pp. $22.95.

In the past Mulisch has posed ontological questions that border on the ludicrous in their enormity, then proceeded to answer them successfully through his clever and munificent fictions. In *Siegfried* Mulisch seeks to solve the lingering problem Hitler holds for humanity through his protagonist, Herter, a character that bears more than a passing resemblance to the affably arrogant Mulisch, who manages to be megalomaniacal and self-effacing at the same time. When Dutch novelist par excellence Herter visits Vienna to read from his masterwork, an old couple approaches him with a story concerning the unknown son of Hitler. Herter hears a tale so bizarre from Hitler's pair of former servants that he never doubts its veracity, nor that the couple raised the child of Hitler and Eva Braun as their own. Mulisch's exploration of Hitler yields unexpected results, not the least of which is that it manages to humanize him, as the author's ability to render a flesh-and-blood Adolf diminishes Hitler's great terror while impressing that the Führer was nothing more than a man, perhaps even less. The tone is unexpected, given that Hitler is the subject matter—the novel is jocular and cerebral, with equal parts devoted to life and death. Much like Mulisch's previous novel, *The Procedure, Siegfried* is aesthetically satisfying in its economy, resolution, and philosophical inquiries, which culminate in a recklessly brilliant proof of Hitler's evil that relies heavily on Nietzsche and Herter himself. The novel is its own problem and solution—*Siegfried* takes "nothingness" as its literal creed, and leaves no players or problems at its conclusion. Mulisch desires the Nobel Prize in Literature, but the chief beneficiary of such an award would not be the Dutchman, but his readers, who would receive more of his incomparable work in translation were the Prize bestowed upon him. [Jason Picone]

Lyonel Trouillot. *Street of Lost Footsteps*. Trans. and intro. Linda Coverdale. Univ. of Nebraska Press, 2003. 115 pp. $45.00; paper: $16.95.

Trouillot's book has three narrators. These include a militant taxi-driver and a poetic retired brothel-keeper. But the middle one, in age and temperament, is crucial. He is an intellectual postal worker, in love with a woman named Laurence, who is as conscious of the obstacles presented by "middle-brow culture" as of the "zone of utter oblivion" in the violence that surrounds them. In this book's night-map of Haiti he represents judgment that links the old woman's memory and the driver's geography. Trouillot is an aggressive writer. He seizes the moment, and he is not afraid to render carnage and domesticity side by side. The colloquial monologues are scalding. They light up the reader like a torch. Corruption and despair do not faze our trio. The old madam achieves a wistful catharsis. The postal worker and Laurence make everyday living exquisite. And the taxi driver turns the Street of Lost Footsteps from a nightmare zone into a destination. One would call Trouillot a Kreyòl Céline or Montherlant, except that he is far more humane. This year sees the bicentennial of Haitian independence. As Coverdale says, "Ever since that glorious independence in 1804, Haiti's history has been dominated by disorder and political oppression." The sadistic specter of "the great dictator Deceased-Forever Immortal"—the senior Duvalier, but also the seemingly inescapable brutality of power as a function in Haitian society—is hard to evade. Andree Polynice, a young woman, a child of promise, falls down. Perhaps like "pretty girls a people sometimes picks the wrong road"? The U.S. was the first country in the Americas to become independent, Haiti the second. Despite sharply different social trajectories, the same dreams remain alive in both. [Nicholas Birns]

Moacyr Scliar. *The Centaur in the Garden*. Trans. Margaret A. Neves. Intro. Ilan Stavans. Univ. of Wisconsin Press, 2003. 216 pp. Paper: $15.95. (Reprint)

First published in 1980 as *O Centauro no jardin* and translated in 1984, *The Centaur in the Garden* is clearly a work of what's been called magic realism. Yet the obvious comparison is not with García Márquez but with Kafka, and the image itself (of a centaur in a garden) recalls *Maternity with Centaur* (1957) by Marc Chagall, yet another Jewish Russian émigré. The character of Guedali, the centaur born of Jewish parents who moved from the shtetls of Russia to the streets of Pôrto Alegre, Brazil, has distinct similarities to Kafka's Gregor Samsa, who also tends to be isolated from friends and family based on his "appearance." But whereas Gregor becomes alienated, despised, and ignored by his family, Guedali's family is very supportive (especially his sister and mother), even though having a centaur as a son does, in the first instance, make for a difficult circumcision and, in the second instance, make for an equally difficult Bar Mitzvah, since being a centaur is like being Jewish in Brazil, at least in 1980. Scliar has said that "As much as possible I live in peace with my Jewishness. . . . I have extracted from it what it has of the best: fantasy, ethical substance, and above all, humour . . . melancholy, bittersweet, the humour of the persecuted fighting against desperation." Clearly, that combination of emotions is present in the novel as Guedali goes through the metaphoric experiences of being Jewish in Brazil. That is, of being Jewish, of not being Jewish, of marrying a non-Jewish centauress, making love to a non-Jewish sphinx, and, eventually, of discovering what his identity actually is. Stylistically, the novel exhibits a kind of restrained inventiveness in that the reader never questions the validity of Sclair's imaginary world, and the dialogue, even in English, shows a consistency of voice that is exceptional. [Mark Axelrod]

Dallas Wiebe. *The Vox Populi Street Stories.* Burning Deck, 2003. 308 pp. Paper: $15.00.

When Gottlieb Otto Liebgott, the narrator of Dallas Wiebe's collection *The Vox Populi Street Stories,* announces his intention to chronicle the activities of Dallasandro Vibini, private investigator of petty crimes, the narrative evokes allusions to a long tradition of picaresque tales. However, the narrator can never really be trusted. His version of reality is one infinitely refracted and reflected through fairly self-conscious lenses, wherein each paragraph, even each sentence, shimmers with allusions, references, and interjected phrases of Latin, Italian, and German. One does not need to understand every allusion or appreciate each inversion, subversion, or perversion to enjoy the humor of these stories. To start, the very notion of Liebgott, a 300-pound retired medical doctor dedicating himself to the study of post-Mussolini Italian military history, is absurd enough. The narrative's informing quest is not to catch criminals or solve crimes, but, as Wiebe puts it in "Vibini and the Virgin Tongue," a search for a new language that "will not mislead me or pervert my feelings." Although he cites Joseph Conrad, Wiebe is more reminiscent of Colombian writer Alvaro Mutis, whose tales of the misadventures of Maqroll, the lookout, illustrate the human condition. When seeking language to express Vibini in love, the narrator explains that he, for the first time, understands the absolute inadequacy of language to directly represent a thing. Instead, it has to be told "slant" and to "avoid direct confrontation with the ecstatic moment and divert the reader's gaze to Italian military history." This is, not coincidentally, the essence of metaphor and figurative language. Dallas Wiebe's *The Vox Populi Street Stories* is a labyrinth of play, allusion, and illusion—a carnivalesque world of characters trapped in their "thrownness" yet ultimately liberated by their self-consciousness—the self-reflexive, tongue-in-cheek perversity that strips away the comforting facade of predictable characterization and, in doing so, deliberately confronts the challenge of writing to capture "the ecstatic moment." [Susan Smith Nash]

Robert Bolaño. *By Night in Chile.* Trans. Chris Andrews. New Directions, 2003. 130 pp. Paper: $13.95.

Considered one of Chile's best writers, Robert Bolaño published nine novels, two story collections, and five books of poetry before his death in July 2003. Aside from a short story that appeared in *Grand Street* some years back, this is the first time his work has been made available to an American audience. *By Night in Chile* is the deathbed meditation of Sebastián

Urrutia Lacroix, a Jesuit priest, poet, and literary critic, who lived the prime of his life around the time that General Augusto Pinochet seized power from Salvador Allende. Using a classic set-up reminiscent of Fuentes's *The Death of Artemio Cruz,* Lacroix's monologue is a supposed defense against the claims of a "wizened youth" (a part of his own consciousness) regarding his occasionally suspect behavior. He recounts his friendship with the famous Chilean literary critic Farewell, the time he met Pablo Neruda, and his tour through Europe to investigate the deteriorating churches, but at the dark heart of this novel are Lacroix's interactions with Pinochet and the happenings that occur in the basement of a Pinochet sympathizer during numerous literary house parties. Acerbic, subtle, hallucinatory, and moving, Bolaño's novel is an interesting depiction of Chile's literati and, in a way, an indictment of their insular nature during the nasty political history of contemporary Chile. Chris Andrews translation is adequate, although at times he doesn't quite get the prose into a recognizable American idiom, such as in the final sentence, "And then the storm of shit begins." [Chad W. Post]

Christian Bök, ed. *Ground Works: Avant-Garde for Thee*. Intro. Margaret Atwood. House of Anansi, 2002. 236 pp. $28.95; paper: $18.95.

In the last few decades mainstream literature has been quite successful in incorporating various innovations that were first tried out in experimental fiction, usually, however, without any form of explicit recognition or attribution. The anthology *Ground Works* is a laudable attempt to map the literary avant-garde in Canada between 1965 and 1985, a period characterized by an energetic activity in anticlassic, antimimetic writing. There is an element of nostalgia in this historical approach that neutralizes much of the defamiliarizing quality that this fiction originally had. But since mainstream literature often sponges unscrupulously on the accomplishments of the avant-garde, it is important that authors of experimental fiction are finally given the credit they deserve. As editor Chistian Bök points out in his afterword, this anthology "does not pretend to represent a particular aesthetic viewpoint, nor does it attempt to distinguish between practising modernists and their postmodern successors." It does, however, give an excellent insight into an unfortunately short-lived period of innovative potential. Even though many samples are taken from larger works, the short introductions to each of the contributions provide the necessary information to put the pieces in context. In her general introduction Margaret Atwood defines experimental fiction as "fiction that sets up certain rules for itself." Since these rules differ from those of mainstream fiction, obeying them implies a subversion of the very conventions that determine what is considered to be "literature" in a certain period. For instance, Audrey Thomas evokes the trauma of giving birth to a stillborn child, using ellipses to mark the pulses of breath. The act of giving birth to a literary creation becomes thematic in several other metafictional contributions. In Chris Scott's Sternean prose the author loses control of his characters. Michael

Ondaatje's "Billy the Kid and the Princess" is a literary outlaw: in this readymade, Ondaatje addresses the issue of plagiarism head-on by quoting the complete text of a comic strip and presenting it as his own "found story." Stream-of-consciousness, dehistoricization, the use of lipograms in the manner of the Oulipo: the experiments collected in this anthology are much more than useful tools for Stephen King's "toolbox"—as he calls it in his book *On Writing*—and prove to be fascinating pieces of fiction in their own right. [Dirk Van Hulle]

Dmitry Bakin. *Reasons for Living.* Trans. Andrew Bromfield. Granta, 2002. 143 pp. Paper: $14.95.

Winner of the 1996 Anti-Booker prize, Dmitry Bakin's first collection, *Reasons for Living,* presents a mélange of fabulism and estranged realism. In the grim, postwar folktale "Leaves" an orphan attaches himself to a blighted village where relationships among family, companions, and lovers offer him tenuous, makeshift shelter from the damaged landscape. This story, perhaps the finest in the collection, moves us through the orphan's life. The detached child forms attachments, but as a man he struggles with the confusion and pain of these bonds until in the final moments of the story he seems to be consumed in a leaf fire. "Hare's Eye" is about a soldier and his plaguing dislike of another member of his company. Ultimately he finds himself having to decide whether or not to give up his life to save his adversary. Though more conversational and less dreamlike than "Leaves," in its ending "Hare's Eye" picks up some of the same surreal qualities as the narrator fades in and out of consciousness. "On Going to Hell" oscillates between events on a mysterious train journey and the future lives of the men on that train. Switching between past tense and future tense, with the present moment elided, the story implies an infinite gap between what has been and what will be. Generally these stories evoke a nearly overwhelming sense of despair, yet somehow Bakin manages to convey a remarkable, and remarkably human, resilience nonetheless. Wonderfully bleak, Bakin's prose is complex and densely metaphorical; though the stories display many of the trappings of Russian modernism, his structural gestures, use of undecidability, and refusal to define the parameters of the world he creates clearly places him in a contemporary space. Incredibly original, *Reasons for Living* supplies a valuable and fresh addition for English-speaking readers. [Joanna Howard]

Pavol Hudík, ed. *In Search of Homo Sapiens: Twenty-Five Contemporary Slovak Short Stories*. Trans. Heather Trebatická. Bolchazy-Carducci/The Publishing House of the Slovak Writers Society, 2002. 264 pp. Paper: $29.95.

These fine stories, most written over the last two decades, culled from a body of literature largely unknown to Western readers, represent a sampling of the best Slovak writers at the height of their craft. Pavol Hudík, a leading figure in disseminating the growing body of writing by his countrymen to the rest of the world, provides a short essay on the historical context of Slovak literature as well as brief biographical sketches and a short prefatory passage or two by each author on his or her sense of mission, craftsmanship, or nationalist sentiment. Some of the most compelling of these stories include Etela Farkašová's "A Sky Full of Migrating Birds," in which the patterns that birds create in flight take on the nature of poetic enchantment to her female protagonist's awakened sensibility; Andrej Ferko's "Intra Muros Populis," in which jaded Gregor attempts to find something in his decadent society for which he can sustain enthusiasm, despite his dilettante's skepticism; and Luboš Jurík's "The Road Sweeper," in which, after turning up a surprise package in some rubbish, an old man stung with sudden purpose labors to overcome infirmity in behalf of new life. Yet Peter Ševčovič's "Near to Eternity," another fable of advancing age, best captures a characteristically elegiac note detectable even in the tales of a more experimental insouciance. When Gizelka and her Jozef reach a crossroads while planning their future together, Jozef's arrangements for his wife's trip to Greece, along with his final rest, lend her courage to defy convention in an act of devotion. Although the style of each author may be somewhat obscured in translation by the same hand, these stories offer stimulus and enjoyment in illuminating haunting scenes from a culture emerging from oppression into the light. [Michael Pinker]

Corey Mesler. *Talk: A Novel in Dialogue*. Livingston, 2002. 208 pp. $27.00; paper: $14.00.

As its title suggests, *Talk: A Novel in Dialogue* is both written entirely in dialogue and concerned with establishing a meaningful "dialogue with the world." Unlike the rollicking, maximalist dialogue found in Gaddis's works, in *Talk* Mesler opts for a minimalist and streamlined approach to speech, closer to an Americanized Henry Green without the class issues. The microrants that Jim, the novel's in medias life-crisis protagonist, delivers throughout the book are directed at the dreck of popular culture and frequently revolve around sex and women. Jim tends to revolve around women too (and has his whole life), even though he's currently "happily married" with two children and supposedly content with his life. But his clinical depression and inability to cease flirting (yet another kind of "talk") gets him into an ambiguous "affair" with a woman resembling Ally McBeal. Jim's yearning for raw sexuality untainted by the media and advertising, coupled with his desire not to "really" cheat on his wife, leads to some rather creative and interesting romantic rendezvous. Since Jim is an intelligent bibliophile, however, his observations on contemporary life are often witty, quirky, and amusing and help to balance a portrait of a character that at times may seem a bit of a womanizer and a solipsist. In this respect the novel has the charm of *The Tao of Steve,* with a Woody Allenesque quality. Yet the question remains: *Is* this all just talk? Is Jim simply a self-obsessed neurotic, or are his complaints legitimate? By illustrating through Jim's struggles how dialogues with the self, others, and the world may be the only way of grasping meaning in our lives, Mesler says that it is and isn't all just talk. [Ralph Clare]

———————

James McCourt. *Queer Street: Rise and Fall of an American Culture, 1947-1985: Excursions in the Mind of the Life.* Norton, 2004. 577 pp. $29.95.

Although this "extravagant edifice" (Harold Bloom's words) will probably be classified as a gay-studies text, it deserves to stand alone. McCourt gives us an autobiography, a social history, a critical appreciation of movies, opera, poetry. This original book can't be easily classified because it cuts across, like a diagonal, various "straight," mindless categories. McCourt offers an epigraph from Robert Calasso: "In storytelling there is an element that is deeply opposed to mortal judgment, that skirts its coercive side, eludes the descending knife. Storytelling is a going forward and a turning back, a wave-like movement in the voice, a continual cancelling of borders, a dodging of sharp spears. (And of *horror vacui.*)" McCourt's consciousness eludes definition (including his own). The very first chapter gives us "echoes of years of overheard and vis-à-vis opinion and commentary" or "memory" as "inhalation." Thus although we have heard of Water Street (Merrill) and Hollywood (Douglas Sirk) and Stonewall and Jackson Heights, and Rome, we must see these spaces viewed by QT (Queer Temperament). The book is so reflexive that it is a series of mirrors (of mirrors). McCourt suggests that the mind constructs its own borders, its own twisting streets. And its mental language writes this text. Indeed, this text apparently has a life of its own. One section is called "The Book Talks Back." We can learn about "drag acts," activities at the baths, Bette Davis's opinion of *All about Eve,* the "tea rooms" in subway stations, and so much more, but in the end it is the voice of McCourt—the singular one that sings of high and low taste and that offers such sentences as: "Diagonal plan, dynamic in itself in spite of the evident fixedness of an apparently accidental composition." Not only is this sentence a masterful description of this edifice—Oedipus?—but it is, in the end, a commentary on earthly lives. Aren't we all shaped by—and shaping—our composite lives? And that is why we stand in "awe of the out-of-body experience"; we are transported to a higher plane by this remarkable book. [Irving Malin]

———————

Ulla E. Dydo with William Rice. *Gertrude Stein: The Language that Rises: 1923-1934.* Northwestern Univ. Press, 2003. 686 pp. $49.95; Steven Meyer. *Irresistible Dictation: Gertrude Stein and the Correlations of Writing and Science.* Stanford Univ. Press, 2001. 450 pp. $65.00; paper: $24.95.

These two valuable studies seem to dovetail neatly. Meyer, in a three-part study that originated as a dissertation, contextualizes and recontextualizes

Gertrude Stein's writing and theorizing about writing in kaleidoscopic fashion, moving from her undergraduate scientific studies and the Johns Hopkins medical school through Emerson, Whitehead, William James, and, due to his late interest in James, Wittgenstein. Dydo writes out of her thirty-year experience of struggling directly with the *carnets, cahiers,* and manuscripts at the Beinecke Library, not always, as she gracefully admits, successfully.

Building on "radical empiricism," which, "divorced from the idea of the primacy of sense-data . . . stresses the decisive role of processes and procedures, of conjunctive as well as disjunctive relations, in the composition of experience," Meyer's method leads to set-pieces of his main figures on consciousness and language, necessitating the insertion of long discussions of the individual thinker, at times only finally linked to Stein's ideas. Meyer close-reads, leading him to interpret, sometimes definitively, Stein's thought and intent, e.g., the discussion of "Mrs. Emerson," in which he states: " 'Now then,' Stein continues, needing just these two words, framed as a discrete utterance, to equate present with past and join presentational immediacy and causal efficacy in the mixed mode Whitehead suggested was both native to human perception and responsible for the experience of pathos." Later, discussing a passage in *The Making of Americans,* he extends his analysis to the placement of a comma, attempting to capture the feeling he believes Stein wished to convey. *Irresistible Dictation* offers a lode of information, with one hundred pages of notes and bibliography. Meyer knows his subject through and through and offers an invaluable work in placing Stein for Americanists and in describing the difficult process by which she attempted to embody the objects of her perception in language. Still, the bibliography, which includes more recent scientific references, does not show much attention to critical approaches applied to American literature after 1975; Stein's work also offers interesting possibilities to the theories of Barthes or Deleuze, among others.

Dydo, whose work follows Stein's composition from "An Elucidation" (1923) through *Lectures in America* (published 1935), allows the reader to look over her shoulder as she reads, reflects upon, and responds to them within their own context. With "An Elucidation" we receive a clever introduction that shows the process of "decontextuating" that Stein used to free language from particular associations, to distinguish between "real writing" and "audience writing." Close reading here allows inconclusive analyses and judgments but does not deny us the excitement of discovery as we are led across the versions of a text: "Stein's is a world—a space—of unending process, which does not unroll toward a climax or conclusion but *goes on,* steadily and simultaneously, in many forms." True of composition of both experience and writing for Stein, it requires Dydo to attempt to measure the flow across years, revealing interconnections between and illumination from the texts and their sources. Her close reading, based on minute observations of Stein's writing process, shows the act of grasping intent in the elusiveness of that process, gives the reader a share in the *feeling* of "understanding." Dydo's footnotes comment on the scholarly work, further uncover detail, and support the careful rendering of her Steinian reading experience. The whole offers a stunning view of a first-rate scholar at work and an indispensable study of this most difficult of the great modernist writers. [Richard J. Murphy]

———————

Gaddis. *Fiction Jones*. 2003. 51 min. CD: $10.00 postpaid (c/o Ed Mish, 621 Emerson St., Madison, WI 53715; www.gaddis.us).

The nexus of music and literature has seemed rife with creative possibilities from the very start—lots of the early epic ballads were likely passed from person to person in some speech-song combo—but no one's ever really capitalized on that potential. There have been lots of crossovers, from musicians trying their hands at serious writing (Nick Cave, Richard Hell, er, Jewel) to writers posing as musicians (the Stephen King/Dave Barry/Barbara Kingsolver/et al. sort-of-super group, the Rock-Bottom Remainders), but nobody accomplished in one field has ever produced something mind-blowingly good in the other, besides maybe Edward Sanders of the Fugs and *1968*; and other than educore outfit BlöödHag, all of whose songs are death-metal biographies of famous science-fiction authors and who throw paperbacks at their audiences, there aren't many bands whose raison d'etre is so principally literary. Enter Madison, WI's Gaddis, whose name every reader of this journal will probably recognize and whose literary influences are generally right up our alley as well. Their second full-length release includes songs inspired by the works of William H. Gass (including a spoken-word excerpt from *The Tunnel*), Don DeLillo, Philip K. Dick, Sven Birkerts, Jonathan Lethem, and William Gaddis himself, and a reading list directs listeners to the likes of Thomas Bernhard, Alasdair Gray, Shelley Jackson, and David Markson. Points for literary taste, as well as for having a nifty handmade package and for copylefting (stupid word, but great concept) the whole thing. So how's the music? Really good—quiet, sparse guitars and percussion, wavery, plaintive vocals, and quirky sound accoutrements create off-kilter melodies that build to moments of rumbling noise, keeping things nicely tense throughout. Unusual arrangements and textures make this hard to classify—it's sort of postrock, maybe postemo (no surprise, since the members of Gaddis were formerly in the emo group Josef K. [not to be confused with the seventies Edinburgh art-punk band of the same name]), possibly something for which there isn't a name yet. *Fiction Jones* sounds like Lester Bangs's "horrible noise," twenty-five years on, meeting the literary scene of today: world-weary, pausing to look inward a little, and wary but hopeful of what may come tomorrow. [Tim Feeney]

Books Received

Abrams, Sam. *The Old Pothead Poems*. Creative Arts, 2003. Paper: $15.00. (P)

Adler, Frances Payne. *The Making of a Matriot: Poetry and Prose 1991-2003*. Red Hen, 2003. Paper: $13.95. (P)

Alexander, Goldie. *Body and Soul*. Indra, 2003. Paper: $17.50. (F)

Allen, Brooke. *Twentieth-Century Attitudes: Literary Powers in Uncertain Times*. Ivan R. Dee, 2003. $26.00. (NF)

Allen, Ed. *Ate It Anyway*. Univ. of Georgia Press, 2003. $24.95. (F)

Arias, Arturo. *Rattlesnake*. Trans. Seán Higgins and Jill Robbins. Curbstone, 2003. Paper: $15.95. (F)

Azzopardi, Trezza. *Remember Me*. Grove, 2004. $23.00. (F)

Balaban, John, trans. *Ca Dao Viet Nam: Vietnamese Folk Poetry*. Copper Canyon, 2003. Paper: $15.00. (P)

Barr, Marleen S. *Oy Pioneer! A Novel*. Univ. of Wisconsin Press, 2003. $19.95. (F)

Baxter, Charles. *Saul and Patsy*. Pantheon, 2003. $24.00. (F)

Binyon, T. J. *Pushkin: A Biography*. Knopf, 2003. $35.00. (NF)

Bioy Cesares, Adolfo. *The Invention of Morel*. Trans. Ruth L. C. Simms. Prologue Jorge Luis Borges. Intro. Suzanne Jill Levine. Illus. Norah Borges de Torre. New York Review Books, 2003. Paper: $12.95. (F)

Blackstone, Charles. *The Week You Weren't Here*. Flame, 2004. Paper: £9.00. (F)

Boym, Svetlana. *Ninochka*. State Univ. of New York Press, 2003. $26.50. (F)

Brady, Catherine. *Curled in the Bed of Love*. Univ. of Georgia Press, 2003. $24.95. (F)

Breton, André. *Selections*. Ed. and intro. Mark Polizzotti. Univ. of California Press, 2003. $50.00; paper: $16.95. (P)

Brockmeier, Kevin. *The Truth about Celia*. Pantheon, 2003. $22.00. (F)

Bunting, Basil. *Complete Poems*. Assoc. ed. Richard Caddel. New Directions, 2003. Paper: $16.95. (P)

Byrd, Max. *Shooting the Sun*. Bantam, 2004. $23.95. (F)

Camp, James, X. J. Kennedy, and Keith Waldrop, eds., notes, and intro. *Pegasus Descending: A Book of the Best Bad Verse*. Burning Deck, 2003. Paper: $10.00. (P)

Carlson, Ron. *A Kind of Flying: Selected Stories*. Intro. by the author. Norton, 2003. Paper: $15.95. (F)

Chapin, Ted. *Everything Was Possible: The Birth of the Musical "Follies."* Foreword by Frank Rich. Knopf, 2003. $30.00. (NF)

Clarke, Maeve. *What Goes Round.* Tindal Street/Dufour, 2003. Paper: $14.95. (F)

Connolly, Joseph. *The Works.* Faber & Faber, 2003. £16.99. (F)

Connor, Pat. *History Lessons.* Univ. of Massachusetts Press, 2003. $24.95. (F)

Conroy, Pat. *My Losing Season.* Bantam, 2003. Paper: $14.95. (NF)

Coulson, Joseph. *The Vanishing Moon.* Archipelago, 2004. $24.00. (F)

Crace, Jim. *Genesis.* Farrar, Straus & Giroux, 2003. $23.00. (F)

Creeley, Robert. *If I Were Writing This.* New Directions, 2003. $21.95. (P)

Curtis, Gregory. *Disarmed: The Story of the Venus de Milo.* Knopf, 2003. $24.00. (NF)

Daigle, France. *A Fine Passage.* Trans. Robert Majzels. Anansi, 2003. Paper: $14.95. (F)

Davenport, Guy. *The Death of Picasso: New & Selected Writing.* Shoemaker & Hoard, 2003. $26.00. (F, NF)

Davies, Tristan. *Cake.* Johns Hopkins Univ. Press, 2003. Paper: $15.95. (F)

Dierbeck, Lisa. *One Pill Makes You Smaller.* Farrar, Straus & Giroux, 2003. $24.00. (F)

Dodge, Trevor/Michael Hemmingson. *Yellow #10/My Fling with Betty Page.* Eraserhead, 2003. Paper: $14.95. (F)

Dostoevsky, Fyodor. *The Adolescent.* Trans. Richard Pevear and Larissa Volokhonsky. Everyman's Library, 2003. $23.00. (F)

Dowson, Ernest. *Collected Shorter Fiction.* Ed. Monica Borg and R. K. R. Thornton. Birmingham Univ. Press, 2003. Paper: $17.50. (F)

Duffy, Jean H. *Signs and Designs: Art and Architecture in the Work of Michel Butor.* Liverpool Univ. Press, 2003. Paper: $29.95. (NF)

Dunn, Mark. *Welcome to Higby.* Touchstone, 2003. Paper: $14.00. (F)

Dybek, Stuart. *I Sailed with Magellan.* Farrar, Straus & Giroux, 2003. $24.00. (F)

Egan, Timothy. *The Winemaker's Daughter.* Knopf, 2004. $24.95. (F)

Ely, Scott. *Pulpwood.* Livingston, 2003. $25.00; paper: $14.95. (F)

Esterházy, Péter. *Celestial Harmonies.* Trans. Judith Sollosy. Ecco, 2004. $29.95. (F)

Federman, Raymond. *Here & Elsewhere: Poetic Cul-de-Sac.* Six Gallery, 2003. Paper: $9.99. (P)

Fishman, Boris, ed. and intro. *Wild East: Stories from the Last Frontier.* Justin, Charles & Co., 2003. $24.95. (F)

Fowler, Christopher. *The Devil in Me.* Serpent's Tail, 2002. Paper: $15.00. (F)

Gabriel, Hayden. *Where the Light Remains.* Touchstone, 2003. Paper: $14.00. (F)

Galodnik, Rudy Wilson. *Take Heart! True Stories of Life, Love, and Laughter.* Broad Horizons, 2004. Paper: $12.95. (NF)

Gao, Xingjian. *Buying a Fishing Rod for My Grandfather.* Trans. Mabel Lee. HarperCollins, 2004. $17.95. (F)

García Márquez, Gabriel. *Living to Tell the Tale.* Trans. Edith Grossman. Knopf, 2003. $26.95. (NF)

Gardiner, John Rolfe. *Double Stitch.* Counterpoint, 2003. $25.00. (F)

Gay, Jackie. *Wist.* Tindal Street/Dufour, 2003. Paper: $14.95. (F)

Gibson, Graeme. *Five Legs.* House of Anansi, 2003. Paper: $21.95. (F)

Ginzburg, Natalia. *It's Hard to Talk about Yourself.* Trans. Louise Quirke. Ed. Cesare Garboli and Lisa Ginzburg. Univ. of Chicago Press, 2003. $25.00. (NF)

Gist, John. *Lizard Dreaming of Birds.* High Sierra, 2004. $24.95. (F)

Goodyear, Sara Suleri. *Boys Will Be Boys: A Daughter's Elegy.* Univ. of Chicago Press, 2003. $22.00. (NF)

Graves, Robert. *"Antigua, Penny, Puce'" and "They Hanged My Saintly Billy."* Ed. and intro. Ian McCormick. Carcanet, 2003. $60.00. (F)

Green, Angela. *The Colour of Water.* Peter Owen/Dufour, 2003. Paper: $23.95. (F)

Green, Lohren. *Poetical Dictionary (Abridged).* Atelos, 2003. Paper: $12.95. (P)

Gregory, Julie. *Sickened: The Memoir of a Munchausen by Proxy Childhood.* Foreword Marc D. Feldman. Bantam, 2003. $24.95. (F)

Grimaldi, Laura. *Suspicion.* Trans. Robin Pickering-Iazzi. Univ. of Wisconsin Press, 2003. $19.95. (F)

Guilloux, Louis. *OK, Joe.* Trans. and intro. Alice Kaplan. Univ. of Chicago Press, 2003. $22.50. (F)

Gunjaca, Drazan. *Balkan Farewells.* Moondance, 2003. Paper: $17.95. (F)

Hamann, H. T. *Anthropology of an American Girl.* Vernacular, 2003. $30.00. (F)

Hamblen, Charles F. *The Dawn Timers.* Vantage, 2003. Paper: $13.95. (F)

Hébert, Anne. *Collected Later Novels.* Trans. Sheila Fischman. Intro. Mavis Gallant. Anansi, 2003. Paper: $24.95. (F)

Hegi, Ursula. *Sacred Time.* Touchstone, 2003. $25.00. (F)

Hogan, Michael. *Man out of Time.* Delta, 2003. Paper: $11.95. (F)

Hopkinson, Nalo. *The Salt Roads.* Warner, 2003. $22.95. (F)

Howe, Fanny. *Tis of Thee.* Atelos, 2003. Paper with CD: $12.95. (P)

Howells, Coral Ann. *Contemporary Canadian Women's Fiction: Refiguring Identities.* Palgrave, 2003. $59.95. (NF)

Hunt, Jeff. *Eduardo Aquifer and the Great Tanning Incident*. Livingston, 2004. $25.00; paper: $14.95. (F)

Jaeggy, Fleur. *S.S. Proleterka*. Trans. Alastair McEwen. New Directions, 2003. Paper: $17.95. (F)

Jaffe, Harold. *15 Serial Killers*. Visuals Joel Lipman. Raw Dog Screaming, 2003. Paper: $13.95. (F)

Jergović, Miljenko. *Sarajevo Marlboro*. Trans. Stela Tomasevic. Intro. Ammiel Alcalay. Archipelago, 2004. Paper: $14.00. (F)

Johnson, Roberta. *Gender and Nation in the Spanish Modernist Novel*. Vanderbilt Univ. Press, 2003. $69.95; paper: $29.95. (NF)

Kalam, Murad. *Night Journey*. Simon & Schuster, 2003. $23.00. (F)

Kaufman, Andrew. *All My Friends Are Superheroes*. Coach House, 2003. Paper: $14.95. (F)

Kennedy, Christopher. *Trouble with the Machine*. Low Fidelity, 2003. Paper: $11.00. (P)

King, Adele, ed. *From Africa: New Francophone Stories*. Univ. of Nebraska Press, 2004. $40.00; paper: $15.00. (F)

Lardner, Ring. *Ring around the Bases: The Complete Baseball Stories of Ring Lardner*. Ed. and intro. Matthew J. Bruccoli. Foreword Ring Lardner, Jr. Univ. of South Carolina Press, 2003. Paper: $24.95. (F)

Laurence, Patricia. *Lily Briscoe's Chinese Eyes: Bloomsbury, Modernism, and China*. Univ. of South Carolina Press, 2003. $59.95. (NF)

Llamazares, Julio. *The Yellow Rain*. Trans. Margaret Jull Costa. Harcourt, 2004. $22.00. (F)

Luntta, Karl. *Know It by Heart*. Curbstone, 2003. Paper: $15.95. (F)

Major, Clarence. *One Flesh*. Kensington, 2003. Paper: $15.00. (F)

Mark, Ezra. *Intention*. Nine Muses, 2003. Paper: $7.50. (P)

Markson, David. *Vanishing Point*. Shoemaker & Hoard, 2004. Paper: $15.00. (F)

Mason, Daniel. *The Piano Tuner*. Vintage, 2003. Paper: $14.00. (F)

Maugham, W. Somerset. *The Razor's Edge*. Vintage, 2003. Paper: $13.00. (F)

May, John. *Poe & Fanny*. Algonquin, 2004. $25.95. (F)

Mazzini, Miha. *Guarding Hanna*. Trans. Maja Visenjak-Limon and Mark White. Scala House, 2003. Paper: $15.50. (F)

McCarthy, Dermot. *Roddy Doyle: Raining on the Parade*. Liffey/Dufour, 2003. Paper: $25.95. (NF)

McCarthy, Susan Carol. *True Fires*. Bantam, 2004. $23.95. (F)

McGregor, Jon. *If Nobody Speaks of Remarkable Things*. Mariner, 2003. Paper: $13.00. (F)

McMahon, Thomas. *Ira Foxglove: A Novel*. Brook Street, 2003. $21.95. (F)

McMorris, Mark. *The Blaze of the Poui*. Univ. of Georgia Press, 2003. Paper: $16.95. (P)

Menéndez, Ana. *Loving Che.* Atlantic, 2004. $22.00. (F)

Merriman, C. A. *Brotherhood.* Parthian/Dufour, 2003. Paper: $13.95. (F)

Mundler, Helen E. *Homesickness.* Dewi Lewis, 2003. Paper: $13.95. (F)

Muñoz Molina, Antonio. *Sepharad.* Trans. Margaret Sayers Peden. Harcourt, 2003. $27.00. (F)

Murkoff, Bruce. *Waterborne.* Knopf, 2004. $25.00. (F)

Ober, K. Patrick. *Mark Twain and Medicine: "Any Mummery Will Cure."* Univ. of Missouri Press, 2003. $47.50. (NF)

Orr, Mary. *Intertextuality: Debates and Contexts.* Polity, 2003. $62.95; paper: $27.95. (NF)

Papazian, Mary Arshagouni, ed. *John Donne and the Protestant Reformation: New Perspectives.* Wayne State Univ. Press, 2003. $39.95. (NF)

Parise, Goffredo. *The Smell of Blood.* Trans. John Shepley. Northwestern Univ. Press, 2003. Paper: $17.95. (F)

Patterson, J. Hunter. *The Banks of Hunger and Hardship (A Map of Time).* Spuyten Duyvil, 2003. Paper: $12.00. (F)

Pine, Red, trans. *Poems of the Masters: China's Classic Anthology of T'ang and Sung Dynasty Verse.* Copper Canyon, 2003. Paper: $18.00. (P)

Pineau, Gisèle. *Macadam Dreams.* Trans. C. Dickson. Univ. of Nebraska Press, 2003. $50.00; paper: $20.00. (F)

Preston, Richard. *The Boat of Dreams: A Christmas Story.* Illus. George Henry Jennings. Touchstone, 2003. $15.00. (F)

Proust, Marcel. *Swann's Way.* Trans., intro., and notes Lydia Davis. Viking, 2003. $27.95. (F)

Railsback, Brian. *The Darkest Clearing.* High Sierra, 2004. $27.95. (F)

Ramos, Manuel. *Brown-on-Brown: A Luis Móntez Mystery.* Univ. of New Mexico Press, 2003. $21.95. (F)

Rathbone, Julian. *The Indispensable Julian Rathbone.* Intro. Mike Phillips. Do-Not Press/Dufour, 2003. $36.95; paper: $19.95. (F)

Rea, Ermanno. *A Mystery in Naples.* Trans. Thomas Simpson. Guernica, 2003. Paper: $13.00. (F)

Ría, Ana María del. *Carmen's Rust.* Trans. and intro. Michael J. Lazzara. Afterword Diamela Eltit. Overlook Duckworth, 2003. $19.95. (F)

Rivera-Garza, Cristina. *No One Will See Me Cry.* Trans. Andrew Hurley. Curbstone, 2003. Paper: $15.95. (F)

Sabina, María. *Selections.* Ed. Jerome Rothenberg. Commentary Alvaro Estrada, et al. Univ. of California Press, 2003. $50.00; paper: $16.95. (P)

Sciascia, Leonardo. *The Day of the Owl*. Trans. Archibald Colquhoun and Arthur Oliver. Intro. George Scialabba. New York Review Books, 2003. Paper: $12.95. (F)

——. *Equal Danger*. Trans. Adrienne Foulke. Intro. Carlin Romano. New York Review Books, 2003. Paper: $12.95. (F)

Schnitzler, Arthur. *Desire and Delusion: Three Novellas*. Selected and trans. Margret Schaefer. Ivan R. Dee, 2003. $28.50. (F)

Shah, Saira. *The Storyteller's Daughter*. Knopf, 2003. $24.00. (F)

Sharpe, Matthew. *The Sleeping Father*. Soft Skull, 2003. Paper: $14.00. (F)

Sheehan, Aurelie. *The Anxiety of Everyday Objects*. Penguin, 2004. Paper: $14.00. (F)

Shepard, Jim. *Project X*. Knopf, 2004. $20.00. (F)

Sparrow, Rebecca. *The Girl Most Likely*. Univ. of Queensland Press, 2003. Paper: $19.95. (F)

St. Aubyn, Edward. *Some Hope*. Open City Books, 2003. Paper: $14.95. (F)

Suleiman, Susan Rubin, and Éva Forgács, eds. *Contemporary Jewish Writing in Hungary: An Anthology*. Univ. of Nebraska Press, 2003. $60.00; paper: $24.95. (F, NF, P)

Tagore, Rabindranath. *The Lover of God*. Trans. Tony K. Stewart and Chase Twichell. Copper Canyon, 2003. Paper: $15.00. (P)

Tate, Bronwyn. *Lily's Cupola*. Univ. of Otago Press, 2003. Paper: $29.95. (F)

Taylor, John. *Paths to Contemporary French Literature*. Rutgers Univ. Press, 2003. $44.95. (NF)

Thirlwell, Adam. *Politics*. Fourth Estate/HarperCollins, 2003. $22.95. (F)

Toker, Franklin. *Fallingwater Rising: Frank Lloyd Wright, E. J. Kaufmann, and America's Most Extraordinary House*. Knopf, 2003. $35.00. (NF)

Toutonghi, Pauls. *Live Cargo*. Livingston, 2003. $25.00; paper: $14.95. (F)

Tuten, Frederick. *The Green Hour*. Norton, 2003. Paper: $13.95. (F)

Tyler, Anne. *The Amateur Marriage*. Knopf, 2003. $24.95. (F)

Vallejo, César. *The Black Heralds*. 2nd ed. Trans. Richard Schaaf and Kathleen Ross. Latin American Literary Review Press, 2003. Paper: $12.95. (P)

Van Cauwelaert, Didier. *One-Way*. Trans. Mark Polizzotti. Other Press, 2003. $18.00. (F)

Van Straten, Giorgio. *My Name, A Living Memory*. Trans. Martha King. Steerforth, 2003. Paper: $14.95. (F)

Vargas Llosa, Mario. *The Way to Paradise*. Trans. Natasha Wimmer. Farrar, Straus & Giroux, 2003. $25.00. (F)

Vaughan, Dai. *Totes Meer*. Seren, 2003. Paper: £6.95. (F)

Wagner, Bruce. *Still Holding*. Simon & Schuster, 2003. $25.00. (F)

Waldrop, Rosmarie. *Blindsight*. New Directions, 2003. Paper: $15.95. (P)

Wallace, David Foster. *Everything and More: A Compact History of* ∞. Norton, 2003. $23.95. (NF)

Washington, Peter, ed. *Haiku*. Everyman's Library, 2003. $12.50. (P)

Weaver, Brett. *Calling Up the Dead*. Livingston, 2003. $25.00; paper: $14.95. (F)

Weber, Katherine. *The Little Women*. Farrar, Straus & Giroux, 2003. $23.00. (F)

Wesley, Marilyn C. *Violent Adventure: Contemporary Fiction by American Men*. Univ. of Virginia Press, 2003. $55.00; paper: $18.50. (NF)

West, Paul. *The Immensity of the Here and Now: A Novel of 9.11*. Voyant, 2003. $23.00. (F)

Wilton, Caren. *The Heart Sutra*. Univ. of Otago Press, 2003. Paper: $29.95. (F)

Wolff, Tobias. *Old School*. Knopf, 2003. $22.00. (F)

Yarbrough, Steve. *Prisoners of War*. Knopf, 2004. $23.00. (F)

Yaxley, Richard. *The Rose Leopard*. Univ. of Queensland Press, 2003. Paper: $19.95. (F)

Woodbury, Heather. *What Ever: A Living Novel*. Faber & Faber, 2003. Paper: $15.00. (F)

Zaid, Gabriel. *So Many Books: Reading and Publishing in an Age of Abundance*. Trans. Natasha Wimmer. Paul Dry Books, 2003. Paper: $9.95. (NF)

Zárate, Jesús. *Jail*. Trans. Gregory Rabassa. Aliform, 2003. Paper: $14.95. (F)

Živković, Zoran. *The Book / The Writer*. Trans. Aleksandar B. Nedeljkovic and Alice Copple-Tosic. Trans. ed. Tamar Yellin. Prime, 2003. $29.95; paper: $17.95. (F)

Zolin, Miriam. *Tristessa & Lucido*. Univ. of Queensland Press, 2003. Paper: $20.00. (F)

Contributors

JEFF BURSEY is a Hansard editor and a Commissioner of Oaths in Canada. His articles and book reviews have appeared in the *Review of Contemporary Fiction, Books in Canada, Nexus: The International Henry Miller Journal, Quarter after Eight,* and the *Literary Review.* In addition, he is regional editor for Canada of the online environmental journal *Common Ground.*

ROLANDO PÉREZ was born in Cuba in 1957. He is the author of a number of books, including *The Electric Comedy* (Cool Grove, 2000); *The Divine Duty of Servants: A Book of Worship* (based on the artwork of Polish writer/artist, Bruno Schulz; Cool Grove, 1999); *On An(archy) and Schizoanalysis* (Autonomedia/Semiotext(e), 1990); *The Odyssey* (Brook House Press, 1990); and *Severo Sarduy and the Religion of the Text* (UP of America, 1988). His latest book, *The Lining of Our Souls: Excursions into Selected Paintings of Edward Hopper,* was published in 2002 by Cool Grove Press.

BRUCE STONE teaches writing at the University of Wisconsin-Green Bay. His fiction and essays have appeared most recently in *Northwest Review, Hunger Mountain,* and *Salon.*

Robert Creeley • Gertrude Stein
dous Huxley • Robert Coover • Jo
rth • David Markson • Flann O'Bri

www.dalkeyarchive.com

uis-Ferdinand Céline • Marguer
ung • Ishmael Reed • Camilo José C
Gilbert Sorrentino • Ann Quin
icholas Mosley • Douglas Woolf
aymond Queneau • Harry Mathews
kki Ducornet • José Lezama Lima
dan Higgins • Ben Marcus • Colem
owell • Jacques Roubaud • Dju
rnes • Felipe Alfau • Osman Lins
avid Antin • Susan Daitch • Vikt
klovsky • Henry Green • Curtis Wh
Anne Carson • John Hawkes • Fo
adox Ford • Janice Galloway • Mich

Your connection to literature.
DALKEY ARCHIVE PRESS

NOON

NOON

A LITERARY ANNUAL

1369 MADISON AVENUE   PMB 298   NEW YORK   NEW YORK   10128-0711

EDITION PRICE $9 DOMESTIC $14 FOREIGN

Studies in American Fiction

A journal of articles and reviews on the prose fiction of the United States

Published semiannually by the Department of English, Northeastern University

Mary Loeffelholz, Editor

Recent numbers include

Clifford E. Wulfman, *Sighting / Siting / Citing the Scar: Trauma and Homecoming in Faulkner's* Soldier's Pay

Laura Korobkin, *Legal Narratives of Self-Defense and Self-Effacement in* Their Eyes Were Watching God

Tom Allen, *Mellville's Factory Girls: Feminizing the Future*

Claire Chantell, *The Limits of the Mother at Home in* The Wide, Wide

Annual subscriptions: $10.00 for individuals, $13.00 for individuals outside the United States; $16.00 for domestic institutions, $18.00 for institutions outside the United States. **Send subscriptions and inquiries to** *Studies in American Fiction*, Department of English, 406 Holmes Hall, Northeastern University, Boston MA 02115-5000. Phone: 617-373-3687;fax617-373-2509;e-mail: a.pikcilingis@neu.edu. **Visit**

the minnesota review

a journal of committed writing

Forthcoming:

n.s. 58-59

with a special section

The Legacies of
Michael Sprinker

n.s. 60-61

with a special section

Smart Kids

Jeffrey J. Williams, Editor
the minnesota review
Department of English
107 Tate Hall
University of Missouri
Columbia, MO 65211

http://www.theminnesotareview.org

Have fun, be lucky

The Center for Writers has three dozen students working toward M.A. and Ph.D. degrees in fiction and poetry. These writers come from all over the country, all kinds of schools, a variety of backgrounds. They study with Frederick Barthelme, Mary Robison, Angela Ball, Steven Barthelme, David Berry, and Kim Herzinger, and with visitors such as Rick Moody, Amy Hempel, Lucie Brock-Broido, Dana Gioia, Padgett Powell, Michael Waters, Mary Gaitskill, Julia Slavin, C. Michael Curtis and others.

The program is casual, and the results are good. Recent graduates have won the Whiting Award, the Transatlantic Award, the *Playboy* Fiction Contest, and the Flannery O'Connor Award and have published widely. Seven recent graduates published books in 2003. We edit and publish *Mississippi Review*, run workshops, entertain visitors, and help our students become better writers.

The Center for Writers

For information contact Rie Fortenberry, Center for Writers, The University of Southern Mississippi, Box 5144, Hattiesburg, MS 39406-5144, or rief@comcast.net, or look for us on the Web at www.centerforwriters.com.

(AA/EOE/ADAI)

other voices

FICTION FROM *OTHER VOICES* WAS INCLUDED IN *BEST AMERICAN SHORT STORIES OF THE CENTURY*, EDITED BY JOHN UPDIKE AND RECENTLY CITED IN *THE NATION* AS A LEADING FORUM FOR WRITERS OF COLOR.

"LOOKING FOR THE BEST IN SHORT FICTION? [*OTHER VOICES*] CHALLENGES JUST ABOUT ANYTHING YOU WILL FIND IN BETTER-KNOWN COMMERCIAL MAGAZINES."
–Library Journal

"NATURAL, IMPULSIVE, THE ANTITHESIS OF SELF-CONSCIOUSNESS, THESE ARE AFFECTING AND ACCESSIBLE STORIES WITH A STRONG DRAMATIC TENSION AND NARRATIVE DRIVE." *–Small Press Review*

"*OTHER VOICES* IS A CACOPHONY OF EVERY KIND OF VOCALIZATION, FROM LOVING WHISPERS TO MURDEROUS SCREAMS, FROM MURDEROUS MUTTERINGS TO PASSIONATE SCREAMS, FROM HUMMING TO OPERATIC SOPRANO, FROM MONOTONE TO SYMPHONIC CLIMAX TO A SINGLE BUGLE BLOWING TAPS." *–Cris Mazza*

DIVERSE, ORIGINAL FICTION BY PAM HOUSTON, AIMEE BENDER, JEFFREY RENARD ALLEN, STEVE ALMOND, JOSIP NOVAKOVICH, DAN CHAON, WANDA COLEMAN, MOLLY GILES... IN-DEPTH INTERVIEWS WITH JUNOT DIAZ, MICHAEL CUNNINGHAM, ALICE SEBOLD/ GLEN DAVID GOLD, IRVINE WELSH...

4-issue (2-year) Subscription

❏ Individual: $24   ❏ Library/Institution: $28
❏ Canada: $26   ❏ Foreign: $34 (surface) $38 (air)
Start with issue #_____ (#1 is not available)

❏ **Sample Issue** (current #): $7.00 (includes postage)

Name_____

Address_____

City_____ State_____ Zip_____

Enclosed is my   ❏ check   ❏ money order   for $_____

other voices
Department of English (MC 162)
University of Illinois at Chicago
601 South Morgan St.
Chicago, IL 60607-7120
(312) 413-2209

Borderlines.
Autobiography and Fiction in Postmodern Life Writing.

Gunnthórunn Gudmundsdóttir

Amsterdam/New York, NY 2003. VII, 294 pp.
(Postmodern Studies 33)

ISBN: 90-420-1145-9   EUR 60,-/US $ 71.-

Borderlines. Autobiography and Fiction in Postmodern Life Writing locates and investigates the borderlines between autobiography and fiction in various kinds of life-writing dating from the last thirty years. This volume offers a valuable comparative approach to texts by French, English, American, and German authors to illustrate the different forms of experimentation with the borders between genres and literary modes. Gudmundsdóttir tackles important contemporary concerns such as autobiography's relationship to postmodernism by investigating themes such as memory and crossing cultural divides, the use of photographs in autobiography and the role of narrative in life-writing. This work is of interest to students and scholars of comparative literature, postmodernism and contemporary life-writing

USA/Canada: One Rockefeller Plaza, Ste. 1420, New York, NY 10020,
Tel. (212) 265-6360, Call toll-free (U.S. only) 1-800-225-3998,
Fax (212) 265-6402
All other countries: Tijnmuiden 7, 1046 AK Amsterdam, The Netherlands.
Tel. ++ 31 (0)20 611 48 21, Fax ++ 31 (0)20 447 29 79
Orders-queries@rodopi.nl   **www.rodopi.nl**
Please note that the exchange rate is subject to fluctuations

THE MASSACHUSETTS REVIEW

LEONARD BASKIN

A QUARTERLY REVIEW *of* Fiction, Poetry, Essays, and Art, *since 1959*
single copy: $8 ($11 *International*)
Subscriptions: 1 Year $22; 2 Years: $34; 3 Years $52

The Massachusetts Review

editorial office: South College, University of Massachusetts, Amherst, MA 01003 ph: 413-545-2689
e: massrev@external.umass.edu • www.massreview.org

Studies in Twentieth and Twenty-First Century Literature

Volume 28, No. 1 (Winter, 2004)

A Special Issue on

Writing and Reading Berlin

Guest Editor:
Stephen Brockmann

Contributors include:

Erhard Schütz
Sabine Hake
Peter Fritzsche
Ulrike Zitzlsperger
Katharina Gerstenberger
Katrin Sieg
Christian Jäger
Anke Biendarra
Carol Anne Costabile-Heming
Siegfried Mews
Barbara Mennel

Silvia Sauter, Editor
Kansas State University
Eisenhower 104
Manhattan, KS 66506-1003
Submissions in: Spanish and Russian

Jordan Stump, Editor
University of Nebraska
PO Box 880318
Lincoln, NE 68588-0318
Submissions in: French and German

Please check our Web site for subscription and other information:

http://www.ksu.edu/stcl/index.html

30 Years of Excellence:
1974-2003

Kostas Myrsiades, editor
www.collegeliterature.org

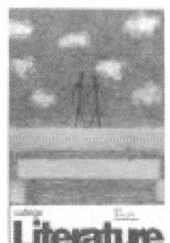

College Literature

Dedicated to the promotion and advancement of the study and craft of translation, translators, and publishers of translated works since 1978. Annual conferences, newsletters, and the journal *Translation Review* and its supplement, *Annotated Books Received*, provide members of this professional association with the latest information in the field of translation.

American Literary Translators
Association
The University of Texas at Dallas
Mail Station MC35, Box 830688
Richardson TX 75083-0688

972-883-2093
Fax: 972-883-6303

www.literarytranslators.org

Dalkey Archive Press

New Releases

The Inquisitory
by ROBERT PINGET

Zero
by IGNÁCIO DE LOYOLA BRANDÃO

Pillow Talk in Europe and Other Places
by DEBORAH LEVY

Mountain R
by JACQUES JOUET

The Inquisitory

ROBERT PINGET

Translation by Donald Watson

John F. Byrne
  French Literature Series
A Novel
$14.95 / paper
ISBN: 1-56478-327-8

Considered Pinget's masterpiece, *The Inquisitory* consists entirely of the interrogation of an old, deaf servant regarding unspecified crimes that may or may not have taken place at his master's French château.

The servant's replies—which are by turns comic, straightforward, angry, nostalgic, and disingenuous—hint at a variety of seedy events, including murder, orgies, tax fraud, and drug deals. Of course, the servant wasn't involved with any of these activities— if the reader chooses to believe him. In trying to convince the inquisitor of his innocence, the servant creates a web of half-truths, vague references, and glaring inconsistencies amid "forgotten" details, indicating that he may know more than he's letting on.

"One of the most important novels of the last ten years."

—Samuel Beckett

"Pinget's very avant-garde novel of the absurd incorporates the full French novelistic tradition. Like Proust, he has a curé who dabbles in the etymology of place names; like Balzac, he avidly traces the fortunes of little provincial shops through all their vicissitudes of gossip."

—John Updike, New Yorker

—— *Now Available* ——

Dalkey Archive Press

Zero

IGNÁCIO DE LOYOLA
BRANDÃO
Translation by Ellen Watson
Introduction by Thomas Colchie

Latin American Literature Series
A Novel
$13.95 / paper
ISBN: 1-56478-331-6

With the help of the Happy Heart Marriage Agency, José meets his wife Rosa. They seem to have an understanding: José isn't bothered by Rosa's dishonesty, extra weight, and fantastically promiscuous past; Rosa isn't too put off by José's clubfoot, periodic blackouts, or lack of direction. She simply wants to buy a house. Pragmatic, José sets out to get the money necessary to make that possible. In doing so, he manages to become a robber, sniper, and political subversive wanted by the government.

Deploying fast-paced, short chapters in a number of styles, Brandão deftly presents an array of engaging characters and conflicts, vividly depicting the absurdity of a repressive political regime with exceptional daring and humor. Initially banned in Brazil, *Zero* went on to win one of Brazil's most prestigious literary prizes and become a controversial best-seller.

"A wild, surreal novel, vulgar, funny, self-conscious, painful. It is done in short takes, each with a headline; a kitchen sink kind of book, envisioning the hideous nature of life under a repressive regime of the 1960s."
—E. L. Doctorow

——— *Now Available* ———

Pillow Talk in Europe and Other Places

DEBORAH LEVY

British Literature Series
Stories
$12.95 / paper
ISBN: 1-56478-333-2

From the author of *Billy and Girl,* this collection of stories explores how men and women interpret and reinvent what freedom means in their relationships with one another.

In "Pillow Talk" everyday rules about decency and kindness are broken and repaired as a Czech man and an English woman search for enduring love in a world that offers them little certainty.

"Vienna" is the story of a man who has sex with an enigmatic woman, despite knowing that she despises him.

In "Cave Girl" a man relates the story of his sister's sex change, not to become a man, but rather to become "less of a real girl and more of a pretend woman." Her surgery transforms her into a woman desired by all men—including her brother.

Throughout these remarkable stories Deborah Levy continues to question and reflect on the ways in which we create our identity and attempt to achieve an elusive sense of fulfillment.

"Levy's strength is her originality of thought and expression."
—*Jeanette Winterson*

"Levy is the genuine article."
—*Harvey Pekar*

———— *Now Available* ————

Mountain R

JACQUES JOUET
Translation by Brian Evenson

French Literature Series
A Novel
$12.95 / paper
ISBN: 1-56478-330-8

The president of the Republican Council, wanting to "do something big," proposes building a 1,500-meter-high mountain as a monument to the nation's greatness. Employing political double-talk at its worst, the president convinces the Council to proceed with this insane, grandiose plan by heralding its hoped-for benefits: the project will reduce unemployment, attract hordes of tourists, solve the problem of garbage (the filler for this artificial mountain), and increase revenue by licensing the idea to other countries.

Told in three distinct parts and from three different points of view, *Mountain R* records the disasters that result from political corruption and manipulative leaders.

An incisive satire about the dangers of government and power, *Mountain R* is a disturbing, funny novel about the times in which we live.

"Jacques Jouet, the distinguished Oulipian, gives us a parable about Government that is both exquisite and alarming: leading a country is not a game."
—*Dominique Durand*, Le Canard enchaîné

"Mountain R is a serious, disturbing novel, which can be read as a fable of communism's shortcomings, or as a parody of liberal illusions."
—*Hugo Marsan*, Le Monde

—— *Available in February 2004* ——

ORDER FORM

Individuals may use this form to subscribe to the *Review of Contemporary Fiction* or to order back issues of the *Review* and Dalkey Archive titles at a 10-20% discount.

Title	ISBN	Quantity	Price

Subtotal_____

(10% for one book, 20% for two or more books) Less Discount_____

Subtotal_____

($4 domestic, $5 foreign) Plus postage_____

1 year individual subscription ($17 domestic, $20.50 foreign)_____

Total_____

Ship to _____

_____

_____

_____

> *mail or fax this form to:*
>
> Dalkey Archive Press
> ISU Campus Box 8905
> Normal, IL 61790-8905
> *fax:* 309.438.7422
> *tel:* 309.438.7555

Credit card payment   ☐ Visa   ☐ Mastercard

Acct #_____ Exp. Date_____

Name on card_____ Phone Number_____

Please make checks (in U.S. dollars only) payable to *Dalkey Archive Press*